I0025282

Securing Sexuality

Securing Sexuality equips therapists and clinicians with the latest information about tech ethics, privacy, cybersecurity, and cybersexuality, providing practical tools to navigate the myriad ways in which their lives and the lives of their clients are lived online.

What does safe sex mean in a digital age? From dating apps and digital consent to deepfakes, AI companions, and online surveillance, this compelling volume examines how intimacy is evolving—and what we risk losing along the way. It provides mental health professionals with tools they need to help their clients safely explore a variety of intimate scenarios across a wide range of apps, websites, and technologies. Award-winning sex therapist Stefani Goerlich discusses hot topics in technology, and each chapter ends with an accessible lesson on a specific aspect of technology by leading cybersecurity expert, J. Wolfgang Goerlich.

Enriched with practical tools and interviews by industry specialists, this book helps therapists mitigate risks while guiding clients through the process of making personal choices in this domain. This book is a vital resource for marriage and family therapists, sex therapists, counselors, scholars, and curious readers who want to understand how technology is reshaping our most intimate spaces.

Stefani Goerlich is a multi-award winning author of four books focusing on alternative sexualities and mental health.

J. Wolfgang Goerlich is an internationally recognized cybersecurity expert and Chief Information Security Officer. Together, Wolf and Stefani co-host the Securing Sexuality podcast.

Securing Sexuality

Emerging Issues at the Intersection of Intimacy and Technology

Stefani Goerlich and
J. Wolfgang Goerlich

Routledge
Taylor & Francis Group

NEW YORK AND LONDON

Designed cover image: Getty Images

First published 2026
by Routledge
605 Third Avenue, New York, NY 10158

and by Routledge
4 Park Square, Milton Park, Abingdon, Oxon, OX14 4RN

*Routledge is an imprint of the Taylor & Francis Group, an informa
business*

ISBN: 978-1-032-48852-3 (hbk)
ISBN: 978-1-032-48851-6 (pbk)
ISBN: 978-1-003-39112-8 (ebk)

DOI: 10.4324/9781003391128

Typeset in Times New Roman
by Apex CoVantage, LLC

Stef and Wolf dedicate this book to Russell Stambaugh (1949–2025)- our friend, mentor, and guardian curmudgeon, who devoted his life to fighting for personal privacy, bodily autonomy, and a more just and loving world.

You are not obligated to complete the work, but neither are you free to desist from it. You just need to make a dent.

Contents

Acknowledgements

Wolf and Stefani would like to thank everyone who has supported our work to bridge the gap between the worlds of privacy/security and sexual health. We are especially grateful to those who contributed their time, passion, and expertise to the inaugural Securing Sexuality Conference, Our "O.G.'s in the D."

Biana Alba
Rachel Arnold
Laura Boyle
Maya Brooks
Ley David Elliette
Venessa Farn
Kurt Fowler
Albert Fox Cahn
Eva Galperin
Elyssa Helfer
Amanda Jepson
Jasmonae Joyriel
Midori
Erika Miley
Ben Miller
Helen Patton
Nicole Prause
Renderman
Aunshul Rege
Nicole Schwartz
Shakun Sethi
Brian Stearns
Markie Twist
Johnny Xmas

As well as our amazing conference team:
Chelle Green, David "Ska" Green, and Frank Mons

From medicine to criminology, finance to psychotherapy, each one of them is committed to building a stronger, safer, sexier society. Healers and hackers, artists and activists, the world is a better place—a *kinder* place—because they are in it.

Introduction

"I'm a therapist, not an engineer."
"I'm a software developer, not a sex ed teacher."
"If it has sex in the name? My company won't touch it with a ten-foot pole."
"I think what you're doing is great . . . but it's not my problem."
"Thank goodness nothing I do touches the human!"

These are just a few of the comments we heard when we first floated the idea of doing a Securing Sexuality live event. We'd been doing the podcast for over a year at that point—inspired by the U.S. Supreme Court reversal of *Roe v. Wade* in America. To be honest? We'd never planned to do a podcast at all. After all, there are over five million podcasts published these days—many of which don't last more than a handful of episodes (Poddster, 2023). That changed when the Dobbs ruling came out in the summer of 2022. We knew that as a Hacker and a Sex Therapist, we were uniquely positioned to try and mitigate some of the harm that loomed on the horizon. So, we did two episodes: "Privacy in a Post-Roe America," parts one and two, hoping to provide immediate, actionable security information to folks whose lives were about to get a lot more complicated. After those first two episodes, we high-fived ourselves on a job well done and started to pack away the microphones. We'd responded with a sense of urgency, and we had helped! Yay us! We were unprepared for the response that we received. Mental health providers, doctors, social workers, and everyday people started reaching out to us, asking questions. For the first time cybersecurity and data protection wasn't just something they thought about when they received yet another email from a big box store letting them know about yet another data leak. After the Dobbs ruling? Information Security became a serious, potentially life-threatening concern.

That's how a spontaneous response to an emergent social crisis became a weekly podcast with (by the time you read these words) over 100 episodes, a live conference, a busy nonprofit consultancy, and this book. And yet, even after two years spent providing public education, conferences, and academic lectures, as well as tabling at advocacy and industry events, we are always surprised by

DOI: 10.4324/9781003391128-1

the number of people who tell us, "This isn't my problem." They're not using birth control or seeking abortions. They're not trans or gender non-conforming. They're not using online dating apps or fancy sex toys. They're not watching porn. In short? They're not . . . those kinds of people. Technology, social media, and the internet have become so ubiquitous so rapidly that an undercurrent of stigma flows through these conversations. The notion that if you don't want to be exposed to risk, just don't do high-risk things. But this mindset only makes sense if we have a realistic idea of what the risks associated with various technologies actually are. In our experience, most everyday users lack the crucial digital literacy necessary to conceptualize their personal level of risk and to make proactive, informed choices for themselves, their families, and their relationships. That's where we come in.

J. Wolfgang Goerlich has been a leading voice in cybersecurity for over twenty years, advising financial services and healthcare providers on how to protect our most sensitive data. He is a highly sought-after conference presenter and has spoken at events worldwide, helping his peers protect everything from your $5 convenience store debit purchase to the identity records of entire nations. Wolf's area of special expertise is Identity and Access Management—a fancy way of saying that he helps companies build strong systems to ensure that users are who they say they are and that only authorized people have access to private information. As an executive coach and mentor, Wolf has trained cybersecurity experts at all levels of the industry, from the twenty-year-old apprentice beginning her journey into the profession after waitressing at the local burger joint, through the seasoned Fortune 500 executive overseeing thousands of security personnel.

Stefani Goerlich is a clinical and forensic social worker and a certified sex therapist. Throughout her career, she has worked with survivors of domestic and sexual violence—including digital abuse and online trafficking. She teaches courses on sexual trauma, sexual dysfunction/disorders, paraphilias, digital sexuality, and social media in universities around the country and is herself a popular conference speaker and consultant. In addition to her academic work, Stefani advises attorneys who are working on cases with elements of sexual abuse, paraphilias, and/or problematic online activity. She is recognized as a leading expert in working with erotic minorities and has written four award-winning books on BDSM/kink and mental health.

Together, we have specialized in consulting with mental health providers, program developers, industry leaders, and everyday people impacted by these issues. After all, the average person will spend about six years and eight months of their life using their smartphone—a device they unlock around 150 times per day (Rafiq, 2023). We hope that this book will consolidate our respective knowledge and experience into a resource that anyone, clinician or layperson, can utilize to increase their understanding of the issues that exist today at the intersection of intimacy and technology. We aim not to be alarmist—both Wolf and Stefani are technology enthusiasts and early adopters. However, we are not utopian either. We recognize that the pace of technology is rapidly advancing—much faster than our ability to conduct research on the impact and long-term effects of these new developments—and that there is a certain degree of risk in everything we do. *Securing Sexuality* is our attempt to offer a framework for you, the reader, to develop your own personal risk framework for technology use in your life and your relationships—both personal and professional.

Each chapter that follows is divided into three sections. First, the content offers a 101-level introduction to each chapter's theme and an analysis of both the pros and cons of the focused aspect of technology. We will explore the latest human-centered research and offer specific suggestions for maximizing the benefits of this topic while reducing any potential risk exposure. Second, because we know that most of our readers are not technologists, each chapter will include a section called Wolf's Tech Ed, which will provide a high-level introduction to the mechanics and application of each chapter's tech. From the origins of the internet through the basics of blockchain, Wolf will ensure that you understand the science behind the jargon . . . without asking you to earn a second degree in computer science to follow along. Finally, each chapter will end with an interview with another leading expert, giving you additional perspectives from leading voices in cybersecurity, SexTech, privacy protection, and user design. We hope that by the time you finish reading Securing Sexuality, you'll have a holistic, non-alarmist, research-based perspective on the influences that technology can (and does) have in your life, as well as a feeling of empowerment and agency over what information you share, when, and with whom. At the end of the day, whether we're talking about physical intimacy or digital privacy, every choice should be made with risk-awareness and ongoing, informed consent. Until we live in a world of perfect technological privacy? We're here to help you reclaim and protect your digital identity. And perhaps have a little bit of fun along the way.

Chapter 1

The History of Sex + Tech

What Do We Mean When We Talk About Tech?

For many of us, thinking about technology is something akin to alchemy: an arcane skill mastered by a handful of skilled practitioners who possess the secret language necessary to alter reality at will. In the Middle Ages, the goal was the transmutation of lead into gold. Today, it's the transformation of invisible bits and bytes into communities, artwork, encyclopedias, and AI companions. For those of us who don't know our Replika from our Ruby on Rails, this modern magic can feel overwhelming, intimidating, even hostile. The solution for these feelings is often to just tune out, let our devices and websites fly on autopilot, and assume that the Computer Science Alchemists have it all under control. This choice makes sense. After all, we each only have so much mental bandwidth each day and can only choose to focus our energy on so many things.

> Most of us do not stop to ponder technology. It is something we find useful that fades to the background of our world. Yet—and this is another source of wonder for me—this thing that fades to the background of our world also creates that world. It creates the realm our lives inhabit.
>
> (Arthur, 2010).

The world has changed rapidly over the last century. While Ada Lovelace pioneered the field of computer programming back in the 1804s, roughly 90% of all the data in the world has been created in the last two years (Rafiq, 2023). You likely have more computing power in your back pocket than NASA's computers had during the Moon landing. "The astronauts had access to only 72 kilobytes of computer memory—a 64-gig cell phone today carries almost a million times more storage space" (George, 2019). Today, there are 4.95 billion internet users, and within the next five years, they'll have 50 billion internet-connected devices—from smartwatches to sex toys—with 127 more being connected to the web every second (McCain, 2023). Baby Boomers, Gen X'ers, and those who

DOI: 10.4324/9781003391128-2

are sometimes called Elder Millennials all experienced a time (longer for some than for others) in their lives before the internet. But even for those of us who are digital natives—born after the arrival of the internet and the introduction of ubiquitous technology—these numbers can be overwhelming.

Yet, when discussing technology, we're not just talking about supercomputers and social media algorithms. If we were to assume that only the most complicated processes and devices "counted" as technology, the 95% of us who do NOT work in the tech sector would feel utterly hopeless: lacking the knowledge, tools, and influence to shape the world around them and held captive to the whims of those aforementioned alchemists who decide what our social media profiles look like and how secure our health records are. Thankfully, that's not the case because each of us is already a technologist.

Christopher Roosen, the co-founder of Cognitive Ink, a human-centered research, mapping, and design consultancy, observes,

> Even the most primitive tools, like furs, sharpened sticks, fire, and roughly shaped stones represent collections of technology. This more primitive list . . . could stretch back as far as 2 to 3 million years. These earliest technologies might seem unimpressive, but they still mediate our interaction with and experience of the world.
>
> (Roosen, 2022)

Economist and complexity scientist W. Brian Arthur offers four ways to conceptualize technology:

- A means to fulfil a human purpose
- An assemblage of practices and components
- A collection of devices
- A phenomenon captured and put to use

> (Arthur, 2010)

Roosen synthesizes these into an integrated definition that will inform our understanding of technology throughout this book: "*Technology is an assemblage of practices and devices, available to a culture, that captures a phenomena, putting it to use to achieve some purpose*. This aggregate definition clearly includes the ancient, like a drinking gourd; to the modern, like a microprocessor" (Roosen, 2022, emphasis in original).

You don't have to know how to code a website, build a data center, or even reset the time on your microwave to be able to own your power as a technologist. If you've created a spreadsheet, you have done some computer programming. If you've set up an automatic bill payment through your bank, you've created an algorithm. If you've connected your phone to your digital doorbell or your printer to your home Wi-Fi, you've built a small computer network. Much of what we talk about when we talk about tech can feel massive. After all, they're called SUPER-computers for a reason. But each of these machines and each of their component technologies can be understood by laypeople and applied to our everyday lives . . . even our sex lives!

Intimacy Drives Innovation

We can't talk about technology without exploring what drives humanity's constant need for the next different, better, cooler thing. As a species, we are constantly innovating—from clay and sticks to holograms and nanoparticles. But why? Understanding what drives this impulse can help us understand a lot about human behavior and human relationships. Is the urgency that pushes us to upgrade our cell phones the same as that which tempts us to "trade up" our partners? When technologists and digital ethicists consider this question, they typically point to four key drivers of innovation:

- Incremental improvements
- Disruptive innovations
- Institutional influences
- Organizational pressures

As our most basic technologies run through incremental improvements, new services and products become possible (Ross, 2015). These are punctuated by disruptive innovations like the user interface, the smartphone, and generative AI (Lyytinen & Rose, 2003). Remember your first BlackBerry or iPhone? The possibilities felt magical. The broader context technology is used within also provides additional innovation-drivers from broader systems like government regulations and other institutional interventions (King et al., 1994) or more localized pressures, such as corporations and companies demanding processing power for competitive advantages (Melville & Ramirez, 2008). Incremental, disruptive, institutional, and organizational pressures shape the technological world we live in. However, we believe that many researchers and scientists tend to overlook one crucial source:

- The human need for connection

Like a black hole exerting immense gravity but going unseen, this primal human desire drives, shapes, and reshapes our technology.

For reasons both obvious and mysterious—explanations variously cite the work of Newton, Freud, and Beavis and Butthead—sex has had a peculiarly creative impact. . . . Sometimes the erotic has been a force driving technological innovation; virtually always, from Stone Age sculpture to computer bulletin boards, it has been one of the first uses for a new medium.

(Tierney, 1994)

From the telegraph to video calls, from the airport to the Internet, technology over the last century has had a theme of

> bringing people closer to each other or making the world a better place to live in common. With technological advances, however, humans must be aware of their responsibilities. Anything related to the use of technological inventions that will affect their lives is, therefore, a side effect of their full realization and desire to evolve.
>
> (Zhang, 2022)

It is not hyperbole to compare our innovative impulses to an evolutionary urge—specifically, the mating ritual.

Sociologists who study cultural evolution have explored how humans compete for partners and how their sexual and relational priorities shape not only their relationships but society as a whole. They describe this primal competition for companionship as mating games.

> There are many different ways of categorizing these games: some contests are overt, some masked; there are games played by the population as a whole, and there are niche games; there are games of chance (poker, lottery, dice) . . . of skill (running, chess, soccer) . . . of simulation (role-playing) . . . to mention just a few.
>
> (De Block & Dewitte, 2007)

Historian George Basalla ties this same desire for competition and play impulse to the creation of technology as well. What he describes mirrors De Block and Dewitte's description of cultural games of skill, describing technology innovators as gaining "much satisfaction from solving the puzzles they encounter, overcoming the challenges set before them, and pitting their intellects against the nature and human competitors to win" (Basalla, 1988).

In other words, if technology is a competition, our primal drive for intimacy and connection determines the winners. What does this look like in practice? Let's take two examples. In the early 1980s, there were two video formats: Betamax and VHS. Both were introduced in the mid-1970s, and competition was fierce. Betamax was widely regarded as the better format, and yet VHS won (Raustiala, 2018). This market victory has been attributed, in part, to the desire for adult videos and the ease with which camcorders allowed content creators to produce sexy VHS tapes, both for home use and for distribution in stores. Sony (creator of Betamax) prohibited this use for their products and thus sealed their fate

(Coopersmith, 2000). A similar story played out in the 1990s between Prodigy and AOL. Prodigy was arguably the better online experience for users; and, noticing it was families purchasing the service, decided to enforce a family-friendly content policy. AOL allowed adult content and access to the then-wild Internet. By 2001, Prodigy was acquired by SBC and faded into obscurity. "Many people believe that AOL triumphed over Prodigy because of Prodigy's refusal to allow sexually oriented chat rooms or sexual content" (Roberts, 2001).

If Betamax and Prodigy seem like dusty examples, consider Tumblr. The website came into prominence for sharing art, ideas, and interests (Raustiala, 2018). Google Trends show the peak interest in Tumblr, the golden years, from 2012–2017. In 2018, Tumblr enacted an adult content ban to increase advertising revenue. Tumblr's new rules led to 30% of the traffic dropping in the first month. This only continued as people left for websites like Pillowfort and Deviant Art. Google Trends shows interest in the website has remained at the lowest levels for several years. In 2023, the then-CEO Matt Mullenweg shared that Tumblr lost $30 million annually. Another innovative idea crushed by going against our human needs, perhaps.

Tumblr, Betamax, and Prodigy are all real-life examples of how the evolutionary desire for connection (and to be frank, sex) has influenced our cultural progress. But these natural laws aren't the only forces at work. In the tech sector, there are three that have been used to conceptualize the rapid pace of innovation today. First, Moore's Law says the number of transistors in a computer chip doubles every two years. Next, Gilder's Law tells us that network bandwidth triples in pace with Moore's Law. Finally, Metcalf's Law came in, claiming that the value of a network would be proportional to the square of the number of nodes on the network. We know . . . that last one is quite a mouthful! And as the industry has advanced, not all of these laws held. But it is undisputed that computing and networking have gotten faster and cheaper, year over year. As they have, the value of networks like the Internet and social media have also rapidly increased.

Moore's Law, Gilder's Law, and Metcalfe's Law have created new resources to tap to satisfy our basic needs. These are the incremental improvements that lay the foundation for disruptive innovations, which companies take advantage of for competition and which governments follow behind to govern. For example, "the ability to harvest and analyze large datasets enables streaming platforms to make informed decisions about what content to produce, distribute, and promote" (Raustiala & Sprigman, 2019). Take Aylo. Formerly MindGeek, the company is behind such websites as PornHub, RedTube, and Brazzers. Aylo uses data from billions of views to understand consumer preferences, enabling it to produce highly targeted content. This data-driven approach allows Aylo to take creative risks and optimize viewer engagement. Integrating Big Data analytics into its business model, Aylo has set a precedent for other industries, including mainstream entertainment.

Firms like Aylo understand the competitive advantage that comes from better satisfying human needs. We see this reflected in the adoption of human-centered design. This is a product philosophy of placing people first; their needs, preferences, and their experiences are central to the development of interactive systems (Putnam, 2016). Specifically, human-centered design considers engagement and emotion (Bannon, 2005) which is achieved through user interface and user experience (UI/UX) innovation (Djamasbi & Strong, 2019). Interfaces can drive up engagement. Experiences can evoke and amplify emotions. Companies continue to produce products better and better attuned to our primal needs, aligning with our expectations and natural behaviors.

Are we using our technology, or are our technologies using us?

Everything Is Eroticized

Now that we understand how and why sexuality drives innovation, let's take a look at the long history of this phenomenon across human history. . . . Beginning at the very start with mankind's most primitive form of technology: the manipulation of the natural world. From sharpened hunting sticks to wheels carved from stone, humans have taken whatever materials existed around them and transformed them into weapons, tools, and, yes, even sex toys.

> In the history of human inventions, this is one of the oldest and longest-enduring tools. At our current estimate, the oldest known dildo dates back to at least 28,000 years ago. It was discovered by a team of researchers from Türbingen University in 2005, exploring the famous Hohle Fels Cave (near Ulm in Germany's Swabian Jura region). . . . Archaeological discoveries in Eurasia have revealed the existence of suspected dildos that date back to 40,000–10,000 BCE.
>
> (James, 2023)

Using the Hohle Fels discovery as our starting point, let's travel approximately 500 kilometers northeast to Dresden, where one archaeologist found the world's oldest pornographic statues.

Clay—Germany (7200 BCE): Researchers from the Archaeological Institute of Saxony discovered a small clay statue depicting a male figure from the waist down, which they named the Adonis of Zschernitz. A month later, they found a matching female figure. "Adonis is bent forward, and the female figure is bent forward even more. It is strongly believed that the figures were copulating, with the man standing behind the woman. The intent of the sculpture is not established, whether it was for religious or ritualistic purposes or as a means of storytelling or home decoration. This is considered the oldest representation of a man having intercourse with a woman" (Manne, 2019). Dr. Harald

Stäuble, who led the discovery, explains, "these figurines are not stylistic, but realistic. They open up a gateway for historians and anthropologists to discuss whether sex was really a taboo subject in the stone age" (Diver, 2005).

Pigments—Pompeii and Herculaneum (740 BCE—79 CE): A wide variety of artworks—frescos and pottery, mosaics and sculpture—depict the full spectrum of sexual diversity. Images featuring gay/lesbian sex, oral and anal sex, group sex, and more are incredibly common. These are not considered to have been prurient images, hidden away from the delicate eyes of "mainstream" society. Rather, these explicit images decorate homes and the exterior walls of businesses and appear on tokens used at brothels ubiquitous throughout the ancient cities.

Bronze—China (206–220 CE): Bronze strap-on dildos are discovered in the tomb of a king from the Han Dynasty. "They were all definitely made for use, and we can speculate based on their various bases how they were worn. They're all bespoke, and the ones we have here might have been laced into place with leather or silk thongs, though it's not clear if they were designed for men or women" (Waugh, 2017). Anal plugs carved from jade were also discovered in this same trove but seem to have been used more as embalming/funerary devices rather than sex toys.

Stone—India (885–1000 CE): The Kandariya Mahadeva Temple is one of several sacred sites within the Khajuraho Temple Complex. Built during the Chandella dynasty, the complex contains temples belonging to two religions—Hinduism and the Jains. The Kandariya Mahadeva Temple is world renowned for its carvings depicting all matters of erotic activity, from impressively gymnastic partner sex through zoophilic horse orgies, with every possible iteration in between. There are many lovely explanations for why the temple complex features such explicit imagery. Some say that the carvings were a form of sex education for the devotees who came to worship. Others say they are intended as good luck symbols—a tangible wish for the visitors to be blessed with pleasure and ease. There are also more religious interpretations as well. "One of them speaks about leaving your lust and desires behind before entering the temple—which is probably why there are no carvings of sex inside the temples . . . Perhaps you can attain nirvana, once you are done with all your worldly pleasures" (Sharath, 2016).

Parchment/Vellum—Western Europe (1100–1600 CE): Before the invention of the printing press, books were copied word-for-word by scribes, typically affiliated with the Catholic church. Some religious orders dedicated their lives to the reproduction of sacred texts—with weeks of full-time effort devoted to each volume. "A single room of the monastery, called the scriptorium, acted as the workshop for scribes and was usually isolated, mandatorily quiet, and uncomfortable. Monks who worked under these conditions frequently suffered from acedia, a 'foul darkness' that causes the affected to act anxious, apathetic, and hopeless, 'as if the sun was too slow in setting'—in other words, clinical depression" (DABL, 2016). It's no wonder that so many religious texts of this period contain a wide variety of marginalia—small decorative or satirical art sketched in the margins and interwoven into the letters—of the books themselves. Today, we ascribe a high degree of piety to those who—like a monk—devote themselves to a life of religious service. But in the Medieval Ages, religious orders were more akin to a 21st-century non-profit organization: their members ran hospitals and schools, administered social welfare programs, and sometimes aided the local military. Young people who entered a religious order did not always do so out of religious devotion—many were forced into religious life by the need or the circumstances of their birth. This explains why so much of the marginalia we have from this period—even in prayerbooks, Bibles, and other sacred texts—contain illustrations of nuns "plucking penises off a phallus tree . . . a nude bishop chastising a pooping cleric" (Oatman-Stanford, 2014), vulvas aplenty, and lots of explicit fantasies featuring the clergy themselves. Parchment and vellum were too costly to waste entirely on these images. However, with the arrival of the printing press, technology would finally move these silly, sexy, and incredibly explicit doodles onto paper, out of locked libraries, and into the hands of everyday people.

The Printing Press (1450): Often, when we think of the printing press, we tend to think of Johannes Gutenberg. He is the person most of us were introduced to in elementary school as the inventor of the moveable-type press. However, since this chapter is about technological innovation, we want to give credit where credit is due. While carved woodblock printing had existed for several centuries before Gutenberg, what many do not know was that movable type printing—invented in 11th century China and refined by a Korean civil minister named Choe Yun-ui in 1230 AD (Newman, 2019) predated our friend Johannes by approximately 150 years as well! We likely remember Gutenberg and not Choe due to the geopolitical situation at the time: "Notably, Korea was under invasion, which hampered their ability to disseminate their innovation. In addition, Korean writing, then based closely on Chinese, used a large number of different characters, which made creating the metal pieces and assembling them into pages a slow process. Most importantly, Goryeo rulers intended most of its printing projects for the use of the nobility alone" (Newman, 2019). Because of these factors: the relative stability in Europe at the time, the burgeoning movement, inspired by early religious reformers, towards empowering the masses, and the comparable simplicity of the English alphabet created a moment in which Gutenberg's press could take off in a way that Choe's did not. And with the printing press came . . . porn. This led to a social shift as well. Unlike Pompeii, where erotica was the cultural norm, India where it was used as a form of spiritual encouragement, or the chained libraries of the church where it was used to fill time and pages, mass-produced erotic engravings were quickly popularized and just as quickly punished. "Even though Catholic Church clerics commissioned erotic works for their own pleasure, they considered sex and nudity taboo in the dangerously sharable format of print. When provocative illustrations began to circulate widely, the church stepped in" (Palumbo, 2019). Artwork considered lewd was collected and destroyed, and the engravers and writers who produced it were imprisoned. Art historian Andrea Herrera explains that "it was the transition from the highest rungs of society to a broader public that was the cause for concern among the private elite circles of humanists as well as Church clerics" (Herrera, 2018). Unfortunately, it was impossible to put the genie back in the bottle, and within a century, inexpensive, explicit art and writings were proliferating—including Marcantonio Raimondi's 1524 booklet *I Modi*, which depicted 16 partnered sexual illustrations for anyone who had the coins to purchase it and the 1680 book *The School of Venus*—an illustrated sex manual considered the first popular pornographic book.

Photography (1822–1860s): Photography developed (pun very much intended) in France in the early 19th-century. Nicéphore Niépce captured the first photograph in 1827—a process that took eight hours to produce a single image. Within a decade, daguerreotype had reduced this down to just a few minutes, and the medium exploded. While photographs of themselves were still a luxury item for consumers, images of others—including pornography—quickly took off. The sale of erotic images helped fund many early photography studios through the use of artists' models (a common profession in the flourishing art community). However, by 1855, the use of registered artistic nudes had been banned, and the production of explicit photography went underground, even as the popularity of "French postcards" exploded. The moral distinction between photographed nudity versus nude painting and sculpture persists in many places to this day.

The Telegraph (1837–1844): The idea of communicating via electrical impulse was explored by many worldwide, and an early proto-telegraph existed in France as early as 1798. While dozens of inventors attempted to perfect this concept, it was Samuel Morse's model that took off in the mid-1800s. By 1864, Western Union controlled over 44,000 miles of telegraph wire, and the telegraph had become the primary form of communication for those separated by distance. Telegraph operators—skilled workers trained in sending and translating the Morse code telegraph messages—suddenly had access to a great deal of information about their customers and neighbors that would have previously been sent via private letters or personal messages. With the rise of rapid, long-distance communication romance scams and early catfishing schemes appeared. Telegraph operators themselves would flirt with colleagues across the wires or conspire to play matchmaker between their customers. "The telegraph has been called the Victorian Internet. The journey of an email as it hops

Read *Wired Love* on Project Gutenberg here

from server to server mirrors the passage of a telegram from one telegraph office to the next. It allowed people to communicate instantly across great distances . . . A technical sub-culture with its own customs and vocabulary was established. You got hype, skepticism, hackers, online romances, chat rooms, information overload" (Petty, 2017). This "high-tech" subculture went fully mainstream with the publication of Ella Cheever Thayer's *Wired Love: A Romance in Dots and Dashes*, a novel set in the world of telegraph operators, with saucy dialogue spelled out in morse code within the book.

The Telephone (1876): Alexander Graham Bell patented his telephone in 1876, and within a year, Betsey Craddock had not only become both the world's first telephone operator but also the pioneering foremother of phone sex. "She would often talk to customers about how she was unbuckling her shoes, or how her hair felt free from a tight hat she had just taken off. Betsey became the first real sex operator and made millions during a famous six-decade career" (Boudoir, 2024). By 1918, phone sex hotlines were being directly advertised as a service, and by 1920 they had been banned. That ban was formally revoked by Franklin Delano Roosevelt in 1934 but has existed in one form or another ever since. In 1977, Gloria Leonard, adult actress and publisher of the adult magazine *High Society*, had an idea: she would record synopses of each upcoming issue, and readers could call in to listen . . . for a small fee. And the modern 900 number was born. "By the spring of 1983, the line was receiving more than 500,000 calls per day . . . Not surprisingly, the U.S. government perked up its ears. In 1983, the FCC confirmed that no federal law prohibited phone sex. But in 1988, Congress passed the Telephone Decency Act, which criminalized using a 'telephone . . . directly or by recording device' to make 'any obscene or indecent communication for commercial purposes to any person'" (Buck, 2017). It seemed that phone sex might be going the way of Raimondi's engravings, but within a year, the U.S. Supreme Court had ruled that "while Congress could bar 'obscene' calls, it had no power over 'indecent' material" (Buck, 2017). While phone sex hotlines are less popular today than they were in the 80s and 90s, many still exist today focusing on unique fetish markets—reminiscent of Betsey Craddock and her unbuckled shoes—and bring in millions of dollars each year (Kaplan, 2021).

Motion Pictures (1908–1970): You might be picking up on a pattern here. One where a new technology emerges, people eroticize it, and a backlash ensues. When most people think of pornography, they tend to think of video, so, it probably doesn't surprise you to read that this has been the rhythm of the film industry as well. Louis Le Prince recorded the first motion picture (which might be described as a family home video) in 1888. Less than a decade later, in 1895, Louis Lumière released the first commercial short film. And in 1906, the first pornographic movie, a short silent film called *Swimming Forbidden*, debuted. This set off an avalanche of cheaply made explicit vignettes that could be seen in nickelodeon machines placed in saloons, brothels, and boardwalks around the country. Imagine standing in a crowded room and pressing your face into a brass viewfinder to watch a short pornographic filmstrip, surrounded by people who knew *exactly* what you were seeing. By the 1940s and 50s, it was possible to purchase reel-to-reel "stag films" through the mail and under the counter. Often illegal under both the federal Comstock Law as well as a patchwork of local obscenity laws, they were wildly popular and featured fetish performers and strip tease acts and were regularly viewed at bachelor parties and fraternal organizations around the country. In 1969, the Adult Film Association of America was formed, and a period known as the Golden Age of Porn began. Adult movie theaters popped up, and mainstream cinemas screened "prestige" erotica like *Deep Throat, Behind the Green Door*, and *The Devil in Miss Jones*. For a moment, it seemed that porn had truly gone mainstream, but the AIDS epidemic and a backlash against the free love sexuality of the 70s brought the moment to an end. In 1984, the San Francisco Department of Public Health sought to close fourteen bathhouses, bookstores, sex clubs, and movie theatres—ostensibly to curb the transmission of a terrible new virus. One San Francisco regular described this decision as "like shutting off the internet today. Our lines of communication in the war on AIDS were severed here in this city. The solutions were in our faces . . . information, condoms, sanity, but (the Mayor) exercised her power from the basis of her fear, interests, and prejudice . . . AIDS awareness and prevention efforts lost out, but we lost more" (Trout, 2021). While the stigma experienced by erotic minorities such as queer folks and kinksters would continue into the present (we'll talk more about erotica in the modern era in Chapter Four), there was one small consolation: just as the era of public porn was coming to an end, home video cassettes were being introduced, allowing anyone with roughly $25 and one of those fancy new VCR machines to watch all manner of delightfully prurient material in the privacy of their own homes. This was a revolutionary innovation for those who often risked violence or arrest to see themselves and their desires represented on screen. What was lost in collective engagement was gained in personal safety—and that was a trade-off that made sense to many who enjoyed porn.

Try Softporn
Adventure
online here

Video Games (1977–Today): Speaking of revolutionary new home electronics, the late 70s and early 80s ushered in the age of home computers and video game consoles. The Kenback-1 home PC and the Atari 2600 were both released in the 1970s and within a decade, interactive adult software had hit the market. While Atari led the industry in bringing video games into the home, they didn't start releasing sex-themed video games until 1982 . . . a full year after a title called *Softporn Adventure* came out for the home computer in 1981. Advertised as a "computer fantasy game . . . in which players seek to seduce three women while avoiding hazards, such as getting killed by a bouncer in a disco," *Softporn Adventure* was notable for featuring Roberta Williams, one of the world's first female game programmers, naked in a hot tub on the cover (Nooney, 2014). In 1987, *Softporn Adventure* was re-designed and re-titled as *Leisure Suit Larry in the Land of the Lounge Lizards*, launching a bawdy (and rather misogynistic) franchise whose most recent title was published in 2020. From old-school consoles to modern VR-powered immersive environments, "sexcapade" games have been with us all along.

Read the ISO standards for intimate products here

A Brief History of the Future

Earlier in this chapter, we posited five underlying drivers of innovation: incremental growth in our materials, disruptive ideas, institutional and governmental pressures, organizational demands, and our human psychology and physiology. We looked at over two thousand years of technological innovation and the near-immediate "sexification" that followed. But that was the past. Let's look ahead at what the next twenty years may bring should these same trends continue:

We'll see material advancements across all domains. Computing will evolve beyond the transistor, entering the quantum computing era. Connectivity will evolve beyond 5G, making today's speeds look like yesteryear's dial-up Internet. The material world will similarly evolve, as we combine traditional materials with nanoparticles to achieve new composites, becoming more programmable as the programmable world becomes faster and better connected. As these technologies become more immersive and widespread, industries will be revolutionized and reimagined. It's easy to say the future will be more of the present, only faster. But remember, incremental improvements create the opportunity for disruptions.

AI and machine intelligence will build upon these new capabilities, likely combining several currently separate algorithms and techniques. We may see Artificial General Intelligence (AGI) capable of performing tasks that require human-like understanding and decision-making. We can expect Brain-Computer Interfaces (BCIs) to enable direct communication between the brain and external devices, creating new ways to interact with our technology and our environment. At speed and scale, AGI and BCI enable personalization in ways never before seen in everything from entertainment to relationships to healthcare. Other disruptive innovations will occur, things we cannot fathom today that will be possible due to the depth, accuracy, and velocity of information capture of everything we do and think.

This will have legal ramifications. How can it not? Institutions will adopt new digital governance models. As these innovations become more integral to society, new regulations will emerge to address ethical concerns, privacy, and the digital divide. These changes aren't happening in isolation but in the broader context of environmental changes in the coming twenty years. Policies and innovations aimed at combating climate change will drive the development of renewable energy sources, smart grids, and carbon capture technologies. Given the high environmental cost of today's generative AI (Bender, 2021), it is unlikely governments won't put constraints on these future technologies in much the same way that, in earlier centuries, governments restricted pollution from manufacturing.

Companies will continue to strive for market dominance. Directly, this fight will be applying human-centered design and better, richer, faster analytics. If we're unable to find better economic engines than advertising, then cynically, we can imagine our technologies getting even better at monopolizing our attention and converting our time into product sales. Optimistically, this will lead to better products as the Internet leaves the ad-driven days behind. Smart manufacturing—the integration of IoT, Big Data, AI, and robotics—leads to efficient manufacturing processes, making affordable hyper-personalization possible. The interfaces to our devices and products will, through better design, become more intuitive and foster emotional closeness for richer experiences.

What does intimacy mean in this future? Or when everything is tailored specifically for our personality, history, and at-the-moment needs? Will we become ever more selective and pickier about our partners? Polyamory may be the norm, and that norm may include people, AGI companions, and virtual partners. These companions will likely include robots providing physical intimacy and emotional connection tailored to individual desires and preferences. For the humans in our lives, BCI opens new avenues of intimacy and redefines sexual encounters. Immersive experience (augmented reality or virtual reality) will open new ways of meeting, dating, and more. As intimacy becomes more mediated by technology, the issues of privacy, authenticity, and ethical use will become critical.

Making predictions is risky. In the late 20th century, the flying car was a common trope in science fiction. It made sense. In six short decades, from 1908 to 1969, we went from horseback to automobile, from airplane to a rocket on the moon. At that pace, a flying car seemed within reach in twenty years. Futurists failed to account for innovation curves, hidden costs, and other obstacles. We've gone from dial-up internet to a highly connected society where apps, phones, and devices dominate our lives. It's reasonable to assume that we'll have human-level machines in the near future. Or perhaps these will be as fleeting as the flying car.

In the next twenty years, one thing is certain. Technological advancements will reshape human intimacy in ways we can only begin to imagine. While these innovations hold the promise of deeper connections and enhanced emotional experiences, they also present significant ethical and societal challenges. Navigating this future will require a careful balance between embracing new possibilities and preserving the essence of human relationships. Luckily, the rest of this book is here to help provide a roadmap—outlining both the pitfalls and likely benefits of technology—to help guide you on this journey.

TECH ED WITH WOLF
THE EARLY INTERNET, WEB 2.0 & WEB 3.0

TechEd Class: What Is the Web?

The WorldWideWeb (W3) is a wide-area hypermedia information retrieval initiative aiming to give universal access to a large universe of documents. Everything there is online about W3 is linked directly or indirectly to this document.
—Tim Berners-Lee, the very first Web site.

The history of the web is the history of people using emerging technologies to carve out personal rights. This began before the first webpage when the personal computing revolution launched in the 1980s. Personal computing was, well, personal. Put the technology, previously only available in well-funded corporations and universities, into everyone's hands. The promise was technology making people better and freer. This translated directly into the emerging networks on which the Internet and the Web were built in the 1990s.

Web 1.0 was about personal access to information. Every piece of knowledge would be linked and accessible to anyone with Internet access. Information wants to be free was the hacker mentality back then. The free and open-source software (FOSS) movement also began at this time. It was a heady feeling, removing gatekeepers and increasing access. There was a sense that many of our underlying problems would be solved when people had equal access to education and computing. The early Web reached for this promise with a document metaphor. Everything was a page. Every page was linked. Ideally, every page was open to everyone. This would lead to problems in relationships and sexual expression. For example, if everything was open, there isn't an assumption or even a mechanism for privacy. What information should be free? How do we determine the difference between accurate information and disinformation? The optimism of Web 1.0 led to overlooking potential bad actors and bad actions.

If Web 1.0 was about increasing individual access to information, Web 2.0 was about increasing individual access to produce and share information. Starting in the 2000s, social media platforms emerged. The traditional gatekeepers of publishers, newspapers, television, and even radio were pushed aside by tools and websites that enabled people to directly create and share content. Web 2.0 empowers people to engage in conversation and express their opinions. As more of the world joined the Internet, the Web moved from being a solo experience like reading to being a collaborative, communal experience. Our optimism was fueled by changing people from passive viewers to active participants, reshaping culture, democracy, and our institutions. What if everyone was free to share an opinion, what was to stop people from bullying each other? And by whom and how would facts be arbitrated? Rather than bringing people together, social media often creates echo chambers. Sometimes leading to hate groups.

Moreover, the shift from Web 1.0 to Web 2.0 included a shift from universities to corporations. As corporations needed to make money from their audiences, there was a rise in advertising and collecting data on user behavior. Monetizing the Web had the unfortunate side effect of increased surveillance. "If you aren't paying for the product, you are the product," became a common saying describing corporate control of our online spaces. Then in 2008, the Global Financial Crisis (GFC) would further shake people's confidence in large organizations and corporations. Specifically with banking, hackers and technologists alike began conceiving of decentralized ways to replace centralized financial institutions. This led to Bitcoin and Blockchain, which would become the foundations of Web 3.0.

Web 3.0 is about increasing personal control over the fundamental components of the Web. As I'm writing this, Web 2.0 is still very much the world we live in. Web 3.0 is still emerging and slowly being adopted. People should be able to conduct financial transactions between each other with privacy and autonomy. When we create content, be it an image or video or some writing, it should only be readable to those we allow. Any one of us should be able to control what data organizations have on us and revoke that control that consent at any time. Smart contracts would automatically take action to protect the person based on negotiated and agreed-up terms. While Web 1.0 lacked privacy controls and Web 2.0 lacked consent and moderation, Web 3.0 should be consent-based and privacy-first.

You won't be surprised by what I say next. This optimistic take hasn't played out so nicely. Cryptocurrency, so named because of the cryptography behind systems like Bitcoin and the use of these systems as currency, was overrun with scams. Smart contracts and images in non-fungible tokens (NFTs), pitched as our control over our content, were abused in auctions and scams in the early 2020s. This has soured many on the promise of Web 3.0.

The World Wide Web has undeniably improved humanity in three short decades. Information is available like never before, and people can learn new skills and better themselves. Barriers to entry have been lowered, both for consuming and creating content. People are more connected, productive, and able to find each other and themselves. However, it is important to remember that the underlying security controls are often a reaction to risks, not proactively built into the Web. The open information movement didn't consider personal privacy. Social media didn't consider disinformation. The majority of users didn't consider the impacts of harassment the minority would face. And so on, and so on. Specific to sexuality, this pattern of build-first and secure later creates many of the problems we see today with the World Wide Web. Anonymity enables romance scams. Free information lets stalkers find and harass people. Revenge porn wouldn't be possible without content controls and without people being able to post and share content. State surveillance of contested health decisions, from abortion to transgender care, is enabled by data initially gathered for advertising purposes. Blackmail and coercion are made easier with cryptocurrency bypassing financial controls. We've torn down the gatekeepers, only to realize some gates must be held. There's also a deeper problem. By appealing to the individual and driving towards increasing personal freedom, the Web created a situation where these problems are often blamed on the individual. If we personally raise concern about any of the above, the response is often "don't use the technology." Don't want your images shared on a revenge porn website? Don't sext. Alternatively, we're prompted to set our security and privacy settings. (Never mind that there are often dozens of settings across hundreds of apps with descriptions that confuse even the most technically minded person.) An emphasis on individualism lets technology off the hook for failing to provide a safer experience collectively.

Back when the personal computer revolution was heating up, and the Web was science fiction, author William Gibson defined cyberspace as "a consensual hallucination experienced daily by billions of legitimate operators in every nation." The shared experience defines the Web for its estimated five billion users. Gibson was prophetic. Except for the first part. As we continue to work on Web 3.0 and as we can anticipate a Web 4.0, to fulfill the promise cyberspace has to offer, the consensual aspect must take the forefront.

Expert Consult: Byrony Cole

Bryony Cole

Bryony Cole, the world's foremost authority on Sex-Tech, explores how technology influences our most intimate moments. Known for her top-rated podcast "Future of Sex," she advises governments, tech giants, and entertainment leaders on emerging Sex-Tech trends. Cole also founded Sextech School, a pioneering pre-accelerator program, now in its 17th cohort, guiding hundreds of entrepreneurs and innovators in the sexual wellness and technology space. Her innovative research and international hackathons have garnered recognition from events like SXSW, WebSummit and Founders Forum. Featured in the *New York Times*, *Vogue*, and *Wired*, and seen on Netflix, Bryony's work empowers women and redefines the future of sexuality. Today, "Future of Sex" is a central media and resources hub for the SexTech industry. Her vision is to create a world where technology enhances human connection, and she actively works towards this by shaping policy, fostering innovation, and advocating for sexual well-being.

How would you explain SexTech to someone who's new to this field?

Sextech is any technology designed to enhance sexuality. When I'm talking about sexuality, I'm talking about *everything*—not just orgasms, but everything that falls into this big sexuality bucket: education, health, crime and violence reporting, medicine, gender identity, assault of reporting, pain, pleasure, relationships, porn, dating; and how they all intersect with technology. Everything from sophisticated technology—AI and robotics, mixed realities, VR AR, all the good acronyms—right down to simpler technologies like websites, apps, even lubes! Technology being a tool that allows us to go from A to B. With that definition of technology as a tool, the oldest form of SexTech would be the stone dildos being uncovered in caves, made tens of thousands of years ago. In that sense, SexTech is not new. It's been around for a while.

Can you explain what you do and share how you got started in this field?

Like many of us in sex tech, I wear a lot of hats. I come from the tech startup world. I worked in enterprise tech, at a company which was bought by Microsoft. I experienced both the scrappy startup life and the scale of a corporate giant. But I wanted to do something more creative and closer to the humanities. I thought I might become a sex therapist, but the qualifications would take a decade—and I wanted to get moving faster. I started out as an industry analyst, looking at how companies were applying technology to sexuality. I interviewed 100 people about sex and technology. That became the "Future of Sex" podcast, and I found this incredible group in New York called Women of Sex Tech.

That convergence of interests, timing, and location led me into the field. At first, I thought the podcast would be the main thing, but I became more engaged with conferences, speaking, and getting paid to talk about sex tech. That lasted until the pandemic. Once the speaking gigs dried up, I launched an online course, which became Sex Tech School. We're now on our 17th cohort. It's global. The space has grown enormously.

Today, I'd say I'm more of a spokesperson for the industry, advocating for founders and those starting businesses. I also run Sex Tech School, where I help guide people who are just beginning their journey. I sometimes serve as an educator, and I've done podcasting—though less so now—and I'm moving more into consulting with larger companies and coaching founders one-on-one. Founders in this space often come with an idea and are trying to bring a product or service to life under the SexTech umbrella. That could be anything from a sex education app to a new vibrator to something like a sexual wellness product. Some are creating physical products, others services—often digital or app-based. They're typically launching their own thing, not joining a company, and many are hoping to earn revenue and attract investment.

What makes you passionate about this work?

It's the people. For me, sex tech has never really been about the technology; it's about the human side of it. Human behaviors fascinate me, and I'm drawn to how tech intersects with our lives in deeply personal ways. I recently spoke with the team at Polari Labs in the UK about their new product for anal douching. The issue they're tackling—messiness, STI spread—is often felt as a very personal, even shameful, experience. But their work reframes it as a solvable problem that affects millions. That kind of "aha" moment, where someone realizes they're not alone and then builds a solution, is so compelling. And now, with the rise of AI and its impact on intimacy, there's no shortage of topics. It's never boring.

Tell us a bit about the lifecycle of a new sex tech product (toy, app, etc.).

There's a pretty common pattern we see at Sex Tech School. It starts with a deeply personal experience—painful sex, a lack of education, or something transformative—and that leads to a product idea. The first prototype is usually rough. Emily Sauer, who created Ohnut, a product to reduce penetration depth? Her original prototype involved putting donuts on her boyfriend's penis. It eventually evolved into a successful business. But after that initial excitement, founders often hit barriers that aren't covered in typical startup books. Because it's a taboo topic, they run into resistance from banks, CRMs, email services, and manufacturers. These systems label sex tech as high-risk. You might be able to open a bank account one day and have it shut down the next. Email platforms ban you for adult content. Even manufacturers may refuse to work with you. Funding is another huge hurdle. Investors might pass on an idea simply because they find the topic uncomfortable, even if they like the product. I've heard stories where someone's pitch gets rejected because an investor says, "I have daughters—I can't invest in that." So, success often comes down to persistence—fighting for two years through constant setbacks just to get to market.

Why are people embracing technology as a form of intimacy-building?

Because it's easy and convenient. And because technology can take on so many roles. With AI, we're seeing the rise of digital companionship: AI partners, therapists, confidants. People are also turning to tech because of physical limitations—whether due to aging, disability, or mobility challenges. It's also about fantasy. Tech lets us explore scenarios and experiences we might never access otherwise. Humans are incredibly curious, and we have this instinct to eroticize everything. Tech has always promised to extend our minds, our bodies, our experiences. So there's this natural curiosity about what it can do for sex and intimacy. Whether it's putting on a VR headset or using a teledildonic toy, we're using tech to explore consciousness and pleasure in new ways.

What do therapists, educators, and others working in the field of sexual health need to be thinking about when they're talking about sex tech with their clients?

We need to acknowledge both the potential and the risks. There are ethical questions, especially around AI companionship, that we don't fully understand yet. For younger generations who won't know a world without this technology, we need to create educational frameworks. We didn't do great with porn literacy—many people still don't understand how it shapes expectations and self-image. I don't want us to repeat those mistakes with AI intimacy. Therapists and educators should lead this conversation. They should help define what that curriculum looks like. It doesn't have to be fear-based, but it does need structure—some kind of scaffolding for understanding these relationships with technology. We also need more collaboration. A lot of founders have deeply personal stories but little background in business or sex education. Sexologists and therapists could play a huge role in product development—acting as advisors, reviewers, or team members. Apps like Shambhavi or companies developing new sex ed platforms need that expertise. It's a huge opportunity for meaningful impact.

What should consumers look for when they're considering adding a new technology to their intimate life? Are there specific "clues" (materials, ver-biage, use cases, etc.) that can help them parse out the safe sex tech from the unsafe?

Tech literacy is a big issue right now, and it affects everyone. We need to ask the same questions we would with a new partner: What am I hoping to get out of this? What's my intention? What are the risks? There are broad red flags like poor privacy policies or unclear data handling. But also, you need to consider how the product makes you feel. Is it expanding your experience or becoming a crutch? Is it aligning with your values? It's less about checking off specific materials or keywords and more about being self-aware. Ask yourself: Am I okay with the data I'm sharing? Am I in control of how I use this? We need to port over the curiosity and intentionality we bring to real-world relationships into our tech use—especially in intimacy. I talk about this concept of *thrutopia*—where the future isn't a utopia or a dystopia, but somewhere in between. That's probably where SexTech lands too.

Where do you see the future of intimacy + technology heading? What makes you nervous? What excites you?

It's *thrutopia* again. Some of it will be amazing, some of it will be difficult. AI is already reshaping our relationships. A year ago, I said that in two years everyone would have an AI companion, and it's starting to happen. My hope is that we use AI as an *enhancer* of relationships, not a replacement. I worry about losing the spontaneity and mystery that make human connection so magical. We're also seeing a conservative wave that's stifling progress—sex education, business regulations, cultural backlash. But at the same time, that resistance is fueling passion. Founders are even more committed to pushing through and building something better. There's promising movement in areas like midlife and menopausal health, where sex tech is finally getting attention. Supplements and longevity-focused products are growing. But the tech is evolving fast—faster than ever. It's exciting and terrifying. And yes, it does feel like a punk rebellion sometimes—like we're claiming our space and pushing back against systems that want to shut us down. That's energizing.

Chapter 2

Passwords and Privacy

A Brief History of Privacy

Different cultures have differing definitions and expectations of privacy. We apologize to our international reader; this section will be slightly more U.S.-centric due to both the space constraints and the authors' nationality. That said, it is a reasonable thing to say that the American understanding of privacy impacts American innovations. Much of the modern technology (computers, communications, consumer electronics, and content) discussed in this book was designed and developed in the United States, with manufacturing and assembly predominantly occurring in Asia. (Moschella, 1997)

The story begins in the late 18th century during the early days of the United States. Privacy was a relatively limited concept firmly rooted in our physical environment. There was a strong belief in the sanctity of one's home and property. This was tied to the broader Enlightenment ideas of individual rights and liberties, as championed by philosophers like John Locke, who emphasized the protection of life, liberty, and property as fundamental rights. The Fourth Amendment's protection against unreasonable searches and seizures was framed as protecting individual freedoms to material goods. This thinking would begin to shift with the introduction of the Postal Service.

The mailbox and Postal Service initially introduced and later reinforced an expectation of privacy and confidentiality (Igo, 2018). A sealed letter could travel safely across the world without being tampered with, opening new avenues for people to communicate personal information. As personal disclosures have long been a technique to increase intimacy, the mailbox quickly became a tool for establishing and deepening relationships. Sometimes, what we'd call erotica today was exchanged between partners. The law would catch up decades later. The Comstock Act in 1873 made it illegal to send any "obscene, lewd, or lascivious" materials through the mail. This resulted in postal authorities scrutinizing private letters and packages, significantly undermining the confidentiality people had previously associated with the postal system. This is an early example of a recurring pattern in history. A new technology emerges. People erotize it, finding

DOI: 10.4324/9781003391128-3

new ways to flirt, court, and connect. A resultant moral wave goes against this trend. The government extends and expands its powers to bring the seemingly lewd behavior under control.

The so-called Victorian Internet provides an example (Standage, 2014). The telegraph, which came into general use in the mid-19th century, and the telephone, which followed shortly after, provided early communication networks. Ostensibly, these messages were exchanged between the sender and the recipient. The professional ethics of telegraph operators emphasized the importance of discretion and confidentiality. Privacy had business ramifications, too, as the reputation for trustworthiness distinguished telegraph services. But wiretapping, a military practice that began during the Civil War, found new uses by law enforcement agents, private investigators, and even press reporters.

The telegraph and the telephone disrupted traditional notions of privacy. In a century, the idea went from private property to private thoughts. Technology made our communications both accessible and vulnerable and sparked a rethinking and re-examination of privacy. (Igo, 2018). This thinking settled into the consciousness, driven forward in part by sexuality. The origin of the American constitutional right to privacy was set with Griswold v. Connecticut (1965) when the Supreme Court ruled that married couples could use contraceptives based on the "right to marital privacy." *Roe v. Wade* (1973) was the next step in the process, linking privacy to reproductive rights and setting a precedent for individual freedom and autonomy. This happened within the global context of the United Nation's Universal Declaration of Human Rights (1948) with its protection that "No one shall be subject to arbitrary interference with his privacy, family, home or correspondence, nor to attacks upon his honor and reputation." (Note that correspondence has joined home and property here, building on the earlier debates on letters and telegrams.) A series of 20th-century laws codified and reinforced various aspects of privacy as the American civil rights movement went into full swing.

And just as Americans were finally getting a grasp on a shared expectation of privacy, reflected by both international and national law? The stage was set for the Internet Age. The first mouse was clicked in 1965. Douglas Englebart's Mother of All Demos laid the groundwork for the 1968 computer revolution. The first word was sent over the Internet in 1969. Only a few years later, in 1973, in a story often told yet hard to prove, Stanford University students would send a text-based drawing of a naked woman to researchers at the University of Utah on that same early Internet. The early foundations were being laid.

It is important to note that an ongoing argument in America is who deserves privacy (Igo, 2018). In *Bowers v. Hardwick* (1986), for example, the Supreme Court found the right to privacy did not apply to homosexuals. This occurred during the AIDS crisis (1981–1996), where stigma contributed to the deaths of unknown numbers of men and women. Privacy was viewed as a privilege of the middle and upper classes, with little relevance to minorities and the marginalized. And yet? The privacy that the internet allowed opened new spaces for gender, sexuality, and relationship minorities to find each other—safely within their own homes and to rebuild the community that was rapidly being ripped away by reactionary responses to HIV.

"On the Internet, nobody knows you're a dog." Emblematic of the early Internet during the late 20th century, this was the caption of a *New Yorker* cartoon. This also meant that, on the internet, nobody knew your skin color, your gender identity, your sexual orientation, or your erotic preferences. Web 1.0 was about increasing individual access to information while increasing privacy through anonymity. And for a moment, at the end of the century, it seemed that technology would finally put us all on an equal footing. We'll leave the history there on that optimistic note.

The Psychology of Privacy, Part 1

In 1968, seminal legal scholar Alan F. Westin posited a taxonomy of privacy that he described as the Basic States of Individual Privacy. These included **Privacy**, the ability to detach ourselves from other people and be alone; **Intimacy**, the ability to have relationships with close friends, partners, family members, and colleagues without others intruding; **Anonymity**, the ability to move or act freely without being recognized by others or identified by our actions (Westin, 1968); and **Reserve**, which "involves individuals guarding against unauthorized access by controlling . . . the personal information they reveal or withhold" (Psychologs, 2023). Thirty years later, another attorney—this time Jerry Kang at UCLA—defined privacy as

> a union of three overlapping clusters of ideas: (1) *physical space* ('the extent to which an individual's territorial solitude is shielded from invasion by unwanted objects or signals'); (2) *choice* ('an individual's ability to make certain significant decisions without interference'); and (3) *flow of personal information* ('an individual's control over the processing—i.e. the acquisition, disclosure, and use of personal information').
>
> (Solove, 2006)

When we are doing privacy education presentations, we use a much simpler definition:

> Privacy is what allows us to thrive and grow as individuals, separate and distinct from our partners. Privacy is a right that allows us to set and maintain healthy boundaries.
>
> (Goerlich, 2022)

Boundary setting is just as important in digital relationships (including the relationships we have with our devices!) as it is in any other setting—from relatives to sexual partners. However, as a culture, we are still catching up to what this should look like in online spaces.

A need for privacy is hard-wired into us; the evolutionary memory of times when exposure—to the elements, predators, or other groups—could mean death.

> Ancient humans needed personal space to perform various tasks—from caring for their own bodies to crafting tools or nurturing offspring. The ability to retreat into a private space provided safety and security, reducing the risk of theft or aggression. This concept of privacy as a protective barrier against external threats has persisted through the ages.
>
> (Powell, 2023)

When we are deprived of privacy, the impact on mental health can be severe. Stress levels and anxiety increase (Huber, 2018), we experience a loss of individuality (Erickson, 2019) and a pressure to conform to social expectations (Jourard, 1966), lack of trust and genuine intimacy in personal relationships (FHEHealth, 2023), mistrust in the government and institutional systems (Geiger, 2018), and a concurrent feeling of helplessness and lack of control (Anderson & Raine, 2020). When Amnesty International surveyed young people between the ages of 13–24, that feeling of powerlessness was a significant theme. Seventy-five percent of Amnesty's survey respondents felt forced "to choose between the perceived threat of social exclusion or signing up at the cost of their privacy" (Amnesty International, 2023). This forced choice between connection and surveillance now exists for people of all ages across the lifespan.

Cradle-to-grave Surveillance

When we think about privacy, we typically assume a degree of empowerment and choice. We assume that there is a degree of freedom and agency in what information we choose to share and what we keep to ourselves. After all, the most popular social media sites give users a wide range of privacy customizations. On Facebook, for example, "Users have their profiles set to different accessibility levels, they are in contact with friends on Facebook, and they can see the activities of a user on Facebook depending on the accessibility levels of the user's profile" (Zlatolas, Welzer, Hölbl, Heričko, & Kamišalić, 2019). We've got privacy settings that keep those close to us well informed, limit the access casual acquaintances have to our daily lives, and lock out strangers and higher-risk others entirely. Problems solved, right!? Yes . . . if the problem is "how do I limit the information other users can have about me?" If the goal is to limit the amount of information collected about me entirely? We have a slightly bigger issue.

Imagine you are eighteen years old. You're heading off to college and are eager to make new friends and possibly even find a romantic partner as you start your new adult life. So, you download the latest dating app—Bumble or Hinge,

OKCupid, or even Feeld—and you create your profile. You upload some flattering photos, answer the prompts about your interests, desires, goals, and quirky personality traits, and publish your profile for others to review. It doesn't take long before you start getting pings from other users and within a few months, you have met your perfect match. Your new partner proposes a year or two later, and you happily accept. You want to share your wedding updates with those who love you, so you sit down together and create a new online profile—this time on Zola or The Knot. You share the link with your friends and family, ensuring your profile is connected to your wedding registries and venues. After the big day, you use Wedibox, Kululu, or WeddingWire to gather the photos your guests took at the reception and share the portraits provided by your photographer. Everyone, from your Great Aunt Sarah to your boss's former intern, Alyx, tells you how much they love seeing your smiling faces.

You want to enjoy your honeymoon without worrying about starting a family too soon, so you download Clue, Flo, or Luna to track your menstrual cycle and ensure that you're monitoring your fertility. Being able to communicate with your partner about what days are better for sex and which days are more likely to result in pregnancy becomes helpful a few years down the road when you may begin to plan for a family. Thanks to the history of consistent cycle-tracking you've been doing, conception occurs quickly, and now you and your partner need to prepare for a new, tiny human to enter the equation.

Pregnancy can be an incredibly difficult time, and you both take great comfort in the educational resources and community support you find on What To Expect, Peanut, and BabyCenter. It is important to be able to monitor your future child's daily progress, from frequency of kicking to expansion of belly size. When they arrive, BabyTracker and GlowBaby help you and your partner stay on top of feedings and diaper changes, sleep cycles, and growth spurts. As Tiny Human grows up and enters school, you and your partner find apps like Cozi and Maple to help you stay on top of household chores, pediatrician visits, and grocery lists.

As your child grows up, you and your partner agree that you want to limit their screen time and keep them off of social media and other apps. However, by second grade (age seven in the U.S.) their school requires families to use PowerSchool to access information about homework assignments, grades, class events, and school announcements through the app. The school district posts announcements and broader community information via Bloomz, and the teacher requires that all communication be sent via Klassly. By middle school (age 11–13) your child is sending and receiving links to TikTok videos and Instagram posts, even though they do not have accounts on these platforms themselves (as far as you, the parent, know).

As you and your family members age, you experience the same health and well-being issues that impact everyone. Your doctor uploads the records of your annual physicals and well-child visits to your patient portal through a service like FollowMyHealth. When your family loses a grandparent for the first time, you and your child can access therapy through TalkSpace and a peer-to-peer grief support group through GoodGrief and Actively Moving Forward (AMF). As your child grows up and departs for college, you and your partner reconnect with one another as a couple through app-based tools like LoveNudge and Paired. As *you* age, your now-adult child can leverage tools such as Caring Village and CarePredict. Finally, seventy years after you left for college and began this journey, you pass away peacefully at home, surrounded by those you love most. Your partner and child mourn your loss and use EverLoved to communicate your funeral arrangements to others, to gather their memories of your life, and to share your eulogy and burial information with others. From the cradle to the grave, the minute details of every aspect of life are uploaded, curated, shared, and collected. While we might be the ones downloading each app or creating each profile, we are not the ones who own the data we enter or decide where that data goes.

The Terms of Service for many apps allow them not only to collect the information you're providing as a user but also to sell the data they collect to third parties such as advertisers, fundraisers, political parties, law enforcement agencies, and various governmental entities. And the information they do *have* is not limited to the information we knowingly *share*. NYU's Information Technology department describes several of these more subtle data collection points:

Device Identifiers: Apps can track your device through unique identifiers such as International Mobile Equipment Identity (IMEI) or Advertising ID for mobile phones and Media Access Control (MAC) address for network devices.

Cookies and Tracking Pixels: When you use a web-based app or visit a website, cookies may be stored on your device to track your activity. Similarly, tracking pixels embedded in emails or web pages can track user interactions.

GPS and Location Services: Many apps request access to your device's GPS and location data to provide location-based services. This information can be used to track your movements.

User Accounts and Social Media Integration: Apps often require you to create user accounts or sign in through social media platforms. This allows them to track your activity across different devices and platforms.

Analytics and SDKs: App developers often integrate third-party analytics services and software development kits (SDKs) to gather information about user behavior, demographics, and device characteristics.

Permissions: Apps request various permissions to access features and data on your device, such as contacts, photos, and microphone. While these permissions are often necessary for app functionality, they can also be used for tracking purposes.

(NYU, 2024)

How each human interacts with technology, not only in what they voluntarily post but where, how, and on which devices, regardless of their privacy settings, creates a constellation that becomes infinitely more unique than a fingerprint or DNA sequence. A strand of our DNA might reveal our hair color, gender, and propensity towards glaucoma. Our digital footprint—particularly in the form of the metadata described by NYU—reveals everything to those who know how to interpret it.

> Metadata is just as intrusive and, in some instances, can be considered more intrusive than content data. The value of metadata has far surpassed that of content data given the volume of metadata and its ease of access by both public and private sectors. Specifically, greater protections in law are afforded to content data, leaving metadata more accessible to public and private sectors, with a few exceptions (e.g. depending on the data sought from companies, government agencies need a subpoena or court order to access this data; warrants are only needed if content data is sought). The reality is that the metadata, when aggregated, is far more revealing than content data. Content data may reveal a fragment of an individual's life at a particular date and time, whereas the metadata collected, stored, analyzed and disclosed about an individual can create a detailed map of an individual's personal life.
>
> (Mara & Wandt, 2019)

The Psychology of Privacy, Part 2

In 1791, philosopher Jeremy Bentham designed a new kind of building he called the panopticon—designed to allow all inmates within a given institution (prison, asylum, etc.) to be monitored by a single guard without allowing any one individual to know if they were being watched at any given moment. This ambiguity was itself a form of control. While the guard could not physically surveil every resident at once (they still only have one pair of eyes, after all), the possibility that one *might* be being watched led the prisoners to behave as if they *were* being watched, creating a culture of paranoid conformity. As Michel Foucault explains it, "the major effect of the Panopticon (was to) induce in the inmate a state of conscious and permanent visibility that assures the automatic functioning of power" (McCullen, 2022). After twenty years of thinking of the internet as a tool: something we pick up and put down as we need it and decide when and how to use; we are slowly waking up to the ways in which our data-driven lives have become self-constructed panopticons complete with all the carceral-state implications of the original design:

> Private companies in the United States not only enable mass surveillance of the population because of their collection of vast quantities of individuals' data but also engage in this form of surveillance by aggregating and analyzing the data they have and continuously monitoring people to glean more information about them. This mass surveillance occurs to construct profiles

of people, learn about their preferences, habits, and purchases, and use this information to conduct targeted marketing campaigns designed to get the customers/consumers to make more purchases that benefit companies. The data harvested about users can and has been used for criminal justice purposes as well. Particularly, law enforcement agencies have sought and obtained data from medical devices, alarm systems and fitness trackers, among other digital devices, for use in criminal investigations.

(Mara & Wandt, 2019)

Thinking about digital boundary setting not only as a practical task (like locking our car doors or double-checking that we've turned off the stove after dinner) but also as a protective factor for our mental, social, and relational well-being is a crucial mindset shift that we are only just now beginning to explore as a society. Controversial NSA whistleblower Edward Snowden said:

Privacy is what gives you the ability to share with the world who you are, on your own terms . . . and to protect for yourself the parts of you that you're not sure about, that you're still experimenting with. . . . What we're losing is the ability to make mistakes . . . to be ourselves.

(Desta, 2016)

And yet, so many of us chafe at the privacy basics that can ward off threats to those most personal aspects of ourselves: 36% of adults tell researchers that "they never read a company's privacy policy before agreeing to it" (Auxier, et al., 2019). Eighty-nine percent of people understand that reusing passwords puts their security at risk, (Stouffer, 2023) but only 12% say that they switch passwords between accounts (LastPass, 2022). Seventy-seven percent of consumers agreed that tools like password managers and multifactor authorization (MFA) are easy to use (LastPass, 2022), and yet "38% of password users believe that . . . MFA makes their life too difficult" (Stouffer, 2023), and only 36% of people actually use these tools to protect themselves (Ponemon, 2020). Why are we so resistant to taking steps that we know intellectually are both simple to do and vital to implement?

Psychologists who study resistance have identified the "Four Faces of Resistance." These are Reactance, Distrust, Scrutiny, and Inertia (Knowles & Linn, 2004), each of which evokes their own specific cognitive reactions. Let's take a look at each of them in brief:

Reactance is a term coined by Jack W. Brehm in 1966 to describe his theory that resistance to change is caused by a perceived threat to one's freedom of choice. "When a person senses that someone else is limiting his or her freedom to choose or act, an uncomfortable state of reactance results, creating motivation to reassert that freedom. This externally provoked contrariness initiates oppositional feelings and behaviors; the reactant person likes the forbidden fruit even more, and finds ways to enact the banned behavior" (Knowles & Linn, 2004). Reactance evokes the cognitive response, "I don't like it!"

Distrust arises when someone is given guidance or instruction from a source they don't know or find suspicious. Most people are wary about new processes, technologies, or changes, and this natural hesitancy can burgeon into full-grown distrust (or paranoia) when they don't feel that they have sufficient information to understand the why behind the change or the benefit of the new process. Distrust's cognitive reaction is "I don't believe it!"

Scrutiny is a form of resistance in which the proposed new process/change is accepted on the surface but rejected in favor of the status quo when examined with a fine-tooth comb. Someone being asked to adopt a passwordless system within their group practice, for example, might accept that this is a great idea on the surface but get so lost in the comparison of the selected password-less product's drawbacks versus the potential benefits of its competitor that they resist ever actually implementing the new system at all. Scrutiny combines the "I don't like it" and "I don't believe it" mindsets into one seemingly rational yet still resistant response.

Inertia, the fourth face of resistance, is best explained through its companion cognitive response: "I won't do it." It's not that inertia is opposed to change or suspicious of the motivations behind the new system. Inertia simply . . . won't. It has a pace and a routine that works for it and is unlikely to choose to break this pattern, even when the benefits are clear.

Each Face has its own specific pathway towards overcoming the resistance, predicated on framing privacy protections in a way that speaks to their unique needs and concerns. You might recognize yourself—or a client or colleague—in one of these faces. Thankfully, cybersecurity strategist Lourdes Turrecha offers us a new way of conceptualizing privacy that we can use to push back on these resistant tendencies. For our distrusting responders, Turrecha suggests framing *privacy as secrecy;* for the scrutinizers, *privacy as control;* for those experiencing reactance, *privacy as power;* and for those who simply don't want to move, *Privacy as integrity* (Turrecha, 2021). What does that mean in practice for privacy to be a form of integrity? Let's take a look.

Privacy in Glass Houses

"All my information is out there so why even bother," people sometimes say to us. Why indeed?

In two short decades, we went from "nobody knows you're a dog" on the Internet to everyone knowing your breed, appetite, and habits. It is tempting to say that privacy is dead. But then, it wouldn't be the first time. Privacy died in the 1860s when wiretapping of telegraphs came to light. It was said we lost our privacy when mail started being intercepted in the 1870s and again with photography in the 1890s. Privacy died several times in the following century due to telephones, government surveillance, and the rise of personal computers. *The Death of Privacy* was declared in a book published in 1969. At the time of this book, privacy again is facing significant challenges due to emerging technology at a time when we look with nostalgia at previous centuries.

Never stop believing in privacy. Never stop fighting for privacy. Every significant technological and sociological change led to us rethinking privacy. We went from property to correspondence to personal decisions. Now, the current battleground is privacy for our behavior. We are able, even today, to personally make small changes and collectively to make systemic changes. Privacy need not die on our watch.

When determining what changes should be made, you should begin by defining what acceptable privacy is for you. This can be framed as a question of personal boundaries. What associations, friends, relatives, or coworkers would you want to be kept private? What thoughts and feelings are you alright sharing, and which are you not? Which of your correspondence (postal mail, email, text messages, chats) should remain private? What about your beliefs? Decisions? And what about your personal data? Simply thinking through various types of information and communication channels can give you a quick gut check. Don't forget about private property, too. You may find that there are more things you want to keep to yourself than you initially thought.

The next step is to figure out what could go wrong and what to do about it. Within the cybersecurity domain, this is called threat modeling (Shostack, 2014). Shostack offers us a four-step process:

1. "What are we working on?" Sharing our family vacation with close friends.
2. "What can go wrong?" Someone who's not our friend sees we're on vacation and burglars our house.
3. "What are we going to do about it?" Well, perhaps we set our vacation trip to private, or perhaps we lock down our social media, or maybe we share it only after we get home.
4. "Did we do a good job?" After making these changes, we check to make sure no one can view our photos except those we allow.

Following this process opens the door to many other actions we can then take. We may use aliases instead of our real names on public accounts. We can limit the profile information to not share our location or birthday. We can configure privacy settings on our social media accounts or create new accounts for different audiences. If we're blogging, we might selectively censor what we share in our articles. We can crop our photos to not share information that might give away our location or hide our kids' faces. We can also regularly clean up old posts, emails, or accounts to reduce the amount and type of information we may have left open in the past but that no longer fits our newly established boundaries.

When we find websites with our personal information, we have a few options. If we have an account, regulations like the General Data Protection Regulation (GDPR) and the California Consumer Privacy Act (CCPA) mandate the "right to be forgotten," and most sites have the option to delete all of our information stored there. Services like DeleteMe (https://joindeleteme.com) can automate the removal process for others, like telephone or real-estate directories.

When it comes to keeping our behavior private, things often get trickier and more technical. Some websites and services allow you to opt-out of data collection and targeted advertising. For others, services like the Network Advertising Initiative's opt-out page or browser extensions can be used to block online trackers. We can also use privacy-focused Web browsers and Web-based search engines, like Brave and DuckDuckGo.

The above also applies to clinicians, of course. Our threat model is different, however. What can go wrong? Stalking, protesting, harassment, and violence towards clinicians when those clinicians are from a marginalized group or are serving a marginalized group, such as transgendered therapists (Shipman & Martin, 2019). Moreover, clinicians must balance being accessible to existing and potential clients (by phone, by email, by office location) with their need for privacy. For that reason, we may want to use professional privacy services. Black-Cloak (https://blackcloak.io) and Hush (https://www.gohush.com) are examples of these. It is possible to reduce the information out there to a manageable level, though, with requirements for licensure, it is impossible to opt out entirely.

The NPI (National Provider Identifier) license requirement is a good case study in changing risks and views of privacy. The NPI is a single identifier for every healthcare provider in America. It was mandated by the Health Insurance Portability and Accountability Act (HIPAA), and the NPI requirement went into effect between 2005 and 2007 (Pickens & Solak, 2005). The purpose was to streamline services, and NPI required, among other things, the place of work to be listed. The office or practice location wasn't a private home in the 2000s, and less than 5% of people worked from home before 2019 (Huyler, 2021). NPI was convenient for the patient, the insurer, the biller, and the license bodies.

But then two things happened. The COVID-19 pandemic meant many providers moved to home offices, along with 35% of the U.S. workforce (Bick et al., 2021). Then, there was a rise in violence against providers of contested services, such as gender-affirming care (Santoro, 2022). "What are we working on?" and "What can go wrong?" changed, and many clinicians no longer felt safe exposing their home address (where work is now often done) on the very public NPI registry.

The concern was that public information would be weaponized against therapists and doctors. For four years, practitioners across several healthcare industries voiced this concern. Then, in the spring of 2024, the rules were updated to allow a post office box or a mail service as the practice location in lieu of home offices. The collective pressure to bring the service in line with current expectations of privacy was heard.

"Did we do a good job?" is the final question in the threat modeling process. It may be too soon to tell with the NPI changes. However, it certainly is a significant step forward for American providers. But a quick Web search of our name, our home address, and other information we wish not to share can be enlightening. And disappointing. Working to keep the Internet aligned with our values and perspectives on privacy is the work of a lifetime.

TECH ED WITH WOLF
WHAT ARE KEYLOGGERS?

TechEd Class: What Are Keyloggers?

"What do you mean they can tell what I'm typing?" Something we have been asked several times during the work of Securing Sexuality. From social media sites tracking what we type (even if we don't post) to jealous spouses installing software on people's computers, this always raises the question, and it makes sense. We type some of our most intimate thoughts into our screens. Search engines know about our medical fears before our partners do. When we've got an idea or a thought, our second nature is to pick up a phone or sit down at a computer and type it up. The trouble is that this can be captured and logged.

Enter the keylogger. A keylogger is a small piece of software that records keystrokes. These then go into a log or running record that others can review. This record is often run through pattern matching to surface the good bits. For example, rather than review every single keystroke, an adversary may want to know when you've typed a password, a credit card number, or other sensitive information. Generally, there are three recognized types of keyloggers. The first works by intercepting the signals within the device itself, between the keyboard and the application. The second works by intercepting the keystrokes within the web browser. A final type, outside of the scope of this book, is used by corporations to record what administrators and privileged users type while on servers. How does it work? Well, let's get geeky.

Suppose we have a USB keyboard and a computer using a Web browser. Each keystroke gets interpreted as electrical signals on the USB bus. The operating system, Windows, in our hypothetical example, then does error-handling to ensure we haven't accidentally hit the key too many times or to otherwise handle any electrical noise. Windows then converts the keystroke into a character. In this example, we're sending the character over the Internet using a Web browser. This is done by wrapping the characters into a network traffic sent to the Web site. We're about to go one level deeper, but we're almost through the techiest part. The critical thing to know is everything done on a computer follows a similar pattern. Here, we're talking about keystrokes. The electrical signals get converted to a bit (on or off), bits get bundled into bytes, and bytes get encoded in protocols. Each time we jump from one part of the interaction to another, we decode the protocol and encode it in the next protocol. Here, we went from the keyboard (Human Interface Device or HID protocol) to Windows characters (Unicode Transformation Format or UTF-16), and then over to Web traffic (Hypertext Transfer Protocol or HTTP). The same pattern plays out whenever we're clicking or swiping or otherwise interacting with devices and apps, only the protocols and way the data flows changes.

Why is this a problem? Well, let's get back to keyloggers. We expect a degree of privacy in our conversations and in our private thoughts. We generally have a sense of whether or not that privacy is there, built up over a lifetime of experiences resting on a foundation of generational knowledge. It gets much more challenging to know whether our bits and bytes are being kept private. Ask yourself, do you have a keylogger running on your computer right now? Are you sure?

This, of course, extends beyond keylogging. Anything on computers follows this pattern. Therefore, anything on a computer may be intercepted and monitored. It could even be tampered with. For example, with keyloggers, some allow an adversary to send keystrokes as if the person at the keyboard had typed it. Keylogging can quickly become logging all facets of our digital lives. This personally plays out with partners and parents. Pitched in a variety of ways, from catching your cheating spouse to protecting your children, these applications run behind the scenes and often include keyloggers, website trackers, and more. Under the covers, they intercept the bytes to decode the protocols and store the results in logs. The result is an invasion of privacy under the guise of protecting relationships.

This isn't restricted to our personal lives, of course. The pandemic shifted many in the workforce into performing remote work. Many corporations responded by demanding increased monitoring from their employees. Some required tools to be installed on computers and phones, similarly collecting data on what people are doing. Because of corporate privacy laws, this tends to be limited to providing only the highlights (like prohibited websites or suspicious messaging). Nonetheless, many people are pushing back on employers' demands to protect their personal privacy.

The nature of bits, bytes, and protocols also makes it surprisingly easy for mass surveillance. This is playing out at multiple levels, from nations under the auspices of national security to corporations looking for an edge in advertising to local communities and citizen groups. It's a prevalent human bias to believe that more information equates to less risk. Think back to the last time you were scared about something. What did you do? We wager you picked up your phone and read everything you could. It is also very human to believe more information gives a competitive advantage. This seems to be true to a point in the human prediction and influence industry, otherwise known as marketing and advertising. At this point, you may be wondering who has the time to read millions of people's keystrokes. If so, stay tuned for our next segment on Big Data.

If you're wondering what we can do to stop this, let's work through that. The personal or professional side share something in common: someone had to install stalkerware software onto your device. Limit what software runs on your computer, and periodically check to see what's running. If you're concerned about spyware being installed, reinstall Windows (or reset Macs to factory settings) to remove all software, then add only what you need. What about passwords that can get stolen from keyloggers or other ways? Using multi-factor authentication on a device that's not your computer is the control here. That way, if someone does have your password, they cannot use it without you providing a code or making a gesture on your MFA device. MFA works so well against so many different types of attack that it is a must-have for any account. Another common protection here is encryption. Bytes encoded in protocols sent over a network or the Internet can be intercepted and read. But, what if the bytes are encrypted? Then, only those with the decryption keys can read the content. With any luck, only the intended recipient has the key; only they can decrypt and decode the bytes into keystrokes and data. The green locked icon on our Web browsers, indicating encrypted Web traffic (encrypted Hypertext Transfer Protocol or HTTPS) is something we all can look for. Using encrypted messaging tools like Signal is another. The keylogger provides a great example of the problem of privacy in the digital age. This problem is pervasive and extends to how a person interacts with a device, phone, or computer. Please remember that whatever goes digital may be intercepted, logged, and manipulated. Use MFA with passwords to limit the impact of stolen passwords. Remember that encryption means privacy. And please, for the love of all things holy, don't install spyware on the devices of your kids, your partners, or your employees. Privacy is a human right that's all too easy to undermine with technology.

Expert Consult: Jodi Daniels

Jodi Daniels is Founder and CEO of Red Clover Advisors, a privacy consultancy, that integrates data privacy strategy and compliance into a flexible, scalable approach that simplifies complex privacy challenges. A Certified Information Privacy Professional, Jodi brings over 25 years of experience in privacy, marketing, strategy, and finance across diverse sectors, working and supporting startups to Fortune 500 companies. Jodi is a national keynote speaker, host of the top ranked "She Said Privacy/He Said Security" Podcast and *WSJ* best-selling author of *Data Reimagined: Building Trust One Byte at a Time*, and she also has been featured in CNBC, *The Economist, WSJ, Forbes*, Inc., and more. Jodi holds a MBA and BBA from Emory University's Goizueta Business School.

Jodi Daniels

Can you explain your what you do to us and share how your work relates to the way everyday users experience the internet?

Data privacy is about the use and collection of personal information. This can be as simple as just a name, email, phone number or even IP address. Unlike security, it doesn't have to be two elements already tied together. It's that the possibility of them could be and therefore alone are considered personal information. Data privacy is then about how data is used. Just because it is collected does not mean it should be used and under some privacy laws that it should be processed.

A data privacy officer is someone who sets the strategy for data privacy in the organization is likely the person responsible for compliance with privacy laws. A privacy officer sits in different places depending on the culture of the organization. In some it sits in the legal function, others compliance or risk, others data or security. I work with companies to help them create and maintain their privacy program and for smaller organizations this is potentially serving as a fractional privacy officer. Companies need to build trust with customers and that trust is based on how their data is collected, used, shared and stored. This at the core is data privacy. Therefore, companies that have strong privacy programs are showing their customers they are a trustworthy brand of not only their products and services but also of their data.

What makes you passionate about this work?

I feel very strongly about the connection of trust between companies and consumers. So many companies look at privacy as just a compliance activity. Complying with privacy laws should be the foundation and where companies can start. That's not the end. Companies that understand the connection between data and trust appreciate that a privacy notice that is easy to read, a website that clearly answers what type of data is collected and how it's used and shared, gives consumers choice, and considers privacy by design in their products will have a longer lasting relationship with their customers based on trust. I love helping companies see this value and build programs that work for them. It is not a one size fits all approach and what works for one company may or may not work for another. I love educating companies on building trust through privacy, making privacy simpler to understand, and working with them on their own privacy journey.

What do therapists, educators, and others working in the field of sexual health need to know about privacy risks and ways in which they (or their clients) are vulnerable online?

Those in the medical or related field need to know that not all personal information is covered by HIPAA and that there are other privacy laws like in Washington (My Health My Data Act) that might cover that data. More importantly, no matter the size of the practice, consumers expect strong data privacy measures and to not have their data used in a manner they did not expect. It is critical that companies evaluate technology vendors, especially in the health field, to understand their security measures and adherence to privacy laws. Any tech vendor you're considering should have a privacy policy that's within the current year. It should also list somewhere on their site (often in the support section) something about their privacy and security measures. If the software vendor doesn't have a statement or seal verifying that it's HIPAA compliant? It's not a safe tool for personal health information.

There are also many technology companies that collect more data than they really should. Companies have collected data through forms and asked for more information than they need at the time of collection, because they think they might use that data someday. Some companies also use advertising or analytics pixels which can collect appointment information like doctor name, service rendered, and more and then send that to social media or advertising companies. This can be considered a data breach by sharing personal health information to a third party without consent.

What advice do you have for someone whose daily work requires them to be public facing in a way they might not otherwise choose to be?

The more public facing a provider is, the more vulnerable their website is to attack and their practice is to scrutiny. It's important to have your own privacy policy updated and strong security measures on your site. They need to find a balance between the business reason to provide information about themselves more public versus privacy concerns. We live in a world now where building a personal brand requires participation in LinkedIn, doing webinars and other public speaking all of which result in a higher public profile. You have to decide what activities you wish to participate in to drive your brand that may expose you from a privacy perspective. That is a very individual choice.

What steps can someone take to protect our privacy online, beyond the usual "protect your passwords?" What about offline privacy?

You have to change your mindset to one where the default is skepticism until proven otherwise. Make sure that you're only providing information that makes sense for the purpose you're wanting it to be used for. If a question or request doesn't make sense to you? Don't answer it. Screen the vendors and people you're interacting with and make sure they have the least amount of information necessary to accomplish the task you've set out to achieve. Use strong passwords and multi-factor authentication everywhere you can. Decide on a secret code to use with your family to avoid deepfake scams. An email you don't expect from someone you have not corresponded with in a while immediately trigger skepticism instead of excitement to click on an attachment. At the end of the day guard who and when you wish to give others, even friends, access to your digital identity.

What can everyday users do to advocate for stronger privacy protections and more safety for themselves and others?

The foundation of advocacy is educating regular people about how important their data is and what's done with it. Too many people accept the fact that there is nothing they can do about their data. Education about your data leads to empowerment and ultimately to advocacy around what third parties should collect about you and what is done about it. For people wanting to educate their kids to be smarter digital citizens, I recommend a nonprofit called Savvy Cyber Kids. I recommend that everyone read company privacy notices before sharing data with them. When there is a concern? Reach out to their privacy office—It's usually listed in the company privacy policy. Companies need to hear from individuals that privacy matters to them. It also leads to being more vocal to state and federal government about better regulations that protect individual consumers.

Chapter 3

Surveillance and Stalking

The New Domestic Violence

While "wife-beating" was a crime in all fifty states by the 1920s, domestic violence was, for the most part, an internal family issue that police were disinclined to prevent. This began to shift with the rise of the Women's Liberation Movement (Second Wave Feminism) in the 1970s when activists opened the first crisis hotlines and domestic violence shelters. By 1984, the attorney general's "task force on family violence declared that intimate partner violence was a criminal justice problem that required a criminal justice solution" (Goodmark, 2019). Ten years later, the Violence Against Women Act was passed, and the notion of abuse being something that society has an interest in preventing and prosecuting was thoroughly normalized. And yet, even with millions of funding dollars poured into prevention efforts, intervention programs, recovery services for victims, and increased prosecution of offenders, nearly 20 people are abused by their partner in the U.S. every minute (NCDAV, 2024). Unfortunately, this pattern of institutional neglect is repeating itself with the law, and public policy is failing to keep up with advancing technologies and the ways in which abusers weaponize these solutions.

In 2017, the Center for Innovative Public Health Research released a report on the prevalence of digital abuse. At that time, 12% of study respondents told researchers that they had experienced at least "one form of online harassment . . . at the hands of a current or former romantic partner. More than twice as many people, 26% had been targeted by someone else . . . (while) 14% of digitally abused individuals reported not knowing who their perpetrator was" (Ybarra, Price-Feeney, Lenhart, & Zickuhr, 2017). Within three years, the prevalence of online violence against women around the world had risen to 85% (EIU, 2021). Abusive online behaviors identified by researchers include:

- Monitoring online activities
- Monitoring text messages and phone calls
- Hate speech and name-calling
- Defamation, embarrassment, or spreading misinformation
- Doxxing

DOI: 10.4324/9781003391128-4

- Stalking
- Impersonation
- Harassment via social media or messaging apps
- Video- and image-based abuse
- Threats of violence
- Hacking

While in the past, victims were most likely to be abused by a family member or intimate partner, the rise of social media has more recently shifted the profile of abusers. Now, most victims report that they do not know their perpetrator. One crucial exception thus far seems to be the act of sharing non-consensual intimate images or videos. In one Australian study, 71% of image abuse victims reported that a current or prior romantic partner posted their intimate images, while only 16% said a stranger had shared them. Aside from partners, other perpetrators included friends and family of the victim, as well as people who are total strangers to them (Henry, Flynn, & Powell, 2019). The COVID-19 pandemic seems to have also affected the rise of this specific form of digital abuse. The UK's revenge porn Helpline reported that calls "shot through the roof during the pandemic . . . In 2019, the revenge porn Helpline worked on a *total* annual number of 1,685 cases. In March 2020 alone, it had a total of 520 cases . . .

Explore your state's cyber-safety laws here

(and) expected its monthly caseload to increase to 2,700 cases *per month* (TISP, 2023; Council on Criminal Justice, 2024). Because you don't need to leave the house to perpetrate—or to be attacked—online, digital abuse rates will only continue to rise until adequate laws are in place to protect victims.

Currently, the legal protections for digital abuse survivors are spotty. While all fifty U.S. states now have laws against non-consensual image abuse, protections against cyberstalking and cyber harassment are still evolving.

> Many states don't have specific criminal laws that differentiate between online and offline conduct. Your state may have harassment and stalking laws, but not *cyber*-harassment or *cyber*stalking laws. Fortunately, standard harassment and stalking laws typically apply broadly to communications—including online communications. In order for cyber-harassment or cyberstalking to be punishable as a criminal offense, it must cause the victim disturbance, substantial emotional distress, or place the victim in reasonable fear of death or serious bodily injury, or in fear that the same thing might happen to a member of their immediate family or an intimate partner.
>
> (PEN, 2024)

These standards can be difficult to prove to law enforcement agencies when your abuser is on the device you hold while sitting alone on your couch. Because of this, most victims of digital abuse—86%—do not report the online violence they experience to offline agencies (such as local law enforcement or their local domestic violence organization) at all (EIU, 2021).

Most victims of online abuse turn to the technology companies themselves for assistance, by flagging harassing posts and reporting the profiles of their abusers. While nearly all social media platforms have some form of Terms of Service (TOS) that users must agree to when they sign up to use the site, these can vary widely in what content they allow and what options are available to those who are being harassed or abused on their platforms. Likewise, the punishments for unacceptable conduct can range from simple removal of the offending comment to banning the abusive user from the site. The protections from online abuse, exploitation, and harassment afforded to online users are so inadequate that five of the National Center on Sexual Exploitation's 2023 "Dirty Dozen" websites are some of the popular social media platforms today: Discord (150 million monthly active users), Instagram (2 billion MAU), Reddit (1.212 billion MAU), Snapchat (800 million MAU), and X/Twitter (500 million MAU). Roblox, the popular immersive online building platform, also makes the list at 196 million MAU, with 60% of them under the age of 18 (NCOSE, 2024).

Part of the problem is that social media platforms have every incentive to retain their users, after all, user clicks on online ads drive a considerable portion of their revenue. There is no serious reason to banish bad actors. Section 230 of the Communications Decency Act of 1996 is perhaps the most essential piece of modern legislation that most of us have never heard of. Section 230 "protects internet platforms from civil liability for the content posted on their sites by users. With Section 230 immunity, online platforms have no incentive to police illegal or harmful activity on their sites" (Bokzam, 2022). One might argue that the simple solution would be to reform or undo Section 230—an argument made repeatedly and often by activists outside the tech sector. Unfortunately, this solution would have far-reaching ramifications that make it unworkable for digital abuse. The Electronic Frontier Foundation explains:

> The free and open internet as we know it couldn't exist without Section 230 . . . Without Section 230's protections, many online intermediaries would intensively filter and censor user speech, while others may simply not host user content at all. . . . Without Section 230, the internet is different. In Canada and Australia, courts have allowed operators of online discussion groups to be punished for things their users have said. That has reduced the amount of user speech online, particularly on controversial subjects, in non-democratic countries, governments can directly censor the internet, controlling the speech of platforms and users.
>
> (EFF, 2024)

Repealing Section 230 to address online abuse would be the equivalent of burning down a house because a burst pipe has flooded the basement. The flooding issue—torrents of cruelty, harassment, and surveillance—is very real, but the structure itself can be preserved. One of the most significant public policy challenges of our day is finding the balance between protecting the essential freedoms that the internet affords while simultaneously addressing the danger of digital abuse because the harm is VERY real.

The Impact of Digital Abuse

"Sticks and stones might break my bones, but words can never hurt me." We teach children this playground rhyme early in life, and yet, we know both from data and from our own experiences that words can be incredibly painful. From panic disorder and low self-esteem to substance use and "risky sexual behavior," (Armitage, 2021) multiple studies have shown that bullying has an impact not only on the social lives of young people but their mental and physical health as well. And yet, we continue to send the message that words are less hurtful than more overtly physical forms of abuse. This is not something we can dismiss as a playground concern:

> Approximately 29% of the adulthood depression burden could be attributed to victimization by peers in adolescence, and bully victimization by peers is thought to have a greater impact on adult mental health than maltreatment by adults, including sexual and physical abuse. Finally, these consequences reach beyond the realm of health, as childhood bullying victimization is associated with a lack of social relationships, economic hardship, and poor perceived quality of life at age 50.
>
> (Armitage, 2021)

People who report being bullied in childhood and adolescence are at greater risk of experiencing domestic violence/IPV compared to their non-bullied peers. Those who bully their classmates are more likely to perpetuate violence against their partners in adulthood as well (Adhia, et al., 2019). Digital abuse "grants potential anonymity to the aggressor, which can correspond to a diminished sense of prosocial remorse and the inability to avoid attacks without fully detaching from online media" (Schonfeld, McNiel, Toyoshima, & Binder, 2023).

One of the classic examples of how IPV perpetrators abusers control their victims is surveillance/monitoring of the abused partner, following them, demanding that they check in or report movements to them, and leveraging information gathered from others to create an atmosphere of all-seeing, all-knowing omnipotence within the relationship (Fontes & Miller, 2022). The internet, smartphones, and easy access to affordable geolocation tracking services, such as Apple Airtags, have brought bullying home from school, allowed the abusive partner unprecedented access into their victim's private lives, and expanded the geographic reach of abusers across the lifespan. Digital abuse is described as "degrading, embarrassing, coercive, controlling and **unavoidable**" (Urban Institute, 2024, emphasis added). As information sharing becomes normalized as a form of intimacy building, the risk of exploitation and abuse expands exponentially beyond the walls of our real-world classrooms and bedrooms. In addition to cyberbullying and digital domestic violence, more and more victims are being targeted for abuse by acquaintances or even total strangers—and the consequences are deadly.

Victims of digital abuse and online harassment are at increased risk of suicidal ideation and suicide attempts (Schonfeld, McNiel, Toyoshima, & Binder, 2023). When this abuse is sexual in nature, experiences of stigma, shame, and victim-blaming exacerbate the trauma considerably (Adler & Cooper, 2022). For those who have sensitive images shared without their consent (NCSM), victims report experiencing "both depression and posttraumatic stress (PTSD) . . . similar to the outcomes of sexual abuse. Furthermore, difficulty with emotional regulation responses is a profound outcome . . . among cyber-sexual assault survivors" (Holladay & Lardier, 2021). Unfortunately, social media and the ability to readily weaponize one's followers against a target (stochastic terror) have resulted in many cases wherein the trauma survivor did not have one perpetrator but many—sometimes hundreds. Online abuse, particularly when perpetrated by multiple abusers, compounds the trauma with feelings of hopelessness, lack of control, isolation, self-doubt, and low self-worth and self-objectification (Iroegbu, O'Brien, Muñoz, & Parsons, 2024).

> When harassment is online (it) . . . may be felt more pervasively . . . due to the permanence and speed at which online material is shared; threatening messages can be instantaneously communication through online means and sent to an unlimited number of people unexpectedly and often anonymously.
>
> (Iroegbu, O'Brien, Muñoz, & Parsons, 2024)

This rapid spread of abusive information and exponentially increased harassment has been referred to as doxxing, dogpiling, and in some instances, "being cancelled."

Doxxing, Dogpiling, and Cancellation

These are the stories whispered in fear around the modern campfire: doxxing, dogpiling, and cancellation. Doxxing involves the malicious act of collecting and publishing someone's personal information online, leading to a loss of anonymity and potential harm to the victim's personal and professional life. Dogpiling, on the other hand, refers to coordinated online attacks aimed at overwhelming a target with hostile comments from multiple accounts. Cancel culture subjects individuals to social and economic repercussions for their actions or statements, often seen as a form of public accountability or, conversely, as censorship. But how real are these risks, and what can we do about them?

When someone gets doxxed, someone else must spend time searching the Internet for information about them, pulling out personal data and identifying information. The resulting documents (or docs or dox) may cause the doxxed person to lose anonymity, obscurity, legitimacy, or even lose a job or competitive advantage (Anderson & Wood, 2021). Dogpiling, meanwhile, means "bombarding a targeted individual or space with ad hominem attacks from multiple accounts" (Matthews & Goerzen, 2019). We can contextualize dogpiling as a form of vigilantism or mob justice (Pantumsinchai, 2018). These often go hand-in-hand with someone getting dogpiled and then doxxed.

Meanwhile, the related cancel culture phenomenon is where individuals are subjected to social and economic disinvestment due to their writing, speech, or actions (Clark, 2020). Cancel culture is often equated to censorship and silence by the media. However, by those doing the canceling, it is experienced as an expression of agency. Those canceled are experiencing consequences of their actions, it could be argued, much the same way someone doxxing or dogpiling may feel the other party deserves it. This comparison certainly breaks down in scenarios where a historically marginalized community holds a person in a position of power (celebrities or the wealthy) accountable.

In the political landscape, those on the conservative right often express fear of being cancelled while those on the progressive left have fears of being doxxed and dogpiled. "It would be incorrect, however, to characterize doxxing as a weapon solely wielded by right-leaning groups. Although doxxing has been regarded as one of the alt-right's weapons of choice, the technique has also been employed against members of this group" (Anderson & Wood, 2021). Similarly, cancel culture isn't solely a progressive tactic. Right-wing activists have attacked

> the moral behavior of liberal icons, such as Hillary Clinton, Barack Obama, George Soros, and Bill Gates, as well as mobilizing support for US state lawmakers seeking to ban teaching of critical race theory, the Hungarian government's restrictions on homosexuality, and UK Conservative government legislation tightening protection of free speech in higher education.
>
> (Norris, 2021)

In the last chapter, we discussed threat modeling. What are we working on? What can go wrong? What are we going to do about it? And, are we doing a good job addressing the threat? There are three aspects to consider when thinking about what can go wrong. The first is the motivations of the adversary. With doxxing, for example, common motivations include silencing or controlling the target, as well as retribution or extortion (Anderson & Wood, 2021). Cancel culture is often driven by demands for accountability, moral outrage, and collective expression of values (Clark, 2020). The next question is the likelihood of the risk scenario. The conversation around cancel culture tends to be based on anecdotal evidence and high-profile cases, making hard numbers difficult to come by. For doxxing, around 4% of people in a recent study reported being personally attacked (Sheridan, 2024).

The final question is one of impact. Understanding the motivations, likelihood, and impact behind these threats is crucial for developing effective safety planning and coping strategies to mitigate their effects. We need to identify warning signs that a crisis may be developing. Other than waiting to see it in our email or on our socials, how will we know if we're being doxxed, dogpiled, or canceled? We need internal coping strategies. Perhaps it is as simple as unplugging or just setting our accounts to private. The authors know someone who went through online dogpiling and took a week online sabbatical to let it blow over, spending their nights with friends. On occasion, we may need professional support. There are helplines and resources available, depending on the situation. Additionally, we can work with our company's HR (especially when the online attacker contacts our offices to get us fired). By giving cursory thought to these ahead of time, we can form a simple crisis plan for scenarios that are likely to occur and would be impactful. These steps are more manageable if taken earlier and before an online attack, and by doing so, we have created a more private presence on the internet.

Protecting Yourself from Online Harm

Technology and laws don't necessarily work in our favor. Search, online advertising, and Big Data collect much more about our activities than we often know. Data brokers regularly package and sell our personal information (ironically, advertising our names and tracking our visits all along the way). Social media incentivizes us to share, speak up, and engage. This provides the materials for those seeking to stalk, dox, or cancel us. When adverse outcomes do occur, the law is often silent or powerless.

So, what can we do? Begin by doxxing and canceling yourself.

There are several guides out there on doxxing (Henry, 2014). Use them to have a sense of what others may find, look at your social media accounts, email addresses, domain names, and physical addresses. Check your voter records, court records, and other criminal databases. For cancel culture, find any of your posts that might be misconstrued (this sometimes requires another person's eye, as we often give ourselves the benefit of the doubt). Be as harsh on yourself as someone who would be going after you. From there? Identify those things that attackers would take advantage of and then seek to have them removed.

A note here: This is a form of self-censorship. On the one hand, it is appropriate to be mindful of what we put out to the world. On the other hand, self-censorship out of fear comes with its own consequences. If Internet vigilantism has a chilling effect on our speech and behavior, has it won? The solution to this won't be found in these pages. For now, the aim should be to seek a healthy balance.

When we find data, we can request it be taken down. In many cases, this will be handled as most Website administrators, online services, and data brokers are good operators. It may be difficult, labor-intensive, and it may take a long time (Take, 2022). The Internet continuously collects data from various sources (government records, social media, data brokers, searches, and more). This perpetual collection makes it difficult for us to achieve a final state of privacy because new information is always being added, and older information often resurfaces. But at least in most cases, if we can navigate the instructions or if we have subscribed to removal services, most will remove it. *Most*.

Hunter Moore is an example of a bad operator. As covered in the documentary, *The Most Hated Man on the Internet*, Moore launched a revenge porn website in 2010. Ostensibly, people angry at their exes (predominately women but not only women) could seek revenge by posting explicit photographs. The website would then map those to the woman's social media profiles and, sometimes, to their home addresses. When these women complained and asked for their information to be removed, Hunter Moore would publicly taunt them on the website. Because he wasn't the one posting the content, Section 230 protected Moore from prosecution. It wasn't until the FBI proved some of these photos were obtained from criminal hacking into women's emails that Moore was stopped (Wikipedia, 2024).

Sometimes, removal is complicated by the website's purpose. Take websites where sex workers share and rate their clients, often referred to as "john boards" or "escort review boards." These sites allow sex workers to communicate about their experiences with clients, providing a platform for mutual safety and information sharing. Unfortunately, some have submitted images of exes or people they are harassing to these websites. As you might imagine, these websites aren't set up to determine a legitimate takedown request versus an actual bad actor trying to hide their behavior.

Self-doxxing and self-canceling will increase your safety and reduce the likelihood and impact of online attacks. But they won't provide complete coverage. It would be best to assume that attackers will try to break into your accounts. To thwart that, use unique passwords (and possibly unique email addresses) for each website and service. If this is beginning to be too much to remember, use a password manager (popular ones include 1Password, Dashlane, and LastPass) to keep track of your accounts. Enable MFA wherever possible, preferably with a phone app (such as Duo Security, Google Authenticator, or Microsoft Authenticator). If a phone-based MFA isn't available, use your phone number. This is easier to break into than phone apps, but significantly stronger than no MFA at all.

You should assume attackers will try to break into your devices. Keep your phones, computers, and Internet routers up to date with the latest software and patches. Wherever and whenever possible, set these to automatically update. In the case of smart appliances, thermostats, doorbells, etc., use strong passwords, MFA where possible, and apply patches. (Anecdotally, abusive spouses have taken control over the home temperature and monitored cameras from the doorbell.) Remember to change the home Wi-Fi passwords when people no longer need access, such as at the end of a relationship.

Generally, as we've seen with Big Data and revenge porn and everything in between, the legal protections are behind the ability technology when it comes to scammers, stalkers, and other bad actors. We can wait for better technology; secure-by-default, with higher levels of privacy, better moderation, trauma-informed reporting mechanisms, and more. Some companies are prioritizing consent, safety, and responsiveness in their products and integrating tech abuse considerations into conventional security practices (Penzeymoog, 2021). But it's far too few. Another path is to wait for regulators to catch up, which is where organizations such as Surveillance Technology Oversight Project's (STOP) exerting pressure comes into the conversation. There is only so much personal responsibility we can take before the need for systemic change becomes mandatory. Our proactive measures today are our shield against tomorrow's threats. While we wait for laws to catch up and technology to improve, we can take steps towards online self-defense.

TECH ED WITH WOLF
WHAT IS BIG DATA?

TechEd Class: What Is Big Data?

In the beginning, there was the ad. The ad wasn't particularly good. It was a small image with what we'd now call click bait text. "Have you ever clicked your mouse right here? You will." The ad went to AT&T and was published on HotWired's website. The year was 1994 and no one, not even the brightest of minds or the most farseeing of futurist, no one could predict where this would take us in three decades.

"Data is the new oil" was how Clive Humby summed up the shifting economy in 2006. More data meant better targeting and better messaging. By 2024, in the United States alone, Internet advertising revenues were more than $225 billion dollars. Data starts small. Small datasets are the easiest for us to imagine. Say we are doing a fundraising campaign, and we want to get the word out to donors. We can take a spreadsheet with columns like how much they've given in the past, where they're located, what they're interests are. We can sort and select who to reach out to. It's a nice tidy structured format. You can imagine similar directories for educators, counselors, and therapists. Perhaps this spreadsheet has their specialty, whether they take insurance, and if they're good for referrals. These datasets allow us to pivot and analyze, make basic decisions, and to take action. Even when small, it's easy to find the immoral uses. Add a column for religion and suddenly our small dataset is a list of Jews. Add a column for sexual preferences and we can filter out referrals to LGBTQ individuals. It's easy for data to turn toxic, even at this scale.

A database is a series of small datasets, all in tables, with neatly structured columns describing the data. Imagine a number of spreadsheets all rolled up into one unit. Now at a certain scale, as our data grows, we may need to be pulling data in from multiple databases for analysis and use. This then becomes a data warehouse, a collection of databases from multiple sources. That's often in the background of systems for customer relationship management (CRM), electronic health records (EHR), enterprise resource planning (ERP), and of course marketing databases. These data warehouses track many facets of our lives as we interact with scores of businesses and services.

Let's get bigger. In addition to demographical data, let's include all the other digital footprints we leave. Where have we gone on the Internet? Where have we been recently (as inferred by which cell towers our mobile devices have connected to, perhaps)? What have we typed on social media? What have we bought and, perhaps more importantly, what have we looked at several times but not actually purchased? There's no way we can fit that into a spreadsheet. There's no way a person or even a team could analyze all that information.

Big Data is the term for extremely large datasets that are too complex for traditional data analysis. Big Data is sometimes differentiated from data warehousing by the four Vs: high volume, high velocity, high variety, and high veracity. (The savvy reader will note that privacy does not begin with the letter V.)

Whereas our previous examples were rough approximates of what we wanted to know ("who might donate to our cause?" or "who would be a good referral for this client?"), Big Data seeks to more accurately model and predict human behavior through large scale pattern analysis.

Like oil, the data economy is as series of producers, collectors, refiners, and resellers. Data is generated by organizations and institutions through their interactions with customers, partners, suppliers, and vendors. This means the everyday activities of all of us provide raw materials to be refined and distilled. The next layer is the data brokers who collect data from various sources, correlate it, aggregate it, and resell it. You might have wondered earlier how your phone connecting to a cell tower would relate to what you purchased for lunch and who you were interacting with on social media. These are all separate companies, after all. But they often have third party agreements with data brokers to resell their data.

The data brokers buy it up, combine it, and create detailed behavior profiles. Advertisers, data scientists, and others then purchase access to this data.

By some estimates, the majority (more than 50%) of Big Data efforts are directed towards enhanced marketing and advertising strategies. If that was the only use case, it might be creepy, but it might be acceptable. After all, it's rather pleasant when our phone shows us just the right product at just the right time. Nice feature, like having a personal shopper. However. These data brokers also sell to organizations seeking to manipulate elections. But then, people have tried swaying votes for years, one might think. How about this one? Law enforcement and government agencies can buy from data brokers and effectively bypass legal protections like the United States' Fourth Amendment.

In this way, simple advertising turns into surveillance capitalism. The term, coined by Shoshana Zuboff, describes Big Data's growing use for behavior prediction and behavior modification. There are things we can do to reduce our data footprint. One of the easiest is to look at the privacy and security settings of our common apps and opt out of data tracking and personalized advertising. We can cut some of the chatter by using adblockers in our Web browser (example: AdBlock.) There are also privacy plug-ins for many Web browsers (example: Privacy Badger.) We can also use privacy-focused search engines, like Duck Duck Go, and privacy-focused Web browsers like Brave. Our Internet traffic itself can be protected with VPNs or TOR. These reduce the information on our activities going forward, but what about what's already been collected?

There is also a growing market for services that monitor the Internet for personal information and work with publishers and data brokers to have it removed. DeleteMe and Lifelock are examples here.

For executives or celebrities, there are black car versions of these tools. These reduce the likelihood of attacks like identity theft and harassment (doxing, swatting). There are also things corporations themselves can do. It begins with collecting less data and storing it for less time. If we want an age range for an analysis, perhaps ask for the age range instead of the person's birthdate. We can also push back on the idea of collecting data "just in case it matters later." For retention, we don't need to save data indefinitely, only for as long as is needed from a business and regulatory perspective. If we don't need it, don't ask for it. If we have asked for it but we're not using it, delete it. And then? Resist making third-party agreements to share information for data analytics or AI training.

The trouble with the above is that it may cut into an organization's profitability or business opportunities. For this reason, a longer-term solution must come from legal and regulatory bodies. The privacy regulations like California Consumer Privacy Act (CCPA) in the United States and General Data Protection Regulation (GDPR) in Europe are a good starting point. We will need more pressure to address unexpected Big Data like law enforcement's dragnets. That's what the Electronic Frontier Foundation (EFF) and the Surveillance Technology Oversight Project (STOP) are working on. When a graphics artist created a humble 476 by 56-pixel banner ad in 1994, when HotWired agreed to cash AT&T's check, no one foresaw the impact of advertising on society. Then the Internet scaled up and data processing sped up. Our ability to collect everything people do digitally, at high volume, and then process and analyze it, at high velocity, has made Big Data a reality. For good (thank you for the personal shopper) and for bad (please stop selling me out), Big Data is here to stay.

Expert Consult: Albert Fox Cahn

Albert Fox Cahn is the founder and executive director of the Surveillance Technology Oversight Project (STOP). He is also Practitioner-in-Residence at NYU Law School's Information Law Institute and a fellow at the Harvard Kennedy School's Carr Center for Human Rights Policy and Yale Law School's Information Society Project.

Albert Fox Cahn

You are a Harvard law graduate and an attorney well known for his work on immigrant rights. Tell us about your career trajectory and how you came to work on issues related to technology and privacy.

It really goes back to childhood. I grew up with two hobbies: protesting the NYPD and building computers. From a very young age I saw the intersection of those two worlds. But in the aftermath of 9/11 as a young protester, I saw police holding cameras and recording me, surveilling me for wanting to stand up against the invasion of Iraq. As I grew up, the technology changed by the fear grew, as I became every more certain that this type of surveillance would threaten the bedrock of our democracy. After a brief ill-fated stint in corporate law, I went to the Council on American Islamic Relations, where I was hoping to head up their New York chapter, rebuild it after a period when it had effectively gone out of business. And that job really covered the intersection of so many different types of law and activism and public policy. And I would help with immigration cases and lead work against the Muslim ban, but also was helping people whose family members were accused of terrorism or who were getting a knock at the door from the Joint Terrorism Task force. And I saw how the surveillance systems that quietly map out so many of our lives in such intimate detail, could quickly be transformed into the predicate for state violence that it was this unchecked surveillance that so often led to someone being held in that dark room at JFK or hearing the noise as their door was broken down by the SWAT team. And so, that was part of what inspired me to focus on surveillance, particularly state and local government surveillance because as a privacy nerd and an activist, I saw the amazing work that national groups had been doing to push back against the post 911 surveillance state that tracked so much of the world, but so little had been done to fight the ways that we were being surveilled by police departments that increasingly looked like many NSAs at the state and local level, particularly here in New York with the NYPD.

What makes you passionate about this work?

I feel the technology remaking our communities, moment by moment, the real time loss of the agency and autonomy that's indispensable to an open society. And I just am so deeply afraid that if we don't take action now, we will wake up in a country truly unrecognizable. But I also have this profound hope and this belief that at the state and local level, we actually can make things better in a real way, that we can take action that creates real lasting change. And that even as things remain unbelievably dysfunctional in DC, you know, there's still so much evidence that people power still packs a punch at city hall. And yeah, I really just, for me, it's like the most important thing anyone can do with their life is fight to leave their world better than they found it. And for me, I see this as the way I can sort of affect that change.

This is an area that many mental health and medical providers are already aware of, since telehealth has gained in popularity, but other than issues related to EMR's and industry-specific technology, why should therapists, educators, and others be concerned about privacy issues?

Because a lot of them are going to end up in jail. We see the weaponization of medical treatment along ideological lines, whether it's reproductive care, gender affirming care, or whatever forms of medical care that will be targeted by ideologues in the years to come. And we rightfully fear the way that this will lead to patients in prison. But oftentimes, historically, it's been providers who have been locked away when care becomes a crime. And so, this is something that impacts so much of the medical community. And when I think about the steps that people can take now to protect themselves, to protect their patients, to harden their data and really bring threat modeling into the way they approach patient-centered care, that to me is just the bare minimum for really protecting the people you're seeking to treat. If you're ignoring the threat from this sort of data collection, it would be like treating patients in the middle of COVID-19 and pretending that the pandemic doesn't exist.

How do state surveillance and data tracking relate to sexuality and mental health care?

When we see medical treatment becoming a crime, it's hard to provide treatment without recognizing the threat that surveillance poses to patients and practitioners, whether it's a patient seeking gender affirming care in a state that is trying to wall that off, or whether it's a patient seeking care that for conditions or identities that are stigmatized and marginalized. You know, we increasingly see these surveillance tactics targeted at individuals who are seeking treatment. And it's just quite clear that if you want to treat patients in a risk informed way, you have to keep in mind the risk of how your data, their data will be used. I really worry that anything that reduces the cost and inconvenience of accessing patient records will increase the potential for abuse. You know, historically, the biggest barrier to mass surveillance was un constitution. It wasn't, you know some technical barrier. It was the expense that it took to track people's locations, to track people's activities. But as location tracking and internet tracking became much more effective, much cheaper, you could see that scaled up from dozens to hundreds or thousands. And the idea that putting medical records, confidential patient information in a system where it can easily be scraped, where it can easily be analyzed, I deeply worry about how long it'll take before police and prosecutors start just using analytics tools to try to identify patients whose medical care is controversial or even allegedly criminal. And just like, as someone who's been seeing therapists for more than three quarters of my life, I mean, I just can't imagine how I could ever have an effective therapeutic environment without trust. And how could I have trust without confidentiality?

Would you consider this to be a public health issue as well as a technological concern?

Any time we make it harder for people to get care, any time we make patients feel less secure that their data will be protected, it's going to shield them from accessing care. I really think that, you know, we've seen this in past public health crises, and I'm thinking of the criminalization of HIV status in the past, how, when we treat health conditions as a crime, it drives people underground and chills access to treatment.

What steps can someone take to protect their privacy from the "Big Watchers" like Meta, Google, and the state? What about "small watchers" like surveillance apps and peer-to-peer stalker sites?

It's going to be different for everyone. My privacy philosophy is usually one size fits none, and so really it becomes an active practice of threat modeling. Going through the list of actors who might pose a threat to you and your loved ones, thinking about what data is most harmful to you and valuable to them, and prioritizing protections to really address the low hanging fruit. For some people, that may mean dramatically limiting what content they post on these platforms. For some people, it may mean you know, dramatically altering their digital hygiene practices.

Read STOP's research on the surveillance of vulnerable communities here

But I think that as long as we're putting the onus on individuals to fix these systemic structural threats to public safety and public health, that we're failing. And that's why we need to implement the source of safeguards that everyone deserves through laws, which is one giant way of saying it depends. I think that no matter what form of surveillance we're talking about, the best practices are always going to vary because the trade-offs are always going to hit us differently. I am quite public as part of my work and have to expose a lot of my information just to be vocal against the technologies and the surveillance practices I despise. But there are lots of my clients who can't be that open about how they live their lives and who aren't able to directly engage in the debate the same way. It might be because of immigration status or criminal justice involvement. It might be because of interpersonal dynamics or family situations. There's so many factors that can impact how even the silliest platform potentially impacts our privacy and what that means.

What can we do to push back on the trend towards increasing surveillance and data sharing? How can we advocate for wider change around these issues?

I always say stay local and stay vocal. There are campaigns in just about every state in so many cities pushing for laws to protect against the types of abuses that keep me up at night. We see how it just takes a relatively small number of folks raising their voices in their local communities to push through changes that can really be a matter of life and death. And so, whether it's fighting to prevent abortion surveillance, fighting against gender affirming care surveillance, fighting to block new and even more dystopian forms of tracking; there are those of us on the ground fighting each and every day, and we need their support.

Chapter 4

Pornography

The Internet Is for Porn

The year was 1959. IBM announced the IBM 1401 mainframe. It was a business-oriented computer, meant to be affordable. Though affordable those days was relative. Businesses could lease the computer for $2,500 a month ($27,000 in today's currency), or businesses could purchase an IBM 1401 for around $150,000 ($1.6 million today). It featured a printer and could be programmed with FORTAN. "The 1401 convinced enterprises of all sizes that a computer was essential to their daily operation" (IBM, 2024). This was a serious computer meant for serious business. And EDITH, one of the first computer programs ever written for the 1401 does one thing: it prints out dot matrix pin-up models (Verdiell, 2018).

Let's jump ahead to the year 1995. As described in Chapter One, Tim Berners-Lee's invention, the World Wide Web, went online in 1991. IBM released the Web Explorer browser for the OS/2 Warp operating system. Microsoft's browser, Internet Explorer, had just come out that same year. But the major player was Netscape Navigator. While these early browsers (and others) vied for dominance, the Internet as we knew it was coming into shape. Early innovators were defining protocols and standards, while early adopters were dialing in and exploring. One of the first websites launched in 1995 is online pornography: Danni's Hard Drive (Rosen, 2023).

Watch the EDITH program run on the IBM 1401

Between these two points, lots had changed of course. We went from the crude text available during the IBM 1401's heyday to the full color images available in the 1990s. A suite of techniques and technologies had to be invented. We needed a way to convert binary into visual images, work that led to pixels and image formats. We also needed algorithms and methods for compressing images so that they would fit the limited storage devices of the days, and so that they could be sent across an Internet with limited bandwidth. The creative constraints of floppy disks and dial-up modems drove many of the early work

DOI: 10.4324/9781003391128-5

into digital photography and imaging. In order to validate, compare, and contrast techniques, a standard set of images was agreed upon. It is to one of these images we turn our attention to next.

Lena Forsén was born in Sweden in 1951 and was modeling in the 1970s. Her big break came in the November 1972 issue of *Playboy* magazine. There, as a centerfold, she was credited as Lenna Sjööblom (Playboy, 1972). The photograph has her in front of a mirror, looking over her right shoulder, wearing a hat and holding a burgundy boa. It is a fetching photo and that should have been the end of the story. After all, who remembers October's or December's 1972 centerfolds? Around this time, however, University of Southern California's Signal and Image Processing Institute (SIPI) was doing groundbreaking work into digital images. The engineers were looking for test images with vibrant colors and faces. One had Lena Forsén's *Playboy*, which SIPI scanned and shared, and the rest is history (Hutchison, 2019). The Lenna test image became one of the most referenced images of all time. Researchers continued to use it as the benchmark for image manipulation until 2024, when the IEEE Computer Society decided that they would no longer accept research that used it (*The Guardian*, 2024) and Lena Forsén has been recognized by the Society for Imaging Science and Technology as "The First Lady of the Internet" (Kinstler, 2019). Every image we see on the Internet today uses techniques perfected for and optimized around a pornographic photograph, albeit a tasteful one.

This brings us back to Danni's Hard Drive and other early Internet Websites, like Sizzle or the presumably American Online (AOL) inspired Adult America and Erotica Online. While the images and videos were improving thanks in part to Lena Forsén, very little was understood at the time about how to keep a Website operational. Back then, when a Website received significant traffic, it would often simply become unresponsive. Engineers had to figure out how to optimize and operationalize everything, from the operating system to the Web server, to the pages and the images, right up to the Internet connections themselves. "Overloaded servers, difficulties with video streaming technology, credit card processing—all the problems that web businesses struggle with today were handled in short order by the adult webmasters" (Reed, 1999). Many of these problems had been previously theorized and discussed as part of the standards bodies building the foundational Internet protocols. But here was the opportunity to see this in action, where the hands-on engineering took concepts from the lab into the real world. "Although not necessarily credited with inventing these technologies, adult webmasters were the first to figure out how to put them to profitable use" (Reed, 1999). The lessons learned and shared by these webmasters make the scalable and reliable Internet we know of in the 2020s possible.

Today's pornographic websites continue to see significant traffic well above major non-pornographic sites like Netflix and Amazon (Wright, 2023).

Pornographic content makes up about 25% of all search engine requests and 35% of all internet downloads (Mahmoud, 2012). While numbers vary and it is difficult to get an exact census of the Internet, adult websites have consistently been a significant percentage of all websites on the Internet since the beginning. The public Web now exceeds a billion Websites (Internet Live Stats, 2019), owing in part to the work of early pioneers and early webmasters simply trying to share images and keep servers online.

Moral Panics and Porn Misinformation

As we've seen above, the playwrights of Avenue Q got it right when they sang "the internet is for porn." And where there is ease of access to any illicit object or substance, there are often moral and public health panics that rise up in response. The temperance movement was a response to domestic violence and child neglect, which Carrie Nation and her followers blamed on free-flowing alcohol (Masson, 1997). The AIDS crisis inspired a moral panic around free love and the perceived promiscuity of gay persons that resulted in the passage of a number of laws designed to protect children from seduction and sin (Miller & Kitzinger, 1998). More recently, anti-immigration activists have pointed to migration as an impending moral threat, accusing immigrants of everything from violent crime to subverting democracy (Walsh & Hill, 2022). But no moral issue has held the public's attention quite so long as the topic of pornography and other erotic content. As we discussed in Chapter One, explicit images have been created in every culture and every time period, for as long as humankind has had the capacity to manipulate materials. And in many instances it has been banned or burned almost as quickly as it was created. In modern times, porn has been declared a public health crisis in seventeen states (Samuels, 2020) and eight states have mandated that adult websites require users verify their age by providing identification prior to accessing explicit content (Davis, 2023).

Porn exists in every medium. Watch the first animated erotic short: "Everready Harton in Buried Treasure" released in 1930 here

Anti-porn activists have described adult content producers as racist and homophobic and as de facto sex traffickers. They claim that pornography is addictive, inspires violence, and normalizes objectification and abuse. They tell consumers that watching erotic media damages their brain, diminishes sexual function, and negatively impacts mental health and relationships (FTND, 2024). At first glance, these claims seem to mirror the classic roadmap of moral panic.

During a moral panic, then, a substantial number of the members of a given society harbor and express the feeling that evildoers pose a threat to the society and to the moral order as a consequence of their behavior, and therefore 'something should be done' about them and their behavior. A major focus of that 'something' typically entails strengthening the social control apparatus of the society—tougher or renewed rules, more intense public hostility and condemnation, more laws . . . If society has become morally lax, a revival of traditional values may be necessary; if innocent people are victimized by crime, a crackdown on offenders will do the trick; if the young and the morally weak, wavering and questionable and dabbling (or might dabble) in evil, harmful deeds, they should be made aware of what they are doing and what its consequences are. A major cause of the problem is, some say, society's feeble and insufficient efforts to control the wrongdoing: a major solution is to restrengthen those efforts.

(Goode & Ben-Yehuda, 2009)

And yet! Each of these claims is backed up with extensive source citations and a seemingly vast body of research literature. So what is the evidence-based clinician to do? What guidance do we offer to clients who come to us asking if their online viewing habits are problematic or if they have an addiction? Can the sex therapist or marriage therapist ethically recommend that their clients consume explicit content—online or off? In the midst of mainstream moral panic and the volley of pro- and anti-porn research publications, where does the truth lie? In many ways, we're still trying to parse that out.

In their seminal study *What Do We Know About The Effects of Pornography After Fifty Years of Academic Research*, Alan McKee, Katerina Litsou, et al. came to the following conclusion: "What have we learned from 50 years of research into the effects of pornography? Well, one thing we have learned for certain—in many cases, we've been researching the wrong things" (McKee, Litsou, Byron, & Ignham, 2022). From empirically evaluating the potential risks and benefits of viewing pornography through simply agreeing on what is meant when we say the word "pornography," much of the body of research literature that exists is (in McKee & Litsou's assessment) poorly designed, inaccurately analyzed, and often influenced by external factors such as the author's social or moral positionings. This presents a problem for the everyday clinician who does not have the time to conduct an in-depth literature review but simply needs to know what to tell their clients about pornography, relationships, and mental health. Thankfully, in the midst of the thousands of articles published every year on this topic, there is sound science out there that we can draw from. This is what it tells us:

- Pornography is not a public health crisis. This statement was true when the Nixon Administration's Presidential Commission on Obscenity and Pornography released its findings in 1970 (USCOP, 1970) and was true in 2020 when the *American Journal of Public Health* stated that "pornography is not a cri-sis" (Nelson & Rothman, 2020)

- "Research suggests that there may be adverse health consequences of por-nography for some, no substantial consequences for the majority, and positive effects for others" (Valkenburg, 2016)
- When viewers consume erotic content that depicts higher-risk behaviors such as condom-free sex, casual sex, or rough sex, there is some evidence that it influences their real-life sexual activities; however, this outcome is not con-sistent across studies. "In many cases direct links between mere consump-tion of pornography and sexual risk-taking are not evident" (Grubbs, Wright, Braden, Wilt, & Kraus, 2019)
- Along those same lines, pornography can help to expand the viewer's sex-ual repertoire and normalize activities (such as giving or receiving oral sex or the use of vibrators) or identities (LGBTQIA+, kinky, etc.) which may have been considered outré prior to exposure (Weinberg, Irizarry, & Wil-liams, 2010)
- While religiosity is linked to negative opinions/moral disapproval of por-nography it is not a reliable predictor of behavior around pornography viewing or avoidance. That said, the more religious the viewer is, the more likely they are to perceive negative consequences related to their pornog-raphy consumption—and this is not entirely unfounded. "Research has made a compelling case that pornography use has unique consequences for the religious in terms of relationship quality, sexual satisfaction, psy-chological distress, and religious and spiritual struggle" (Floyd & Grubbs, 2022), which leads many religious pornography viewers to self-identify as addicted to porn, even when the actual amount of time they spend view-ing porn was below the norm (Grubbs, Exline, Pargament, Volk, & Lind-berg, 2017)
- However, most people who view pornography do not experience substan-tial disruptions in their relationships with partners, and when they engage with erotica together with their partner, may even experience positive benefits for the relationship (Perry, 2017). Some of the positive benefits of viewing porn include lower stress levels (Heid, 2013), improved intimate communi-cation (Dickson, Hubby, & Lang, 2020), and increased libido/sexual desire (Prause & Pfauss, 2015)
- "While some studies suggest a relationship between pornography consump-tion and sexually aggressive behaviors, others have reported that pornography use is not associated with negative views towards women and argue that the relationship between viewing sexually explicit materials and real-life vio-lence is not necessarily a causal one" (Shor & Seida, 2021)
- "Existing research has not established an association between general por-nography use and sexual aggression. It does, however, suggest a relationship

between pornography that includes aggression and real-life aggression. Still, scholars remain undecided regarding the causal nature of this relationship and the relationship is further complicated by multiple qualifying and moderating factors" (Shor & Seida, 2021)

- "It is not clear that behaviors that are currently described as sex addition (or pornography addiction) are actual health issues. Humanities researchers insist that these are moral issues; and some data from the social sciences support that contention . . . Often, the term addiction is used as a moral judgement to keep people's behavior 'within socially acceptable boundaries'" (McKee, Litsou, Byron, & Ignham, 2022) (The authors will discuss the notion of process addictions, including viewing pornography, later on in Chapter Seven.)

These findings (such as they are) highlight the limitations in making declarative statements about the benefits or harms of pornography. This empirical uncertainty surrounding a topic that many of us have strong opinions about is one element that feeds the modern moral panic. With the advent of the internet and the ubiquity of online erotic expression, we are entering a new era where both the potential benefits and social consequences of previously private behaviors are magnified. Let's explore what happens when private sexual exploration is mediated by the public internet.

The Authenticity Kink

Over the last three to five years, social scientists who study dating, sexuality, and relationships have begun to notice a new emerging pattern. Young people are delaying their sexual debuts (CDC, 2022), forming fewer relationships (Hauser, 2024), and having less sex with fewer partners (Julian, 2018) than ever before. One in four 18–24-year-olds tell researchers they've *never* had partnered sex (Lehmiller, 2022); and yet? Their engagement with technology—both erotic and otherwise—is rapidly increasing. "The increased availability of online entertainment, including streaming services and social media, plays a role in how often sex occurs" (Naftulin, 2021) and, the authors would argue, the *kind* of sex that is occurring when it does. While 25% of young adults have yet to engage in in real life (IRL) partnered sex, 31% of this group have sexted or had some other form of cybersex; including 6% who report using connected sex toys with a partner (Lehmiller, 2022).

It would be a mistake to assume that these cybersexual encounters are happening between two humans. In 2023, *Forbes* reported that 20% of male dating app users report having used AI to create a girlfriend. Google searches for AI girlfriends increased 2400% in 2023 (Westfall, 2023), driven in large part by loneliness and the desire to have an "easy" relationship with an entity who never argues, pouts, or disagrees about what movie to watch (Vittert, 2023). Even those who are not intentionally opting to create their ideal partner using AI apps such as Replika or Chai are likely to be interacting with artificial intelligence while chatting (and more) online. Cybersecurity firm Thales reported in 2024 that nearly half (49.6%) of all internet traffic worldwide was comprised of bots (Thales, 2024). From intentionally curated relationship simulators through catfishing lures and simple user-created algorithms, it is no longer entirely possible to know if the person you are flirting with online is a person at all.

As we discussed in the previous chapter, this reality-ambiguity fosters a sense of powerlessness and lack of agency that has a dramatic impact on the mental health of those who spend significant amounts of time online. But the conditions for folks offline can feel just as dire. Sixty percent of Americans surveyed told researchers that they feel lonely on a regular basis (PBS News, 2023). We might explain this away as an after-effect of the COVID-19 lockdowns, but these figures were already quite high in the year before the pandemic struck. In 2018, 46% of Americans stated that they "sometimes or always feel alone" while 43% felt "isolated from others" or told researchers that their "relationships are not meaningful" (Jackson & Ballard, 2018). The Coronavirus certainly exacerbated a problem that the Surgeon General has declared a public health emergency (HHS, 2023), but it did not cause the social isolation so many are now struggling to overcome. As Dr. Andrew Weil observed, "there's a great deal of scientific evidence that social connectedness is a very strong protector of emotional well-being, and I think there's no question that social isolation has greatly increased in our culture in, say, the past fifty years" (Lefferts & Dempsey, 2013).

In their analysis of the impact of pornography, McKee, Litsou, eta. al. make the following observation (emphasis ours):

> One important insight about digital cultures is **the increasing importance of 'authenticity' as a virtue** . . . in cultural areas such as social media and online pornography. . . . We can argue that **amateurism is a logic**—one that carries through many sites including social networking, digital dating, television, and pornography—**that conveys intimacy**. It is a preference as well as a genre . . . **(and) can structure** our affective engagement with everyday media as well as **our pleasure preferences**.
>
> (McKee, Litsou, Byron, & Ignham, 2022)

In other words, as it becomes harder and harder to discern reality from artifice, humanity from bots, photos and videos from AI creations, we have begun to crave The Real. This emerging pleasure preference is what the authors have termed The Authenticity Kink. Much like anything that exists just, tantalizingly, out of reach, we have begun to sexualize, perhaps even fetishize, that which presents sexual encounters that feel organic, sincere, authentic. One example of this phenomenon is the annual Pornhub Year In Review, which found in 2022 that "The Reality category grew by +169% . . . while the popularity of the Amateur category has dropped slightly by −19%. Our statisticians theorize that as more amateur models have become full-time performers, the quality of their videos has improved, but visitors are still seeking a real homemade porn experience" (PornHub, 2023). Another way in which The Authenticity Kink manifests is through the ever-increasing variety of niche interest and identity diverse content creators being highlighted on both independent aggregator platforms and their own websites. The benefit of this abundant diversity is access (again) to Realness: "It puts real pleasure first instead of catering to what people think porn looks like, all while emphasizing the female, nonbinary, and/or queer experience" (Quinn, 2024).

For every action, there is an equal and opposite reaction. Just as in physics, when a social shift occurs, we typically see a reactionary response as well. As third and fourth wave feminism embraced sex positivity and the potential for personal empowerment through erotic expression, a smaller community of men have formed a movement that pushes back on pornography use. The "manosphere"—a confederation of social media influencers, bloggers, and online forums—focuses on men's rights issues (O'Donnell, 2022), pseudoscientific theories of health (Cannito & Camoletto, 2022), and peer to peer support for those suffering from pathological loneliness and social isolation: self-described "incels" or involuntary celibates (Helm, Holt, Scrivens, & Frank, 2022). Online communities such as NoFap and Men Going Their Own Way (MGTOW) put forth the proposition that pornography emasculates the male viewer, creating a class of "beta" males who are perceived as physically inferior, less desirable, and less successful than the "alphas" who abstain.

> These men frequently describe themselves as losers—feeling cuckolded by the men they watch having sex with the women they're attracted to—and there's a clear association for these men between narratives of their own abstinence and their sense of self-worth and masculinity.
>
> (Bailey, 2023)

Over the last decade, beginning in 2014 when Elliot Rogers killed six people in Isla Vista, California, at least five mass murders in North America and Europe have been inspired by the manosphere's online hatred towards those they see (or perceive) as "getting" more sex than they are (Barcellona, 2022). These perceptions of pornography as "documentary" seem to prove true the manosphere member's most irrational thoughts of objectification, deservingness, and self-loathing.

As author Dan Brown put it, "each of us is now electronically connected to the globe, and yet we feel utterly alone" (Brown, 2001). Loneliness has been linked to depression, anxiety, addiction, cognitive decline, and increased risk of suicide (HHS, 2023). When one is battling loneliness, it becomes quite easy to confuse information sharing with intimacy building; particularly when so many of us are fostering relationships friendly, romantic, and sexual in online spaces. The Authenticity Kink motivates us to share our genuine selves at quite a granular level with those in our social networks. We want to demonstrate our realness—our images us, our stories true—and prove (consciously or otherwise) that we are not one of the bots. We offer up the minutia of our lives to Instagram followers and Reddit feeds, FetLife profiles and NextDoor apps in the name of representation and connection. Unfortunately, when conspiracy-filtered misogyny (Johanssen, 2022) meets good-faith information sharing, the situation can change dramatically, and the details of our selves can be weaponized in ways we might not ever have imagined.

Sexting and "Revenge Porn"*

The confusion of information sharing with intimacy leads naturally to an increase in sharing sexual images with potential and current sexual partners. In the early 2010s, 43% of young adults in the United States were sexting: "28.2% were two-way sexters, 12.6% were receivers, and 2% were senders" (Gordon-Messer, 2013). By 2020, these numbers had more than doubled, with reciprocal sexting 47.7%, receiving 41.5%, and sending 38.3% (Mori, 2020). This unsurprisingly correlates with teenage ownership of the Apple iPhone climbing from 40% in 2012 (McGlaun, 2013), up to 88% in 2024, according to the Piper Jaffray annual survey (Silva, 2025). Motive, means, and opportunity came together to drive people to share personal photographs now more than ever.

Is this a cause for concern? Revisiting the moral panic conceptualization of risk, we need to ask ourselves three questions of the data. (1) Who is engaging in the harmful practice, and how harmful is it? (2) Is the concern or fear proportionate or disproportionate to the actual threat? (3) Assuming the threat is genuine, is the response appropriate or exaggerated? (Goode & Ben-Yehuda, 2009). The field of cybersecurity risk management would classify this as the likelihood and impact, risk tolerance, and response effectiveness. Often by considering these questions, the risks we identify are not the ones we emotionally respond to, or that the press is covering.

---

* Author's Note: We have chosen to use the phrase "revenge porn" in this section because that reflects the language most commonly used by clients and other lay people. Academics and safety professionals more accurately describe this phenomenon as "image based abuse" or "nonconsensual intimate image sharing."

For example, we might associate sexting with low self-esteem, anxiety, or other negative mental states. Curiously, many studies have found low, no, or negative correlation between sexting and mental health. A closer look reveals a real risk: coercion.

> Receiving unwanted sexts and sending sexts under coercion were associated with poorer mental health. Specifically, when receiving or sending unwanted but consensual sexts, respondents reported higher depression, anxiety, and stress, and lower self-esteem. Another significant finding was that receiving unwanted sexts and sending sexts under pressure were independent predictors of poorer mental health.
>
> (Klettke, 2019).

Suppose a sexually charged image is consensually exchanged between two adults, the research indicates a relatively low negative impact on the participants. This can quickly change if one of the people shares the image without the other person's consent. That's not unlikely, unfortunately. The Data & Society Research Institute and the Center for Innovative Public Health Research found that "4% of men and 6% of women under 30 have had someone post a nearly nude or nude image of them without their permission" (Data & Society Research, 2016). The negative impacts of revenge porn include "experiences of trust issues, posttraumatic stress disorder (PTSD), anxiety, depression, suicidal thoughts, and several other mental health effects" (Bates, 2017).

The conceptualization of the harms of sexting stemming from the loss of agency extends to the creation of the images. As previously discussed, the negative mental health outcomes are the result of people feeling coerced into creating content. But what happens if they don't even have the choice? This is the case with the "example of deepfakes is the superimposing of women's faces into pornographic videos. The implication here is a reification of women's bodies as a thing to be visually consumed, here circumventing consent" (Wagner & Blewer, 2019). This began with celebrities but has quickly moved to regular people, with one recent case of students using smartphones to create nudes of fellow schoolgirls, resulting in "over 30 victims between the ages of 12 and 14 years of age" (Saliba, 2023).

Normal people can do little today to counteract fake revenge porn. The technology platforms need to implement safeguards against creating adult content with the faces of real people. At some level, this is in place for celebrities. For example, Dall-E and Designer AI prohibit creating images with Taylor Swift's likeness (Maiberg, 2024). Many of the websites will have a trust and safety team which will also act to remove the content if shared, especially if it violates the Terms of Service (ToS). Meanwhile, we have to wait for the law to catch up with the technology. Some states in the USA allow individuals to sue people who create deepfakes of them: California AB-972 (2022) and New York Senate Bill S1042 (2024).

People have more personal control over sexting and revenge porn. First, when creating images, carefully crop it to hide details such as location or to make facial recognition impossible. To preserve intellectual property rights over the image, which is key in having it removed or in suing people who distribute it, watermark the image (see tools such as Pixlr, InShot.) Some people may watermark it distinctly for who they are sharing with, so that they can identify who may have posted it elsewhere. Now that we have an image that if shared doesn't give too much information or cause us too many problems, and now that we have a watermarked image that clearly marks it as ours? The next step is to store it discretely. Use a photo vault on the phone (like KeepSafe) or store it offline on a storage drive. This minimizes the likelihood of the photo being stolen from your phone. Finally, share it discretely. Use apps that prohibit the photo from being copied or screenshot, like SnapChat or Dust. Set the photo to only be available for a specific time period (hours or days) which further limits the risk.

Sex-positive safe sexting is possible. We can reduce the likelihood of harm through the above steps. This should be seen within the larger context of teaching the importance of consent, educating on the harm that comes from revenge porn and deepfake porn, and encouraging the formation of better technology and better laws to mitigate these harms.

Exploring Ethical Erotica

Speaking of panic—moral and otherwise—you might have reached the end of this chapter wondering how on earth one can know that the media they choose is ethically produced. If you are one of the 90%+ of folks who consume pornography, you might be questioning your own choices, favorite websites, or preferred erotic plot points . . . or those of your partner. We hope that you're reflecting on how this information informs your understanding of your client's behaviors, from passive viewing to active creation; and considering how your perception of problematic or high-risk behavior influences your clinical practice.

We would be poor educators indeed if we didn't leave you with a roadmap for identifying and enjoying ethical erotic content as well! Thankfully, an international "Delphi panel" comprised of over a dozen of the leading experts on sexual health across disciplines was convened by a research team at the University of Sidney to identify the common attributes of ethical porn, or as they put it, "pornography that can support healthy sexual development" (McKee, Dawson, &

Kang, 2023). They identified six key elements of ethical/health-promoting erotica:

- Consent negotiated onscreen
- Depictions of safe sex (condom use, etc.)
- Ethical production
- A focus on pleasure for all participants
- A variety of sexual practices
- A variety of body types, genders, and races (University of Sidney, 2023)

Some of these are easy for the layperson (or porn-curious clinician) to recognize. We know what body diversity (for example) looks like when we see it. Others can be more difficult to parse out, from outside the world of the porn industry itself. How does one know whether or not their favorite scene was produced ethically, for example? Thankfully, there are a growing number of platforms that are modelling transparency in their production practices. AdultTime, for example, is an online streaming subscription service that offers a variety of channels featuring different themes (such as ongoing affirmative consent in their series "The Yes List"), sexual orientations, and body types. AdultTime publishes information on its website offering transparency about what their on-set experience looks like for performers, including posting their Production Code of Conduct, provides a downloadable consent checklist and mental health resources for adult performers, and verifies that their channel partners adhere to these same production standards. Another great resource—particularly for those who prioritize diverse bodies or an amateur/realistic aesthetic in their erotica is MakeLoveNotPorn.com, a "social erotica" platform that is 100% human moderated. Outside of visual media, Dipsea curates audio-only erotic stories that are created by voice performers specifically chosen because they sound like adults (no faux baby talk!) and have a variety of accents to represent the lives and experiences of their listeners.

Explore AdultTime Performer Resource Center here

Some of the criteria identified by the Delphi panel are a bit more nebulous. What, for example, does negotiated consent look like in this context? Most production studios have a practice of recording a pre-scene interview with the star performer (typically, but not always a cis-female) that asks her what she's excited about in the scene to come and confirms that she is a willing performer in the day's production. These videos can be insufficient, in our minds, to confirm consent—particularly when the clip is featured on a user-uploaded or "tube" site where the viewer can access the video for free. Several adult

performers have shared experiences of financial pressures leaving them feeling pressured to agree, while others have come out to discuss sets where what they agreed to in the pre-recorded consent portion was not what occurred in practice once filming began. We discuss the nature of online sex work in greater depth in Chapter Nine. For our purposes here, we recommend seeking out erotic content where all performers are featured in the pre-scene discussion OR where ongoing, enthusiastic consent is requested and communicated by performers throughout the scene itself.

We love depictions of pleasure for all, but would be remiss if we didn't acknowledge that pleasure takes different forms for different people. In fact, when we think about what "a variety of sexual practices" would include, we must hold space for BDSM and other forms of kink, which may not present a traditional notion of pleasure, but which is enjoyed both by participants and viewers for the sensation and scenarios these scenes depict. The argument can be made that safer sex practices also fall into this category of more subjective ethical criteria. In 2012, Los Angeles County in California (longtime home of the American adult film industry) passed the *County of Los Angeles Safer Sex In the Adult Film Industry Act*. Measure B, as it was called on the ballot, required condom use on porn sets to prevent the spread of STIs (YesOnB, 2024). Adult performers argued vocally both in favor and against the mandate on grounds ranging from constitutional free speech to personal comfort and agency; and many production companies left the county after the measure passed. A few years later in 2016, voters rejected a similar proposal that would have expanded the mandate statewide (Sokol, 2018). The conversation around condoms on professional sets continues today, and performers on both sides of the issue have valid reasons for their stance; which can make identifying ethical content difficult for viewers who consider barrier-free sex to be intrinsically high-risk behavior.

Nothing in life is perfectly safe. Lying outside on a blanket in the backyard exposes us to sunlight and increases our risk of skin cancer. Being indoors too much can put us at risk of Vitamin D deficiency and make us more prone to depression. Pornography, like sunlight, carries both risk and reward. Sending a sexy selfie or video clip to our partner while they are away on a business trip can be a glorious way to strengthen the relationship bond and cultivate intimacy across long distances. Watching anonymous uploads on a free adult site might mean inadvertently boosting the reach of non-consensual sexual material. Each and every one of us has an obligation—to ourselves and to our clients—to understand the potential risks of online erotica and the ways in which these risks are hyperbolized by moral panic. We can educate ourselves about the realities of erotica consumption and learn how to recognize and support ethical porn and its producers. This ethical work begins by destigmatizing the creation and consumption of explicit images, stories, or scenes; particularly given the fact that ubiquitous technology has made many (if not most) of us into amateur pornographers ourselves.

TECH ED WITH WOLF
WHAT ARE DEEPFAKES?

TechEd Class: What Are Deepfakes?

Let's talk deepfakes. As computers have gotten faster, and as algorithms of gotten better, it's easier than ever to manipulate audio and visual images. This can be something simple, like cleaning up the sound file the podcast, or lightning up a photo and re-coloring. We've all long known about Photoshop and the great degree of photo manipulation is possible. But recently this editing of images and sounds has been combined with advances and machine learning. Enter the deepfake. Deepfakes gets their name from a type of machine learning (ML) and generative adversarial networks (GANs). Those are the technology terms for what is basically math competing with math. When you do these competitions several times and you stack on the math, it's pretty deep. That over-simplifies the idea behind deep learning. Now when applied to faking someone's face or faking voices, deep learning becomes deepfakes. That's the one thing you can count on from us technologists: we love plays on words that take paragraphs if not books to describe. But essentially deepfakes are like Photoshop taken to another level.

First an encoder analyzes and learns from a large data set of images or expressions to understand the nuances of an individual. In commercial applications, this can be as simple as a couple photographs. Then a decoder synthesizes those images and creates new content via morphing what it saw onto a source material. These machine learning algorithms work together, refining their output, to produce convincingly realistic results. Because we rely on what our senses tell us, this technology can be particularly troublesome. As is the way with humans and technology, it didn't take very long at all for deepfakes to become sexualized. One of the first ways was to undress people's photographs. It's certainly not a new goal. Last century, "amazing" x-ray glasses were advertised with promises to see through clothing and images of women scantily clad. So wasn't surprising when apps started to appear using deepfake technology with similar claims.

Users would provide a clothed photo, and the app would encode the phone, decode and render a picture of what the woman might look like naked. (And these were definitely for women. If the user fed it a picture of a man, the app would create a picture of what the man would look like with breasts and a vulva.)

Apps like these were quickly taken down from app stores, but the general idea persists. At the time of this writing, there are many websites that will generate pornography off of photographs. Then these websites do ask the person to confirm that both adults are consenting. Although how that consent is determined, well, isn't necessarily something we can have confidence in. After uploading photographs, say perhaps of you and your partner, these pornography websites would generate a scene where your respective photographs will be overlaid with the respective actors. This has raised some serious ethical concerns as you are effectively superimposing the face of a partner, acquaintance, or even unsuspecting individual, onto a pornographic movie. And while there are usually enough clues that this image has been faked, the technology continues to get better, and professional tools can render images that are very difficult to distinguish as faked. On pornography websites that do not advertise themselves as deepfake websites, this leads to additional concerns. The proliferation of deepfake pornography is challenging to detect and remove. Many websites do not have a clear process for handling people's complaints about the misuse of their images. Moreover, the legislative frameworks and privacy laws are behind in this area.

Stepping away from pornography, and stepping towards relationships, deepfakes have created other areas of concern. Relationship scams have been a problem since the dawn of the Internet. In 2010, thanks to a documentary, one type of relationship scams was coined as catfishing. The basic idea is that the criminal poses as a fictional person to lure in the victim, hook them, and then defraud them. Early advice on how to handle catfishing and relationship scams was to request photos or video or a video chat. By confirming that the person looked and sounded like the person they claimed to be, a potential victim could be assured that they were not being scammed. You probably see where I'm going with this. Using deep learning for sound and image manipulation, with enough time and enough computing power, anyone can pretend to be someone else in photos or on video. Scammers can create convincing profiles using someone else's face or inventing an entirely fictional person. They can create multiple different photos, enough to fill a social media profile. Deepfakes then allow scammers to establish a false sense of trust and intimacy with their victims. It's often not until the ask, not until the scam is complete, that the victim realizes what's happened. The emotional damage such scams can be significant, as people feel betrayed, have financial losses, and generally are in psychological distress. You can't blame them. After all, the person they were speaking to looked and sounded legitimate.

In the early days of phishing scams, we taught people to look for signs such as strange grammar or typos or other indicators that the person didn't speak your native language or wasn't from your country. As technology got better, with things like generative AI to write phishing emails, these indicators became rarer. Paralleling this arc, with catfishing and other deepfake attacks, today we teach people to look for signs such as strange movements or audiovisual artifacts that indicate the person isn't a real person. (You can see this firsthand using some of the deepfake pornography websites and your own image. Watch what happens when the light changes or when there are sudden movements.) Technology is advancing quickly, however, and these indicators will likely be gone in the next 5 to 10 years. Another parallel between phishing and catfishing is that we can rely on technology to check content before it gets to us. It is the anti-phishing detection that sends things to your spam or junk mailbox. Similar technology is being developed to detect deepfakes. Cybersecurity is an arms race, and as you might imagine, a technology based on adversarial machine learning has an advantage as, well, an adversary. Deepfakes will continue to improve. From a personal, from a cultural, and from a legal perspective, we simply are not prepared for a world in which we cannot trust our eyes, our ears, and our hearts.

Expert Consult: Joshua Marpet

Joshua Marpet

Joshua Marpet is an entrepreneur and advisor to many Fortune 1000 companies on information and physical security, as well as compliance and risk management. He honed his skills in the police, fire, and surveillance industries as well as the Federal Reserve Bank system.

Can you explain your what you do to us and share how your work relates to the creation and dissemination of deepfake images and videos?

I advise companies on security, compliance, and technology. While I do not typically create or disseminate deepfake videos, I do advise companies on what to do about them, and how they are part of the risks of doing business in today's high-tech environment. One company recently lost $25 million when an employee was convinced to transfer the funds by scammers who used video deepfakes to impersonate several corporate management in a teleconference meeting. I am starting a company that prepares and certifies other companies under various regulatory standards, which have clauses related to identity management, identity verification, and so on. So as part of that, I have to assess and audit and certify that those companies are handling all risks in the identity space properly. Deepfakes are, of course, a huge threat in the identity space. I help companies to remove human judgement from the authentication process entirely. If one employee recognizes their coworker Jimmy's voice over the phone? That employee still can't reset Jimmy's password, replace his laptop, or whatever. If Jimmy lost his laptop on vacation, he gets no email until he shows back up at the office, period.

What makes you passionate about this work?

I enjoy the technology and what it means, I enjoy the idea of standardizing and regularizing processes and protections, rather than treating technology as the Wild West. I am not a cowboy. I am a mathematician and a process-builder. Disorder is offensive (except apparently in my house, where executive dysfunction reigns supreme). I work to make process simple. To define terms, to make everyone work together. When we can increase security universally, we help everyone.

Why should therapists, educators, and others working in the field of sexual health be concerned about this topic? What do deepfakes have to do with mental health?

Deepfakes started with deepfake porn, putting a celebrity head on a porn actor's body. It was done to be funny (not funny), or to satisfy some . . . urges. But then, deepfake got easier to do—significantly easier. So people started doing it to their ex-partner, as revenge porn, or for blackmail, or for many other horrible reasons. When you think about blackmail, or coercion, or destroying someone's life, this is a HUGE mental health issue. Monstrous.

What advice do you have for someone who is concerned about the proliferation of deepfakes online? How can someone know if what they're seeing on their screen is real or not?

No picture or even video is real anymore. It's as simple as that. You *must* check with the person whose image it is. And if it is an image of you? Immediately go public: "This disgusting picture is not me. Someone built it off of this picture of me and some other porn image." Use TinEye to do a reverse image search—if you can find the photos that were portmanteaued? Better yet! There are technologies that purport to be able to see the "touches" of digital manipulation. I think it will be an arms race, where all the current ways to spot deepfakes will be made invisible eventually. I really don't know what happens when we can't trust photos or videos.

TinEye.com is an image search service that will search the web to locate websites where an image has been shared online. Try it here.

What can someone do when they realize deepfakes have been created using their images? Do they have any recourse? Does their relationship to the image manufacturer matter?

As I mentioned above? They can go public. Take the power away from the faker. Other than that, there's not much available for them that they can do. There are revenge porn laws in most states, but proving that the image came from a specific person gets difficult—especially if that person is clever enough.

How can we work to stop the proliferation of artificial images online, and advocate for image-based protections on a wider scale?

We can't. There are no technical controls on this. Imagine a law that says a picture that is altered digitally is illegal. Photoshop gets criminalized? That's ridiculous! Okay, so a law says only altered porn is illegal! (Porn companies use photoshop, too, but ignore that for a second). Prove it's altered. If it's subtle enough, it's hard to tell. And what if the faker says "it's real? She really did pose naked?" How does the person being faked prove a negative? And what if it's almost-porn? Lingerie, or sultry looks, or something. How do we define porn? "I know it when I see it" is not really good enough. Revenge porn laws operate on the motivation. Unless you can show the motivation, I don't know of any way to effectively criminalize this.

Chapter 5

Censorship and Nanny Apps

Won't Someone Please Think of the Children!?

"Beware the Four Horsemen of the Information Apocalypse: terrorists, drug dealers, kidnappers, and child pornographers," the cybersecurity and encryption expert Bruce Schneier once wrote. "You can scare any public into allowing the government to do anything with those four."

(Schneier, 2019)

These four provide a challenging set of conflicting thoughts and goals. Fear-based persuasion works, especially after a high profile and highly publicized event. Take the terrorism example. Following the suicide attacks on September 11, 2001, Americans were very open to arguments of trading privacy for safety. The broad surveillance powers granted by the PATRIOT Act (Congress, U. S., 2001) raised issues about government overreach and the potential for abuse, while the REAL ID Act's standardization and information-sharing requirements raised concerns for the loss of personal privacy (Congress, U. S., 2005). We are primed to do whatever we can to ensure the threat doesn't impact us personally. Moreover, we don't want to be seen as not taking the threat seriously and therefore not being a good friend, a good family member, a good citizen.

The same happens when the topic of child pornography is raised.

If we do not stop the scale and intensity of sexual abuses against children, pedophiles will return again and again and if we fail to block them now, it will not be long before society accepts and tolerates this perverted sexual freedom in the name of freedom of expression.

(Kierkegaard, 2011)

Such framing makes it near impossible we won't agree to take action to avoid the threat (in this case, set precedents for broader Internet censorship and surveillance). The fear-based persuasion gets kicked up a notch when numbers get cited demonstrating how "the advent of new technology has made its circulation

DOI: 10.4324/9781003391128-6

wider and has caused global alarm resulting in various national and international legislation to introduce measures to stop online child pornography."

Think of the children and lock down the web. However, one anecdote to fear is understanding. Specifically, investigating and understanding the sources of our information. With contemporary estimates of the Internet hosting 238 million websites (Internet Live Stats, 2019), around 4 million of which were pornography websites at the time (Internet Filter, 2006), it seems unlikely there were over 4 million websites focusing on child pornography (Kierkegaard, 2011). The article cites Breitbart News Network's coverage of a United Nations report by UNICEF in 2009. (Note the actual report does not contain the number of websites in question.) Perhaps the trade-off is worth it, perhaps it is not.

People may still support the increased government action not necessarily because they agree with the measures themselves, but because they want to avoid the social stigma of being perceived as supporting child pornography or terrorism. This is how we find ourselves listening to calls of banning encryption because of terrorism (Everett, 2016) or requiring state ID to watch certain Internet content to protect children (Burgess, 2023). And how we find ourselves needing to clearly state our positions when not in support of such measures. As Bruce Schneier wrote in the article that opens this section, "Let me be clear. None of us who favor strong encryption is saying that child exploitation isn't a serious crime, or a worldwide problem. We're not saying that about kidnapping, international drug cartels, money laundering, or terrorism." (Schneier, 2019)

The extended parallel process model (EPPM) is useful framework for understanding the persuasive process and outcomes of a broader range of emotion-based messages (Witte, 1992). We do a threat appraisal that's in part informed by our perceptions of severity and scariness. We also do a coping appraisal in which we determine how effective the proposed strategies and measures may be. These two cognitive processes are, in the model, performed serially (is this a threat? What do we do about it?). In reality, both processes inform and interrupt each other. In situations with fear-based persuasion combined with social desirability biases, it can be surprisingly easy to be convinced to take drastic measures that run counter to our longer-term interests.

"In our rush to ensure our population is safe from the harms of Internet, and our reliance on code to achieve this, we might be removing fundamental rights and moving toward the *safeguarding dystopia*" (Brennan, 2019, emphasis added). There are four questions we need to ask to avoid this dystopia. (1) Is the fear realistic in terms of magnitude, likelihood, and severity? (2) Does the current state we're being asked to change provide benefits that we're trading off (in the above examples, encryption, private travel, open Internet access)? (3) Does this trade-off do more harm than good? And finally, (4) what other ways could we protect ourselves without these trade-offs?

Put simply, we need not let fear or social pressure drive us to surrender civil liberties.

Censorship and Society

In 1982, *The Driller Killer* was featured in all its gory glory in full page advertisements in the UK. Complaints flooded the UK's Advertising Standards Agency. Sensing an opportunity to ride the news cycle, the distributors of *Cannibal Holocaust* themselves started a campaign to complain about their movie posters. The Advertising Standards Agency was less than amused.

Stories of the "video nasties" (horror movies on VHS that some people thought were too violent and gory) soon dominated the newspapers. The sensational headlines and exaggerated articles drove up concerns. The resulting pressure from media and family groups on politicians led to discussions in Parliament. Stating concerns for the effect these videos might have on society, especially on children, the UK government passed the Video Recordings Act in 1984, giving the government the power to censor videos. The "video nasties" panic is a story about how a new technology, home video, got caught up in a moral panic, leading to censorship laws (Petley, 2012). It's a cycle that can lead to hasty decisions and laws with unintended consequences that might not solve the problem they were meant to address. Perhaps Betamax should have won over VHS after all, if only to avoid censorship.

But before we blame the tape, let's rewind and look at the broader context of the "video nasties" panic. Decades before, American comic books featuring horror, crime, and violence led to the establishment of the Comics Code Authority in 1954, which imposed strict censorship on comic book content. Concerns over explicit rock and roll albums led to the Recording Industry Association of America (RIAA) forcing the "Parental Advisory" labels in 1990. Violent video games created a public outcry leading to the American Entertainment Software Rating Board (ESRB) in 1994 and European Pan European Game Information (PEGI) in 2003. There is an established trend of broader societal concerns over the impact of technology on society, specifically on youth, resulting in efforts to regulate and manage distribution and content.

Placing restrictions on mainstream mass media (Internet, games, movies, television, music) doesn't always have the desired effect. Censorship can have a negative impact by stifling the free expression of ideas and art, which is a fundamental societal value in many nations (Dalton, 2011). When censorship occurs, the censored material gains more attention and support than it would have otherwise, due to public outrage and the desire to resist what is perceived as an injustice (Jansen & Martin, 2004). It can lead to people using privacy-enhancing technologies to bypass the rules or access banded materials (Makin & Ireland, 2019). Even when it is effective in reenforcing public morality and protecting citizens (Burns, 1990), there is a broader conversation to be had about the impact of enforced morality and norms on society.

The balance between the good that censorship can do in protecting vulnerable groups and potential effects on civil liberties is a complex issue. Take for example the Canadian gay rights movement in the late 1990s and early 2000s (Cohen, 2000). Gay rights activists faced a dilemma when considering the expansion of anti-hate legislation to include sexual orientation. On one hand, there were potential benefits of such legislation in reducing hate speech directed at sexual minorities. On the other hand, such legislation could have led to broader restrictions on civil liberties, particularly freedom of expression, which has historically been useful in their struggle for equality.

Of course, two decades later, the tech companies' moderation approaches and content classification rules would have negative effects on sexual minorities by "promoting notions of a 'good' LGBTQ sexual citizen" (Southerton, 2020). By adopting a nuanced approach, it has proven possible to mitigate these risks while still achieving the goal of reducing hate propaganda and promoting equality. But it isn't easy, and the tech "move fast and break things" mentality doesn't often make time for the slow, thoughtful, methodical exploration of moderation.

Successful censorship and moderation share some commonalities, be it encoded in legislation or platform rules. First, it is narrowly defined and crafted to address specific scenarios from specific harms. That's a difference between imposing blanket restrictions on VHS films and prohibiting specific hate speech phrases on social media. This requires clear definitions and a shared agreement of what is prohibited and why. Second, the response should be proportional to the harm it causes. This means considering the context, the likelihood of inciting violence, and the impact on the targeted group. Developing effective agreements, rules, and responses to speech and content requires open public discourse. Maintaining it requires monitoring and reviews. Both developing and maintaining stages are susceptible to moral panics and influence campaigns, making effective systemic change extremely challenging.

Censorship, Surveillance, and Control

In Chapter Three, we talked about surveillance culture and its impact on both society and the individuals being surveilled. In many ways, censorship is the "flip side" of this same coin, moving from *monitoring* behavior and information towards *controlling* behavior and information. While there are bad actors who engage in both practices, typically the impulse to surveil or censor another person is well intended. We think of this as a protective action and we want to ensure that those entrusted to our care are not exposed to dangerous content, people, or situations. Technology has expanded our loci control, allowing us to choose (for example) not only who comes to visit us at our homes, but whose social media profiles, websites, images, etc. are allowed entry as well. This can be incredibly empowering, allowing individuals to set boundaries around what they want to be exposed to and who they wish to engage with. It can also be a means of avoidance and control, allowing us to outsource our socioemotional regulation skills and create comfortable echo-chambers that never require us to experience frustration or dissonance.

In recent years, a wide variety of tools (both software and hardware) have sprung up that claim to help individuals navigate the world more safely. What this safety looks like will vary depending on the target audience. Parents are sold software such as Bark and NetNanny, which allows them to block access to websites or filter content based on specific keywords. Ostensibly designed to prevent children from accessing violent or explicit material online, many filter services also empower parents to block content such as sexual health information, scientific topics such as evolution or climate change research, and more. Even when parents do not choose to block access to educational information for their children, this is often an unintended "side-effect" of content filtering software . . . a flaw that has been known and critiqued almost for as long as these programs have existed (Kranich, 2004; KFF, 2013). For years, therapists working with children have recommended content filtering/behavior management software to parents. However, the perspective is beginning to shift, with many clinicians now understanding that we cannot simply lock young people out of desirable online activities and call a problem solved; we must help families do the work of identifying and encouraging their children to engage in substitute, offline activities as well (Theopilus, Al Mahmud, Davis, & Octavia, 2024). In other words, censorship software is not a substitute for building skills such as self-regulation, time management, and distress tolerance.

But children are not the only clients this wisdom applies to. Many adult clients are being encouraged by their therapists to use behavior modification and regulation technologies as well. One of the best examples of this censorship-surveillance symbiosis is a tool called Covenant Eyes, which was developed to help users who wished to avoid viewing pornography or, as the founder describes it "remain pure online" (CovenantEyes, 2024). Using artificial intelligence, "the app sits quietly on all of your devices, monitors your screen activity, and provides protection through blocking" (CovenantEyes, 2024). It also allows you to designate someone in your life such as a friend or spouse, who can monitor your online movements and receive alerts from Covenant Eyes when it detects potentially problematic activity via an app on their phone. In the mental health and substance use world, the idea of "accountability partners" is fairly mainstream. Covenant Eyes and similar programs take this to a new extreme, by actively censoring the user's access to content and then reporting on their behavior to others. This changes the notion of accountability, offloading responsibility for positive choices from the person looking to change their behaviors and onto the tool itself.

Originally developed for voluntary use by folks who identified as conservative Christians, in at least five states Covenant Eyes has been mandated by courts for use as a surveillance tool on the devices of people awaiting trial or released on parole. In one instance, "Wired reported on the case of a man whose entire family was required to install Covenant Eyes on their devices as a condition of his pretrial release from jail" (EJI, 2023). Covenant Eyes is not the only software being used by institutional systems to monitor and control those under their care. Schools around the country are mandating that students install software on their phones that would allow them to "collect personal data, add/remove accounts and restrictions, install, manage, and list apps, and remotely erase data" from their personal devices (McCloud, 2022), while behind the scenes, school systems are utilizing programs such as Raptor Technologies StudentSafe software to allow school employees from bus drivers to principals to gather data on students, communicate perceived behavioral trends with one another and "operationalize student wellbeing" in order to reduce district liability. This covert tracking of children by their educators, and the dossier of information compiled on each, will follow the student from school to school within the StudentSafe user system. These records may be available to parents who request them under FERPA (Park, 2024), however most parents are not informed about whether or not their district is using these technologies and therefore do not know what their review and opt-out rights might be.

Censorship offers the illusion of protection. In reality, information control undermines many of the key skills we hope to see our clients develop: discernment and media literacy, the ability to delay or deny temptation, to tolerate distress when contradicted and frustration when challenged, a healthy self-concept able to resist peer pressure and outside influences, and the ability to see beyond the influence of our families of origin in order to form differentiated adult identities. Censorship is a disability rights issue—"internet users with disabilities are more likely than users without disabilities to engage in several activities including downloading videos, sharing their own content, and posting to blogs" (Trevisan, 2020)—as well as a matter of intimate justice and pleasure equity (Knight, 2022). As clinicians, we should never shy away from utilizing (properly vetted!) tech such as digital journals, mindfulness tools, symptom trackers, or goal benchmarking apps that help our clients learn and grow. But we must avoid the impulse to "help" by restricting access to information entirely, thereby diminishing the personal agency, self-control, and emotional maturity that good therapy helps to build.

Censorship of Sexual Health and Medical Information

In the previous section, we explored the ways in which censorship is used by authority figures—from school psychologists to court personal—to "protect" those entrusted to their care. This information control as an authoritarian practice has existed forever, but modern technologies have expanded the reach of authority figures, allowing them to exert control over aspects of life and forms of communication never before imagined. These choices are not just being made by helping professionals, they are being made about helping professionals as well. In this section, we will examine the impact of censorship on those who work to educate others about sexual, medical, and relational health.

In 2022, the Center for Intimacy Justice released a report exploring the ways in which the advertising policies of Meta, which owns Instagram and Facebook, representing 4.41 billion monthly users and 59–73% of all internet users (Shepherd, 2024), impacted access to information about sexual health, women's health, and underrepresented gender identities. They examined 60 small businesses that provide health services/products for women and people of diverse genders and that had attempted to advertise on Meta's platforms. "Every single one (100%) had experienced Facebook/Instagram rejecting an ad (and) 50% . . . reported Facebook suspending their entire ad accounts" (CIJ, 2022). Among the topics covered by these rejected ads were "menopause, pelvic pain, pregnancy or postpartum care, menstrual health, fertility, sexual wellness, (and) education" (CIJ, 2022) most of which were identified by Meta's content moderation systems as "adult products." Rejecting paid advertisements for health-related businesses (including services such as sex therapy and relationship/wellness coaching) is not the only way that large technology companies prevent their users from accessing important information.

There are several ways that platforms can accomplish this. Content moderation teams routinely review and remove posts that do not align with the platforms' Terms of Service. If the same user repeatedly violates these guidelines, the user themselves might have their account deleted. User access restrictions can take other, less direct forms as well. Age requirements are the most common example, however geo-blocking (preventing everyone within a specified geographic area from accessing a service) is also common. In recent years, several platforms have implemented fact-checking notices, community notes, and other interstitial warnings to help users recognize potentially problematic content when it comes across their feeds. For high-profile or professional users (such as content creators or live streamers), the platform may choose to influence their messaging by restricting their ability to advertise (demonetizing) problematic accounts.

> Some of these strategies are not as visible or controversial as removal; others may go unnoticed because they are imposed by different product teams, intervene at different points in the platform, are more difficult for users to identify in practice, or get justified in different ways.
>
> (Gillespie, 2022)

Some of these strategies encompass the practice known as "shadowbanning," wherein an individual user account is allowed to post content, but is not told that these posts are not being made available to others. Their accounts may not show up in searches, for example, and their posts may not be included within the content streams of others. This is a common form of covert censorship. According to the Center for Democracy and Technology, "nearly 1 in

10 social media users believe they've been shadowbanned" (Nicholas, 2022). These censorship decisions can occur at a fairly low level. For instance, on Reddit, the moderators of each individual subreddit have the option to shadowban specific users within their communities (Reddit, 2024). While most of the large social media platforms community guidelines state that sexual health and education information are not a content violation, "in practice, this is not enforced. Many sex educators report having their content be removed or shadowbanned, and some are even removed from the platform entirely" (Plaat, 2024).

The power of geo-location and algorithmic content can create new informational barriers for helping professionals and their clients as well. In response to mandatory age-verification laws that have been passed around the country, Pornhub has taken steps to block access to their websites for users in Texas, Arkansas, Mississippi, Montana, North Carolina, Virginia, Utah, Indiana and Kentucky, with more states to follow in the near future (Albenesius, 2024). Pornhub also allows its content creators (those who are Verified Models) to use geo blocking to prevent the content they share from being seen in certain countries, as well as specific states and provinces within North America (Pornhub, 2022). In theory, these technologies are fabulous, right? After all, no one wants young children to have access to pornography and porn performers should have the ability to consent to where their images are published. And yet, the ability of large corporations to restrict access to information based on geographic location opens up new opportunities for abuse as well.

As of May 2024, half of U.S. states have passed laws restricting or outright banning gender-affirming care for young people, impacting 39% of American trans youth (HRC Foundation, 2024). For many of the children and families impacted by these laws, the solution has been to reach beyond their state lines and to access information, support, and care from providers located in states where gender-affirming care is a protected medical service. It is not difficult to imagine additional laws being passed, similar to Pornhub age-verification laws, which block access to these out of state resources based on the geo location of the searching user. Life for trans youth, particularly those who do not have supportive families to help them navigate these precarious circumstances, is already tremendously difficult. Now, imagine a time in the not-too-distant future when the nonbinary teenager in Oklahoma cannot find information about affirming therapy, support groups, or even general sexual health information because their home state has rendered those websites, videos, content creators, or medical journals invisible to them based on their ISP address. This scenario is already both possible technologically and happening legislatively. Women in Spain, for example, already experience geo-blocking of abortion and reproductive health information imposed by their government (DFF, 2024), a pattern that is expanding rapidly as "a record number of national governments (in 2022) blocked websites . . . undermining the rights to free expression and access to information" (Shahbaz, Funk, & Vesteirnsson, 2022).

Resources exist to help users subvert external information controls, however it is easier technologically to access banned content than it is to share it. These tools can seem labyrinthine to folks who don't consider themselves to be particularly tech savvy, but they are fairly straightforward to learn about and utilize when needed. TOR, for example, is a browser—just like Chrome or Firefox—with some unique differences. When you visit a website using TOR, for example, the site host is unable to "see" your IP address or any other identifying features that might make an individual user recognizable. It accomplishes this by disguising your online movements on TOR from those who might be trying to track (or prevent/censor) your movements online.

> (TOR) makes internet traffic appear completely different than it really is. For example, if someone surfs websites, it may look like a video conference, normal email traffic, or something else. It also changes back and forth all the time. This makes it more difficult for censors to follow.
>
> (Schmidt, 2023)

Someone living in Myanmar can use the TOR browser to access information about democracy and political activism, for example, but educational video about condom use may be taken down by TikTok, even if the sex educator who created it used a virtual private network (VPN) to log in to their account. We love social media. Tools such as Facebook and Instagram, Discord and Slack, Reddit and TikTok have become so integrated into our daily lives and relationships that the idea that there are limitations to what we can (or should) do with them (especially when we are acting with the best of intentions and from a desire to teach, help, and support) can feel fairly dissonant for us. And yet? We have to accept the reality that these platforms are private businesses, not public utilities. There will be limitations for those of us who work in mental, medical, and sexual health. This is incredibly frustrating, but also exciting, because it gives us the opportunity to embrace the wisdom of Supreme Court Justice Louis Brandeis who said "the remedy to be applied is more speech, not enforced silence" (Lawrence, 2022). Perhaps this represents an opportunity not only for the kind of public-private policy advocacy that The Center for Intimacy Justice and the Digital Freedom Fund are doing, but also for entrepreneurship and innovation. Perhaps there needs to be new social media platforms, developed by folks who prioritize access to accurate and inclusive information for all. Mastodon and BlueSky are leading the way in working to create more responsive, less reactionary online communities. Perhaps the next great social media resource will be built by someone from within the mental or relational health world. Who else better understands the power and importance of connection?

TECH ED WITH WOLF
WHAT IS PRIVATE, ANYWAY?

TechEd Class: What Is Private, Really?

Different cultures have differing definitions and expectations of privacy. With apologies to our international reader, this section is American-focused. This can be excused as the American understanding of privacy impacts American innovations.

You might think the problem began in 1994. You'd be wrong. The problem goes all the way back to the 1970s. The first computer programs couldn't remember what happened between start and finish of a program running and couldn't talk to each other. Early systems needed a way to maintain continuity between programs and user sessions, so computer scientists invented the "magic cookie." It was a small piece of data that stored the program's status across interactions. Fast forward to the early days of the internet, and Netscape repurposed this idea. The browser "cookie" helped track users across multiple visits and sites. It was quirky, clever, and quietly revolutionary.

This light-hearted choice baked long-term tracking into the fabric of the Web. 1994 was when the Internet grew a memory, but not when the privacy problem began. And even if you think you have nothing to hide? That doesn't mean you want everything exposed. Privacy isn't simply secrecy. Privacy is context, consent, and control.

For hundreds of generations, privacy didn't need a definition. Privacy was a built-in feature of our physical lives. You saw what you saw. You heard what you heard. A person's intimate life existed in a room, in a moment, and not beyond it. (Putting aside the obvious exception being the stories others told about what they saw and heard.) Our physical presence was consent, and our physical presence was under our own control. This began to change in the early 1960s as governments and corporations began using computers to store and process personal data.

Enter Alan F. Westin. Well ahead of his time, Westin warned that "data banks" and "automated surveillance" could fundamentally alter how society treats individuals. From civil rights to women's liberation to sexual freedom, the 1960s were a time of radical individual empowerment. Westin worked to link privacy to control over one's body, identity, and choices. Privacy, in his view, was especially important for marginalized groups seeking autonomy from societal norms or government interference. Westin defined the problem as one of information privacy, communication privacy, and individual autonomy.

The problems Westin foresaw took a major leap forward from 1960s to the 1990s to today. Now, there's a record of nearly everything: what we search, say, and share. High-fidelity captures of our emotions, our relationships, even our vulnerabilities. It's a shift that goes deeper than tech. It changes what it means to be known.

Privacy, then, is more than a shield. It's a scaffold for growth. It's what allows us to be individuals while still connecting meaningfully to others. It defines the space between us: what we choose to share, when, and with whom. Boundaries, after all, are the foundation for healthy connections. Privacy lets us experiment with identity, navigate closeness, and avoid harm. Without it, we risk overexposure, or worse, exploitation. Especially in relationships, consent and privacy go hand in hand. And yet . . .

Consent and privacy are challenging online: Our browsers accept cookies. Our user accounts tag us and log our activities. Your discount code ties your purchase to your name. Even when we try to stay anonymous, metadata leaks through. It's not just tracked. Worse, it's aggregated. Across platforms. Across devices. Across years. And while that might feel benign at first, it adds up. Especially when what we share was meant for someone we trusted, not for public consumption or corporate profiling.

Let's talk about consent. Just like in healthy relationships, the digital world should give us the right to say yes or no. Who gets to see our data? When? Why? Information privacy is about governing that consent. It includes the right to access, the right to correct, and the right to erase. If we break up with a service (or a person), we should be able to take our data and leave. That's portability. That's agency. And without it, we lose not just clarity about how our data is used, but control over that use. Thankfully, these privacy rights are being enshrined in regulations like the California Consumer Privacy Act (CCPA), the California Privacy Rights Act (CPRA), and the European General Data Protection Regulation (GDPR). These provide legal frameworks to discuss information and communication privacy.

Information privacy hits especially hard when the data in question is intimate. Where we live, our medical history, our search behavior? These are more than facts. They are stories. And if leaked, they become weapons. Think of stalking victims whose addresses were exposed. Or people with

STIs whose records get caught up in a data breach. Think of contested healthcare, such as abortions and gender affirming care, being exposed in states where people can face legal or financial penalties for accessing such care. Or someone who Googled "how to come out" and ended up getting targeted ads before they were ready. These are real harms that grow from invisible systems turning our lives into data.

Then there's communication privacy: what you say, how you say it, and who it's meant for. Westin described this as the right to control interpersonal exchanges (speech, writing, and expression) within chosen boundaries. Today, that boundary is under constant pressure. Messaging apps, texts, and DMs have become the backbone of modern relationships. Every flirtation, confession, or argument is no longer ephemeral; it's timestamped, stored, and sometimes searchable. Sexts can be intercepted. Intimate photos can be leaked or repurposed as revenge porn. Even routine conversations can be dredged up in court, exposed in a breach, or misinterpreted out of context. The belief that digital messages are private often doesn't match the legal, technical, or social reality. And yet, many relationships today are built on those very messages. Today, communication privacy is no longer just about who we trust. It's about what we risk when we do.

We've seen communication privacy violations through FBI subpoenas of DMs during investigations. Celebrities' iCloud leaks exposed their photos and texts. Personal chats have been used in court, including during divorces or custody battles. In a connected world, our romantic lives can be replayed, out of context and out of our control. That's the cost of not encrypting, not deleting, not understanding how deeply our devices know us.

And finally, individual privacy. This one's more personal and covers identity, self-expression, boundaries. Individual autonomy and privacy are the hardest to regulate because they are so deeply contextual. Consider, for example: "How I show up at work versus how I show up with my partner." Your partner sees one version. Your boss sees another. Friends, family, strangers, each gets a slice. That segmentation is normal. Healthy, even. But online, it's harder to do. Systems flatten us into one profile. This is something that we intrinsically feel, but also something that is nearly impossible to codify in laws like GDPR and CCPA or to build into privacy knobs on our phones. Individual privacy includes your gender identity, sexual orientation, and reproductive choices. It protects your quirks, your habits, your kinks. And once a part of you is out, it's hard to put it back in the box.

In recent times, we've gone through three major privacy shifts. The first was the early internet era. Back then, anonymity was baked in. You could be a dog on the internet, remember? That freedom helped queer communities and other marginalized groups explore safely. But it was fragile. There were no real safeguards. If something leaked, it stayed leaked. Still, the internet felt new and liberating. Privacy was assumed, even though information privacy was put at significant risk.

Then came the social media boom. Oversharing became the norm. Platforms encouraged us to perform our lives—relationships, breakups, trauma—all for likes. Geo tagging made it easy for stalkers. Algorithms pushed us to post more, reveal more. Relationship milestones became announcements, and announcements became vanity metrics. And while privacy settings existed, they were hard to find or understand. The dramatic increase in communications over these platforms, and others, put communication privacy at risk. People got burned. Sometimes badly. And often, by people they knew.

Now, we're living in the generative AI era. Our content trains the very models we interact with. AI can infer who we are based on language, tone, and behavior. It can mimic us, impersonate us, guess our secrets, and predict future behavior. It is true that, with social media, our social graph is more revealing than our search history. Even without knowing what we say, who we talk to (and when) predicts everything from mental health to political leanings to sexual orientation. With the rise of AI, the interference abilities of these large language models (LLMs) combined with the conversations we're having with them (having raised ourselves on social media) puts individual privacy squarely in the crosshairs. Generative models can estimate our tone, preferences, tastes, sometimes better than we can describe them ourselves

Let's return to the consent and control aspects of privacy. Privacy isn't just theoretical. It's a muscle we strengthen everyday by our choices. Clinicians already know how to protect personal boundaries in a professional setting: what to share with patients, when to withhold, how to document. That same intentionality carries into digital life. Turn off location tagging on photos before sharing them. Don't let social media auto-tag you in posts. Avoid linking your professional email to apps you use for personal journaling or health tracking. If you wouldn't hang it in the break room, don't give an app permission to collect it. Configure LLMs to not train on your conversations and to not remember your conversations. Are these acts of paranoia? No. They are acts of agency. They keep the personal, well, personal.

The same principle of informed consent applies to your devices. Check your settings to see what your phone or apps can access: microphone, camera, health data, contacts. If it doesn't need it, deny it. Privacy settings on iOS and Android can be adjusted per app: use that. Disable cloud backups for truly sensitive notes or photos. Prefer Signal or iMessage (with disappearing messages enabled) over unencrypted SMS. Set Face ID or biometric access for clinical apps, but consider adding a simple passcode for messaging apps. That way, a stolen glance at your screen doesn't open the whole world.

And when it comes to managing your professional identity? Segmentation is your friend. Use a separate browser profile for work (and separate computer, if that's an option). Keep your personal and clinical calendars in different apps. If you're on social media professionally, strip out metadata from images, and avoid posting in real-time. Consider turning off "contacts syncing" in apps like LinkedIn or Facebook. (It's often how private messages get crossed with public personas.) Technology doesn't automatically honor your boundaries. You have to configure it, and configuring it is a skill like any other. It won't be easy initially. But once you do, it becomes easier to practice online the same care and discretion you use in your work every day.

"If you have something that you don't want anyone to know, maybe you shouldn't be doing it in the first place." So said Eric Schmidt, former CEO of Google. The reality is that privacy—information, communication, individualization—is about asserting control over our lives. It lets us set boundaries. Preserving the right to say "no" is the first step towards saying a meaningful "yes." The internet remembers everything. But that doesn't mean it should. In love, in life, and in data: privacy still matters.

Expert Consult: Mandy Salley

Mandy Salley (she/her) is Chief Operating Officer for the Woodhull Freedom Foundation. In this role, she oversees the foundation's programmatic and policy work. Before joining as COO, Mandy was a longtime volunteer with the Sexual Freedom Summit. Mandy brings her passion for social justice and service to her work at Woodhull.

Mandy Salley

Can you explain what you do to us and share how your work relates to the way everyday users experience the internet?

My job title is Chief Operating Officer at the Woodhull Freedom Foundation. I am in charge of all of Woodhull's programming, so anything educational related to Woodhull's work I plan and execute. I'm also the one who is keeping really close tabs on legislation that Woodhull is following and supporting or opposing. The Woodhull Freedom Foundation has taken a really active role in opposing legislation that seeks to quote, 'make the internet safer for children or keep kids safe online,' but which actually censors our speech, impacts privacy, and increases surveillance. One of the first censorship targets for legislators is anything sexual in nature—even if it is not explicit—anything related to sexuality as a broad category. Our mission is to affirm sexual freedom as a human right. Our human right to free expression and our first amendment right to free speech is very much, I would say, in critical condition both at the federal and state level. So my work is monitoring all of that legislation as best we can, and very frequently writing letters or testifying and educating our lawmakers about the privacy and speech concerns, as well as the consequences related to this legislation.

What makes you passionate about this work?

I'm a social worker at heart. That's my professional identity before anything else, and that's because I really believe in social justice. I believe in meeting people where they are and helping people. I worked in direct service for a long time, one-on-one with people and I have seen firsthand how policies, not just sexual freedom policies, but laws of all kinds affect people's everyday lives. I think in order to be a good advocate, you *have* to understand that. The reason I'm on this side of the fence now, doing macro social work, is because I've always felt like I wanted to be doing more. And this is the way I get to *do more* to help people on an individual level, if that makes sense. I really believe in equality and sexual freedom and this is how I put those values into service.

What do therapists, educators, and others working in the field of sexual health need to know about navigating online censorship?

First and foremost, they need to know it exists. If you ever watch Woodhull's Instagram videos, I'm saying things like "Shmexual freedom" or "Shmabortion." It's so silly, but using the actual words gets our content taken down and gets us censored. Woodhull's Instagram is actually shadow banned! Unless you know the exact spelling of our Instagram handle, for example, you won't be able to find our Instagram page. None of our content comes up in the suggested like page. We'll never be suggested to you to follow. It's really hard to do the public education work we're trying to do, and that a lot of folks are trying to do, when Meta is actively censoring our content.

It's important for folks who are trying to market their business, trying to get the word out about their work, to know that they should not ever rely on these social platforms to store their content. Nothing you put online is yours. If you put it on Instagram and you think that it's going to be there forever for you to share it? No. When folks lose their accounts, they lose everything that was posted to that account. And there's very little recourse with these platforms to get your account—your content—back. So please, store your stuff somewhere that is not cloud-based, like on a desktop on a thumb drive. It's crucial and important.

If want to post content about topics that these platforms are very frequently censoring, you need to know what you're doing and make sure you're following the rules. Those very long TOS policies that we all click to say we've read when we first create accounts on these platforms? Most people don't actually read them, and it's really important that you do. We treat the internet like it's a public square, but these platforms are owned by very large social media companies and corporations; and in the United States, corporations have First Amendment rights. They are well within their rights to host or to hide whatever they want on their platforms. If you're going to take that on and post content on the platform, I would make sure you're following their rules. It may seem a little bit contradictory to say, as a free speech/free expression advocate; but I understand that it's not my platform. I don't own Instagram, I'm just putting content there. Users have to follow the rules, and keep tabs on everything they're doing, so that if you ever to have to appeal a moderation decision, you've got sort of a paper trail of what you're doing.

Scan here to see the "Too Long, Didn't Read" overview of your favorite website's Terms of Service

How does online censorship impact the work of sexual health professionals and their clients?

Oh, it makes it a lot harder! Especially in a post-Dobbs United States, it is extremely hard to find information about reproductive healthcare—even if it's not abortion. Information about contraception, about safer sex—all of that—is really hard to find on social media. We live in a time where people are getting the majority of their information from social media. People have come to rely on these platforms. They're very much a part of our everyday routines and our everyday lives. So, when this kind of information is being removed, it's lot harder to find at all. Or at least, it's a lot harder to find information that is accurate, well researched, good health information.

It's really important for people to start to learn basic media literacy and try to understand what is *researched*, what is *proven*, what is *true*, versus what is just somebody talking on the internet. That can be really hard! It takes work to be informed. It requires going to different sources and reading a variety of things, comparing and contrasting what you find. We live in a time where incredible amounts of information are at our fingertips, but in order to actually get *truthful* information, you have to absorb all of it and figure out what's accurate within each source. Censorship makes that harder, because it creates an access issue to even just basic healthcare information.

From nanny-apps to behavioral management programs, censorship and surveillance software is catching on in the healthcare world. What do helping professionals need to consider before recommending these tools to their clients?

Helping professionals have to be particularly mindful of how HIPAA applies or does not apply with these particular tools. To share like a personal anecdote, when I was deciding to go off my birth control, my primary care provider suggested that

I download an app to start tracking your cycle. It wasn't bad advice on its face, but if I lived in a state that banned abortion and I used an app that was not subject to HIPAA protections, that means I'm putting my very private reproductive health information into a cloud-based app that in many states is not protected.

Beyond HIPAA, I don't think people realize that we do not have any comprehensive data privacy protection legislation in the United States. When I put my information online, there's no law anywhere that says the platform I put that information into has to protect it. That's something that wasn't a consideration ten or twenty years ago, but it's certainly a crucial consideration now. It's important for helping professionals to think about the ways in which the laws that we probably don't think about in our everyday practice—affect the people we're helping. We need to know privacy laws and censorship laws and our local state laws order to recommend the best tool to our patients.

This is something that should be built into continuing ed curriculums. There are ethical concerns around many of these topics and it's important to study up and stay current. In the US, every state is different, and so what is okay or safe in one state could not be in another. We need to be putting in effort on our part to see how those laws could affect our practices.

As a free speech advocate, is there ever a time when you think censorship can be a good thing?

There's a phrase in free speech advocacy: "the best way to fight censorship is with more speech, not less speech." I really believe that people should be presented with all of the information and all of their options, before making a decision. I don't think the way to solve some of the problems that the internet is by mandating or blocking certain terms or topics. I don't ever think censorship is a good thing. That said, I do think that there are some topics and content that are not okay to be shared widely. That comes down to consent for me. Non-consensual images (which is frequently called revenge porn) are not okay because the people involved in that did not consent to be a part of it. Things that are violent or illegal are not okay to be seen, shared, consumed. Because again, this is non-consensual media. But in my mind, that's not censorship. That's consent. If somebody's not consenting to be a part of it—either as a participant or a viewer—then it shouldn't be viewed or consumed.

What can everyday users do to advocate for greater freedom online—both in terms of what they are allowed to post on their social media platforms and what they chose not to share with others?

First off for the average user is to remember unless you're a web developer and you've created your own platform, most of the places where people are sharing their content, their information, their lives are not—they're not public squares. You're not going to be able to go on these platforms and just say whatever you want to say, whenever you want to say it. These platforms are heavily moderated by the companies that own them. And the content that you see is curated specifically for you based on your behavior on each platform. That's another thing to remember—my TikTok feed is totally different than yours. People have to remember that the content you are consuming every day is actually its own little vacuum, personalized to you. That's part of where we're getting all this misinformation—people aren't understanding that what they see is curated and manipulated to keep them on the platform longer, to get them to spend money on the platform, all of those things. So just remember: everything you see, you're seeing based on how you behaved.

Secondly, people need to start paying attention to the laws around social media and the internet in general. There's this rhetoric out there right now that legislators are creating policy to keep kids safe online, to make the internet safer, to protect us. The average person is not reading proposed laws. It's certainly not my favorite reading material—I'd rather be reading smut personally! But I would encourage people to read these bills. I think it will frighten people to see just how much content and regulation is written into these bills that would affect them and their lives. Then? Call your legislator—call them or email them or fax them and make your voice heard around these issues because there's just not enough noise being made to our legislators about what they're doing to our online presence.

Third, know that nothing you're putting in a messaging app is protected unless you're using an app that is encrypted end-to-end. The one I know of that can really be trusted is one called Signal. When you're using Facebook Messenger, Snapchat, WhatsApp—any of these ways that people are communicating online—just assume that you're not the only people seeing it. Your assumption should be that this is basically a public conversation. So if you are going to talk about a healthcare decision, if you are going to do anything private, please don't do it via a tool like Facebook Messenger, or even your phones texting service.

Use a password manager. Protect your information. I think that you can never be too safe when it comes to your own data and information online. I strongly suggest people not share their information on apps at all if they can help it. Even your Google Drive and other (G Suite) files—Google can see all of that information. If people want to protect themselves, protect their content, and protect their privacy, then don't do it on a cloud-based storage system and opt out of facial recognition if you can. It's everywhere today—a lot of times we don't even realize it's happening.

People love the internet and the convenience of all it offers us. But a lot of us haven't taken the time to learn how it all works. I want to say that I'm an optimist. I think when we talk about this stuff, it seems so dark, so bad. But I want to say that sexual expression and freedom of speech are our human rights. Our First Amendment rights. And I really do think that there are a lot of people out there that care about these things. I didn't have hope that things would get better? I wouldn't be doing this work. So please, keep expressing yourselves, because I think when we start self-censoring then the censors have already won—without actually needing to remove our content, our words, and our speech.

Chapter 6

Online Dating

Meet-cute Myths and Misconceptions

In 1828, American painter Sarah Goodridge put a small package in the mail to Congressman Daniel Webster. When he unwrapped the delivery, Webster found a small (2.6 by 3.14") piece of ivory with a watercolor depiction of Goodridge's bare breasts, surrounded by white cloth. The artwork, titled "Beauty Revealed" is sometimes referred to as the world's first sext message. In 2024, the idea of finding a partner by sharing images and personal profiles on public platforms seems thoroughly modern. In actuality, the practice of using mass communication to find suitable romantic partners has existed for as long as adults have been empowered to find and select their own future mates. Rather than being ahead of her time, bold Sarah was embracing the latest in cutting-edge technology (the post box) to "shoot her shot" with one of the leading political figures of her day. We touched briefly on the mailbox in Chapter Two, and the way that it revolutionized private communication. The ability for young people, particularly, to send and receive intimate communication without the oversight of a governess or parent was scandalous and sent the Victorian world into a moral panic.

Publicly announcing that one was seeking a suitable spouse was more socially acceptable. It wasn't the overture itself that carried scandal, so much as the private, "for your eyes only" nature of these propositions. With the dawn of the 19th century, Sarah Goodridge was one of many young adults who were coming of age in a time when society was finally encouraging them to seek out their own potential partners, rather than enter into marriages arranged by their families. Many chose to find their soulmate (or at least a suitable extra pair of hands on the farm) through the use of personal ads placed in newspapers around the country. These short 20–200 words classified ads, placed in weekly papers serving immigrant communities, religious denominations, and small towns around the country, were quite popular and served as a proto-Match.com well into the 20th century (SNPM, 2024). As with all new innovations, marginalized communities tended to be early adopters. Queer-coded personal ads helped isolated or closeted LGBT persons find one another in relative safety (Lee, 2016), while women

DOI: 10.4324/9781003391128-7

who chafed under the social and legal control of parents could feel empowered to verbalize their desires and seek out their own paramours. On the other hand? Catfishing and romance scams were rife within the matrimonial pages and more than one 19th century serial killer used the lonely hearts pages to lure unsuspecting victims into their traps.

The handful of bad actors who used them to exploit others created a suspicion around the whole enterprise.

Like the internet today. Lonely hearts ads were suspected of harboring all sorts of scams and perversities. Because they were often used by homosexuals and sex workers, British police continued to prosecute those who placed personals until the late 1960's when ads became part of the burgeoning youth counterculture.

(Lee, 2016)

And as we entered the 20th century, many saw technology as a way to clean up and modernize the old way of finding love across long distances. In 1960, three computer scientists at Harvard programmed Operation Match on (here it is again!) an IBM 1410, leveraging the behemoth 5-ton mainframe to pair up co-eds who had completed a paper questionnaire and paid a $3 fee.

After the answers were copied onto punch cards, the machine would then match each co-ed with 5 others in just seconds and spit out the results via its massive printer. Workers would then mail them to all those college students waiting impatiently for love.

(Hernandez, 2014)

From there, the intuitive instinct to use emerging technology to facilitate romantic and sexual matches became the norm. Home video emerged in the late 70s and 80s, and video dating—where the seeking single would record a VHS tape answering questions about themselves and their ideal partners—took off. Match. com was founded in 1995 and within a decade, online dating had become the second highest online industry for paid content, second only to pornography (Lee, 2016).

For most of us who were born after Operation Match in 1960, it feels natural—even expected—to leverage the algorithms and the internet to find our future mate (or next date). Online or app-based dating feels ubiquitous today—it's simply how the work of romantic connection gets done, right? The data tells us an interesting story. While younger people (those under 30) certainly use apps and other dating platforms to meet new people, it is still not as common as one might expect. A recent report from the Pew Research Council found that only 53% of people ages 18–30 have *ever* used a dating site or app! That number drops to

37% of 30–49 year olds, 20% of those 50–64 and only 13% of folks over age 65. Continuing our theme of Queer early adopters, LGB (lesbian, gay and bisexual) adults report using dating sites and apps at a rate almost double their straight peers: 51% to 28% (Vogels & McClain, 2023). Queer adults are also more likely to find a long-term partner online, with 24% of LGB users telling researchers that they found their spouse or partner online compared to 20% of straight users under 30 and only 10% of straight users ages 30+ (Vogels & McClain, 2023).

These low success rates may be attributed in part to the fact that our definition of what romantic "success" looks like is also changing. In general, folks today are getting married less and choosing to stay single more (Seariac, 2023). Patrick Yang, a student at Yale University described Gen Z's approach to dating and relationships by saying "I've heard a joke on campus that goes something like this: first base is hooking up, second base is talking, third base is going on a date, and fourth base is dating." One possible explanation for this reluctance to connect deeply with others is the pervasive nature of social media, and the sense of cautious suspicion that it evokes in many users (Wilson, 2019). What does it say about online dating platforms, after all, when nearly half of ALL internet traffic is not coming from other humans, but from bots (Beckman, 2024)? How can someone open up to the possibility of meaningful connection when they can't even be sure that there's a real person on the other end? This concern is not entirely new—the aspirational chamber maid of 1860 who boarded a train heading west to marry was likely just as worried about who she would find when she met her new fiancée at the train station. The proliferation of abandoned profiles, chatbots, and malicious actors on dating platforms today takes that same, utterly rational fear and expands it.

That might be why, despite the ubiquity of online dating platforms for every possible identity group and relationship style, more and more people are opting out of the digital dating landscape in favor of meeting potential partners the old fashioned way. You know . . . in person. One Stanford study found that, of folks who did NOT meet online nearly half met their new partner in public spaces such as a bar/restaurant (27%), at work (11%), or in school (9%), while others were introduced by mutual friends (20%) or family (7%) (Rosenfeld, Thomas, & Hausen, 2019). This is not to say that young adults are opting out of technology-facilitated courtship entirely, just that they're starting to leverage social media and other online services in ways that are both novel and reminiscent of dating practices of eras past.

Historically, many cultures relied on professional matchmakers to find a potential spouse. This often involved compiling a lengthy personal dossier (akin to today's dating app profile, but much more detailed) which was used by the matchmaker to introduce their clients to the parents of a potential "match." Today, many Gen Z daters are using their social media algorithms as a matchmaker. After all, if the algorithm is already designed to suggest other profiles it determines you might be interested in connecting with socially . . . why not take the leap and send that person a message introducing yourself? The data collected by social media algorithm becomes a kind of de facto "dossier," which the platform then uses to suggest potential matches for friendship and (in some cases) beyond. This can become problematic, of course, when social media platforms suggest that two people might have a potential connection in common: only to have one "slide into the DM's" of someone uninterested in being approached romantically by a stranger. Others, recognizing that there are consent concerns involved in blindly messaging folks based on the social media prompt, are making their dating dossiers available to anyone viewing their profile—extending an invitation for those who believe they might be a good fit to approach them:

> Information about yourself and what you're looking for in a personalized Google doc, linked in your social media bio . . . offer(s) more in-depth summaries of what someone is looking for and can include helpful things like past partner reviews and calendar links to add time to meet your prospective partner.
>
> (Battle, 2024)

While the realities of online dating—both usage and success—might be exaggerated, it is a fact that these tools have become a common element of modern intimacy and romance. Let's take a look at what happens "behind the scenes" of these products and how technology is influencing and guiding our most intimate connections.

Matchmaker, Matchmaker, Make Me an App

> The dilemma of contemporary love is that we are invested with full agency to choose in our own interest . . . (but) emotions are not always as clear and stable as one may wish. Powered by user-centered affordances that provide access to potentially infinite partners . . . dating apps offer a potential solution to this dilemma.
>
> (Bandinelli, 2022)

Since Match.com (1995) and Kiss.com (1994) broke new ground, a new website or app has launched every year. It begins with user profiles, including security controls to verify the person is who they say they are, and features for adding photos and sharing personal information. There are a search and discovery mechanism, originally by surveys and search filters, but more recently algorithms looking at behaviors and interests. The platform will have ways to connect (swipes, likes, notifications) and communicate (messaging, calls). There are also security and privacy settings, although as often is the case, these take a back seat to the desire to encourage people to spend more time on the app.

Dating apps can cost up to a million US dollars to launch. Many groundbreaking apps, like the first mobile dating app Grindr in 2009, started with modest beginnings and exemplified the myth of the solo tech entrepreneur. These innovations were often crafted by small, resourceful teams working outside the corporate environment, demonstrating that great ideas can start without substantial financial backing. Most, however, require funding from accelerators. Tinder with Hatch Labs (Ghosh, 2017) and Zoosk with Plug and Play Tech Center are good examples. Of course, private equity money brings pressure to have an exit plan.

Match Group (NASDAQ: MTCH) purchased Tinder in 2017, adding it to the portfolio which includes Match.com, Meetic, OkCupid, Hinge, Plenty of Fish, and others. Zoosk was purchased by Spark Networks SE (NASDAQ: LOVLQ), which also owns such dating brands as ChristianMingle, eDarling, Jdate, JSwipe, AdventistSingles, and LDSSingles. Bumble (NASDAQ: BMBL) merged with Badoo and acquired Fruitz. From a business perspective, large players continuing to acquire upstarts isn't unique to dating. But from a dating perspective, the dozens and dozens of dating choices surprisingly come down to a small handful of companies.

Dating is big business, estimated at $10 billion annually (Grand View Research, 2023). Match Group is the leader with reported $3.36 billion in revenue in 2023 (Stock Analysis, 2024b). Bumble reached the $1 billion revenue mark in 2023 (Stock Analysis, 2024a). Meanwhile, Spark Networks is significantly smaller at $172.36 million (Stock Analysis, 2024c). Other apps that are privately held and not publicly traded are difficult to get revenue figures for. The largest is likely eHarmony, which has annual revenue in the hundreds of millions (Calo, 2023).

Dating apps have inherent incentive mismatches with people, as their business models often depend on keeping people engaged and subscribed. These platforms employ various strategies to prolong user activity, sometimes at odds with the people's goals of finding lasting relationships. The user-centered affordances, mentioned at the start of this section, create a cycle of uncertainty and continuous engagement with the platform (Bandinelli, 2022). Some apps use this uncertainty to signal false love interest to encourage people to purchase paid subscriptions (U.S. Federal Trade Commission, 2019). Algorithms recommend popular users more frequently, creating a popularity bias, resulting in less popular users having lower chances of being matched and prolonging their subscriptions (Celdir, 2023). The platforms often prioritize engagement from the thrill of matches over prioritizing the likelihood of users finding compatible partners (Zytko, 2018), resulting in people interacting with people on the apps rather than actively moving conversations to in-person dates (Carpenter & McEwan, 2016). Of course, when all that fails, dating apps can simply process auto-renewals, a practice which eHarmony settled a lawsuit for in 2018 (Tassin, 2018).

Yet people remain very confident in the dating algorithms. In one study, the method of matching with a partner, whether by algorithm or self-selection, did not significantly change the likelihood of a successful first date. However, those who were matched by an algorithm exhibited stronger beliefs that it resulted in a better first date. Personal disclosures are a proven technique to increase intimacy, and confidence in algorithms is associated with increased self-disclosure during online chat within dating apps (Sharabi, 2020). Curiously, the actual effectiveness of dating algorithms appears to matter less than the user's perception of its effectiveness.

Visit the Mozilla Foundation to read their security report for your favorite dating app

$10 billion in annual revenue is generated from the process of searching for matches rather than from successful matches themselves. People who do well on modern dating platforms are those who are adept at transitioning from matches to authentic in-person connections, avoiding the lure of endless feel-good but ultimately shallow online conversations.

Online Relationship Risks

Almost from the start, as early as the mid-1990s, we knew paradoxically that people turned to the Internet for connection, but the Internet left them feeling more alone (Kraut, 1998). This is counterintuitive as people often momentarily feel better after interacting online. But as we've seen with online dating, people's perceptions do not always align with reality when it comes to outcomes (Sharabi, 2020). We've evolved to look for certain signals when evaluating relationships, and technology is great at sending those signals. There is an evolutionary mismatch, a term defined as how our minds evolved to create conditions that are maladaptive in modern situations (Brenner, 2015). Dating platforms may take advantage of evolutionary mismatches to extend subscriptions.

Likewise, criminals and scammers leverage evolutionary mismatches to earn their own income. The most common online dating romance scam, sometimes referred to as mass-marketing fraud or confidence scams, is regularly on the top of the FBI's Internet Crime Complaint Center (IC3) statistics. In 2023, a reported $652 million was stolen from 17,923 people (FBI, 2024). The word reported is crucial here. Victims of romance scams often face psychological barriers that prevent them from reporting the crime. Moreover, there is often little the FBI can do. The actual number is significantly higher than the official statistics. It is likely that 3% of the general population have been victims of romance scams at least once (Coluccia, 2020).

These mass-marketing romance scams follow a predictable pattern (Whitty, Anatomy of the online dating romance scam, 2015). The criminal creates a dating profile with a physically attractive individual, possibly someone with a high socio-economic status. They manipulate the dating algorithms or matchmaking system to match with the victim. The next stage is grooming, where the criminal builds trust and a relationship with the victim. As a recurring theme in this book, the victim is encouraged to self-disclose personal details to heighten the sense of intimacy. Next comes the sting, where the criminal convinces the victim to send them money. This may be presented as a crisis with a large request, or as requests for small amounts of money without a crisis narrative. In some cases, the criminal may ask victim for photographs or to perform sexual acts on video. The final stage is the revelation of the scam, either by the criminal or by the victim's social support structure convincing them that the partner is fraudulent.

Two of these stages involve widely recognized terms in popular culture: catfishing and sextortion. Catfishing typically refers to the creation of a fake persona, complete with online profiles, for the purpose of engaging in a relationship or interaction with a specific person or group of people (Simmons & Lee, 2020). Catfishing may be a form of online impersonation, or it may involve pretending to be someone entirely fictional. The stage of a romance scam wherein sexual abuse is potentially involved is blackmail or sextortion. "Sextortion is the threatened dissemination of explicit, intimate, or embarrassing images of a sexual nature without consent, usually for the purpose of procuring additional images, sexual acts, money, or something else" (Patchin, 2018).

Returning to the concept of evolutionary mismatches, we can see several points in which the behavior is signaling a partnered relationship. Early relationships often disclose personal details. Sharing sexy images is as old as painting. For as long as we have had access to video, we've used the medium to forge relationships. Finally, in partnered relationships, sharing resources during a crisis is a prevalent and beneficial behavior.

The common perception of these romance scams is of a single dastardly criminal who quickly takes advantage of the victim. In fact, a scam often includes multiple criminals acting in concert. "The majority of the narratives included additional characters who held positions of authority; some examples include diplomats, lawyers, doctors, law enforcement and so forth. For the victims, these personas of authority represented someone they could trust" (Whitty, 2013). These conversations play out over 6–8 months, sometimes longer (Coluccia, 2020).

Sha Zhu Pan (杀猪盘) or pig butchering scams take this to an unfortunate but logical next step (Wang & Zhou, 2023). These can begin on dating apps, but also can originate on social media or over a phone's text messages. Once trust is established and a relationship begun, the criminal introduces the idea of investing in seemingly legitimate but actually fraudulent investment opportunities, often involving cryptocurrency or other financial schemes. Additional characters may be introduced to provide testimonials and fabricated evidence of high returns to entice the victim to invest significant amounts of money. As the victim becomes more deeply involved, the criminal may manipulate them into making larger investments. Eventually, the scam is revealed, leaving them with significant financial losses and emotional distress.

The persistence of romance scams reveals a stark contradiction in our digital age: the same tools designed to bring people together can also facilitate profound deception and betrayal. These scams continue to evolve, leveraging smart phones for sextortion and incorporating elements like cryptocurrency investments. By understanding the psychological and technological dynamics at play, we can better equip ourselves and our clinical clients to recognize and combat these deceptive practices. It's not enough to consider only the risks that lie on the other side of the Wi-Fi connection however—there are also cognitive biases and worrisome behaviors that clinicians should be mindful of in our own clients as well.

Clinical Considerations and Concerns

While long-distance relationships have existed for centuries, the internet and the ability to form deep bonds very quickly without the social vetting processes that existed in the past has given rise to a new set of clinical considerations for the modern relationship therapist. For many, using the internet to meet people and form new relationships ranging from platonic to romantic to erotic feels incredibly convenient. We have access to thousands of incredibly specific online communities, allowing us to curate those voices we encounter with hyper-granularity. Do you want to meet singles in your area? Not a problem! Do you *only* want to meet singles who are Southeast Asian, demisexual, lapsed Catholics who cheer for your preferred sports team and love Italian food? Also not a problem! This abundance of choice (or at least, the illusion of choice) brings with it not just a slew of new apps to download and sites to join, but also some unique mental health impacts that we are just now beginning to understand.

The internet can be the consummate ice breaker. Rather than spend hours at a nightclub on a Saturday evening, paying for drinks and hoping that if you bolster the courage to initiate a conversation with someone they won't reject you publicly, many of us choose to hop online. Here, from the safety of our own living room, we can say hello to dozens of people every hour. If they ignore us? We never have to experience that rejection face to face. If they say something dismissive or unkind? We know no one else will overhear. And if they happen to respond favorably? Well, now we have something to talk about if and when we do decide to meet up with them in person! "Remember that hilarious meme you sent me last Thursday? I showed my cousin and she laughed so hard." This feels like a much safer first-date conversation starter than "So. . . . Tell me about yourself." The internet allows us to protect our dignity while optimizing our efficiency (Clemens, Atkin, & Krishnan, 2015). And if it gives us a pre-installed set of shared moments to explore when we move from the server to the coffee shop? More's the better. This might lead us to conclude that those who use the internet as their primary social networking/relationship formation strategy are more socially anxious or shy than their peers who are mixing and mingling at IRL events. This assumption would be incorrect:

> Contrary to the negative stereotype presenting online daters as shy, desperate and anxious individuals, research has suggested the exact opposite; online daters scored low on dating anxiety and. . . . No differences were found between online daters and non-online daters with regard to self-esteem or self-confidence.
>
> (Pitcho-Prelorentzos, Heckel, & Ring, 2020)

Knowing that the quest to meet new people, or even future partners, is not rooted in the stereotypical "socially awkward loner" trope is important because even in 2024 there are many who still consider online dating to be embarrassing or less than other romantic opportunities. But even within this generally healthy pool of daters, there are some mental and behavioral health pitfalls for our clients to be aware of:

- **Dating Profile as Identity Formation:** We've mentioned elsewhere that famous *New Yorker* cartoon that's captioned "on the internet, no one knows you're a dog." The humor lies in the truth of the observation—truly, we can be anything we want to be on the internet. From AI-created headshots to fictive dating profiles worthy of the Pulitzer, there is nothing preventing a user from creating an online persona that represents who they wish they were—or aspire to be—rather than who they actually are. In the same way that an adolescent might jump from trend to trend, embracing Sex Pistols-style punk aesthetics one month and a homespun Cottage Core vibe the next, so too can we use our online presence to experiment with identity. We can come out on the internet before we feel safe doing so in real life (Hiebert & Kortes-Miller, 2021) or experiment with various political or social identities without fearing a backlash from those who know us offline. This can result in anxiety about beliefs, identities, or attitudes we may have held in the past "living forever" online (Brandtzaeg & Chapparro-Dominquez, 2020) as well as an impulse to create a carefully curated, idealized, (or even entirely fictional) online persona. While in any dating process, there is always an element of "putting ones best face forward," we must be mindful of the potential not only for exploration, but also for exaggeration, experimentation, and outright falsehoods, not only from those our clients encounter online, but potentially those created by the client themselves
- **Covert avoidance:** Researchers who study computer-mediated communication have "repeatedly shown a link between neuroticism and using the Internet to find companionship. This is because the online environment affords neurotics the ability to avoid intimacy, face-to-face confrontation, argumentation, and rejection" (Clemens, Atkin, & Krishnan, 2015). While certainly not

every client or online dater could be considered "neurotic," this is an important behavioral pattern to recognize. For some users, online dating profiles are not a mechanism for facilitating real-life romance, but rather they are a way to have the illusion of those romantic connections, without any of the emotional labor and risk involved in actually connecting with another human being. Many clients who use online dating tools in this way may not be consciously aware of these behaviors. The failure to move these online flirtations into real-life encounters may be attributed instead to particularly high standards or complicated scheduling. Speaking of which . . .

- **The paradox of choice:** The authors once met a couple who told us the story of how they met, but their fairytale didn't begin with "Once Upon A Time." Rather their story started with "thank goodness I took a chance and swiped right, because my usual policy was to say no to anyone who had less than an 80% profile match." Barry Schwartz, the author of the book *The Paradox of Choice*, would describe this as the connection of two satisficers—a portmanteau of satisfy and suffice. "For a maximizer, somewhere out there is the perfect lover, the perfect friend. Even though there is nothing wrong with the current relationship, who knows what's possible if you keep your eyes open. The opposite of maximizers are satisficers, who have the ability to know a good thing when they see it without obsessing over 'what ifs.' It's not the same as settling for a bad option, because satisficing also means having high standards. But it does mean ignoring the temptation of finding out if the grass is really greener on the other side (Dodgson, 2018)." Going back just a few decades, our dating prospects were limited to the people we knew in our immediate area. By the time we filtered out everyone single, of the correct gender, and not immediately related to us? We may only have a handful of partner prospects to choose from. Scarcity made satisficers of us all. Today, dating platforms promise us thousands of choices—filtered not only by geography and other basic demographics, but by details as specific as choice of pet, body shape, and preferred sexual positions. It's not that our standards are higher—most everyone wants a partner who is kind, mature, compatible, and relatively attractive—but that the number of other metrics available to us has expanded exponentially, making it that much easier to swipe left without pausing to consider whether there would be a potential spark of interest present, if we saw this person anywhere else but on our screen. This is an important point of reflection, because not only are our clients battling the paradox of choice, they're also dealing with the illusion of choice. Studies show that 10% or more of all new accounts are fake (WebPurify, 2023). Because 65% of dating apps get deleted within a month (Blake, 2024), there are also a relatively high number of abandoned profiles—accounts that are still visible to other users long after the creator has deleted the app and moved on. And then, there are the married users. While there are many dating sites now that allow users to indicate that they are seeking polyamorous relationships or have an ethically non-monogamous agreement with their partner, huge numbers of married users are still actively using dating websites as a form of recreational flirtation, if not outright infidelity. One study conducted by Stanford Medicine found that 65.3% of active Tinder users reported being in a relationship or married (Kato, 2023). This combination of fake profiles, abandoned profiles, and disingenuous profiles can turn online dating into a Sisyphean task, wherein more time and energy is spent simply trying to find someone real than is spent finding the right someone for us. And when we spend days swiping right or sending messages that go unreciprocated or ignored? It can take a serious toll on one's sense of self

- **Feeling rejected/unwanted:** Because online dating in its present form (primarily "swipe based") is still fairly new, the research on its effects is somewhat limited. There have been several studies indicating that using online dating platforms "is significantly associated with psychological distress and depression" with symptoms worsening the longer and more often study participants reporting using the apps (Holtzhausen, et al., 2020). In another study, respondents told researchers that using dating sites "say the experience left them feeling more frustrated (45%) than hopeful (28%)" (Anderson, Vogels, & Turner, 2020). When their profiles don't generate conversations or their greetings go ignored, it becomes increasingly common for the user to look at themselves as being flawed. The desire to appear attractive to potential profile visitors, for example, has been shown to lead to unhealthy weight control behaviors in dating app users (Tran, et al., 2019)—an internalized self-shame that is often reinforced when "women, minorities, fat people, and people with disabilities have negative experiences like harassment on the apps" (Battle, 2024). "Older generations of daters may have more experience with the discomfort of dating rejection. They may also rebound more easily after an awkward encounter, rather than internalizing it as 'cringe' that can't be overcome. Of course, most of us fear rejection, but in a tech-mediated world where ideas and people are liked, upvoted, attacked or labelled, things can feel simultaneously impersonal and very personal" (Battle, 2024)

- **Loss of IRL connectivity skills:** Historically, "the biggest predictor of how people met previously was physical proximity. . . . Are you near them? Do you go to school near them? Are you in the same tribe? It's not chemistry, it's just about being next to them" (Gritters, 2019). Indeed, for most of human history, in those everyday encounters—buying a loaf of bread, repairing a wheel, or sharing a pew in church on Sunday—there may not have been instant attraction, but there was familiarity and with that familiarity, affection grew. Today many younger adults—digital natives who have grown up with an app for everything—are struggling with how to make romantic connections without the mediation of a screen. When one social scientist

> compared the traditional relationship development model to the process of developing relationships on Tinder. He found that at nearly every stage

the process was augmented by digital technology in a way which reduced spontaneous communication; this was particularly true for the process of initiating a relationship, which traditionally relies on the transmission and decoding of nonverbal messages.

(Rosean, Matic, & Samardžija, 2019)

Fear of rejection, uncertainty about what to say, and a lack of fluency in reading body language and non-verbal cues signaling interest feel like insurmountable barriers compared to simply sending a quick message with an emoji and a "hey."

TECH ED WITH WOLF
WHAT'S AN ALGORITHIM?

TechEd Class: What Are Algorithms?

Algorithms. We buy something for a friend and suddenly our social media is swamped with advertisements for their preferences, not ours. We view too many videos on one topic, and suddenly we can't find anything but that topic on the app. And we blame the algorithms. Pesky little things. But what actually are algorithms?

At the most basic level, an algorithm is simply a set of instructions for a specific problem. Multiplication or division are algorithms. Let's take it up a step. Suppose you're writing instructions for a coworker, creating a process for them to follow. Here's how to do a client intake, or how to do billing with insurance. That's like an algorithm, except, people are much more tolerant of nuance and ambiguity than computers. Computer algorithms tend to be very specific, detailed, and fit for purpose.

Algorithms hit the popular consciousness in the mid 2010s due to social media. But the idea goes way back. Historically, Ada Lovelace created the first computer algorithm in 1843 to compute Bernoulli numbers for Charles Babbage's never finished mechanical computer. Alan Turing published an algorithm in 1936 for a machine that could solve any number of mathematic problems. Then the Information Age hit, and suddenly we needed algorithms for sending, receiving, and processing data. We also needed algorithms or instruction sets for keeping data private and limiting who can access it. Early examples included cryptography (RSA algorithm, 1977), image processing (FFT, 1965), image compression (LZW, 1984), and more and more.

Many companies were founded on their algorithm alone. In the late 1990s, we had Google with its PageRank algorithm for search results. In the late 2010s, we had TikTok's For You Page (FYP) algorithm. Both of these began a shift away from solving math problems and towards addressing people problems. With more data, with more computing processing power, algorithms became more complex and rich.

When people today talk about "the algorithm," they don't mean encryption, processing, or compression. At least, most people. They mean personalized recommendations. That's the in-your-face experience. These use behavior analysis and machine learning to improve the experience. (But improve the experience for who, some might ask, the company, the customer, the advertiser?) Netflix's recommendation system was an early standout in this area. They even ran a series of contests to advance the algorithm, awarding $1 million USD in the Netflix Prize to a team of scientists (with the amazing name BellKor's Pragmatic Chaos) for enhancing the prediction. Thank an algorithm the next time you spend a weekend binge watching television.

Preferences are preferences, and what often works in one domain works in another. So thought the dating companies, who turned to algorithms to match people. The early approaches, popularized by eHarmony and OkCupid, were surveys and questionnaires resulting in compatibility scores. This lent an air of science and intelligence to the search of romance. It also was a lot of work, and soon the shine wore off. The next wave was a pairing using geolocation and online status, seen in apps like Tinder and Grindr. Hinge went with a deep-cut, the Gale-Shapley algorithm originally published in 1962, which is a great joke to tell algorithm nerds as they're applying an approach to the stable marriage problem to actual real-life marriages. Anyways. Today every dating site uses a combination of algorithms and techniques to make matches.

Another use of algorithms is in reviewing photographs and videos. On dating sites, that might put an end to the incessant and seemingly unremittent dick pic. Algorithms form the foundation of the field of computer vision, enabling applications such as image classification, object detection, instance segmentation, and semantic segmentation.

In an ideal world, this would mean that adult content would be automatically classified and potentially censored, and child sexual abuse material (CSAM) would be banned. The reality is often a lot less than the ideal. Vision algorithms in particular, and many algorithms in general, have false positives (mistake something wholesome as adult content) and false negatives (miss some adult content altogether). These can create backlash among users of a product if the algorithms are particularly high in false positives or negatives. Tumblr ran into this in 2018–2019 with their adult content guidelines, which all but killed the platform as users went elsewhere.

But when vision algorithms work, they can open new avenues for sensual experiences. Many SexTech companies have used them to synchronize the movement of toys with video content. Kiiroo is an example company with their Keon and Pearl products. As with dating apps, behind the scenes, this is actually several algorithms working together in concert. Some watching the pornography. Some determining what's movement and what's not. Another translating that movement into what makes sense for the toy's form-factor, capabilities, and function. With the addition of interactive storylines, people using these toys anecdotally report being more engaged and feeling more connected to the performance.

Engagement, of course, is key for many Internet companies. As discussed in other Tech Ed sections, the Information Age embraced advertising as the primary way to monetize content in the 1990s. In the 2010s, this meant engagement numbers. How long was a person on the app or website? How much content did they interact with? Did they come back regularly? The higher the numbers, the more company can charge for advertisements. Some apps use the collective actions of all the users to surface what's hot or useful. That's known as collaborative filtering algorithms, seen on sites such as Reddit or early Twitter. Others, like the aforementioned TikTok FYP algorithm, track the individual's interactions with content to give them more of what they are currently enjoying.

A high level of engagement might be nice in intimate settings. This isn't lost on toy manufacturers. The current stage, at the time of this writing, is using algorithms to provide adaptive patterns. Adjusting the movements or vibrations to meet the person's inputs and preferences is the starting point. Some will take in environmental inputs, like synchronizing or responding to music. We can predict that this will eventually incorporate biofeedback. If Instagram can show more Reels based on thumb swipes, a toy can provide more sensations based on what other body parts are doing.

Algorithms are neutral. Most of the use cases we've described here are beneficial and meant for the primary user. We also see algorithms applied to protect us. Verification processes for dating sites are one example. The techy term is remote identity proofing, but, you've probably seen it as taking a selfie and a photo of your driver's license or national ID. Other examples are fraud detection on our financial services accounts. These also have false positives and false negatives, as the majority of algorithms do, but that's counter-balanced by simply asking. "We saw this charge, was it yours?"

Algorithms are neutral, but how we use them is not. Since the start of the Information Age, from technology to technology, concerns have been raised about user engagement turning into addictive and maladaptive behaviors. Modern algorithms, based on machine learning, require massive amounts of data and raise privacy concerns. (That Netflix Prize? It was stopped after a class action lawsuit over privacy concerns and a U.S. Federal Trade Commission investigation.) Algorithms also reflect training data, so when trained on real-world records, the results often perpetuate discrimination and social inequities. Or at least we think they do, however, the lack of transparency and accountability in algorithms make that hard to determine. We've also seen a rise in polarization and radicalization in people who are exposed to more and more of certain information. It's long been said a lie can get halfway around the world before the truth has put on its shoes, as misinformation is much more engaging. We're seeing that today at Internet scale.

We cannot roll back the clock on algorithms. Everything—from basic mathematics to advanced computer vision—is built upon a series of instructions for the machine. We can decide where we spend our time and purchasing power, and this will shift companies to respond accordingly. But by and large, controls around algorithms will come from legal action and regulation. In the meantime, technology companies making ethical decisions to use algorithms for good is our front-line defense. I wonder what Ada Lovelace and Alan Turing would make of this world?

Expert Consult: Sherrod DiGrippo

Sherrod DiGrippo is Director of Threat Intelligence Strategy at Microsoft. She was selected as Cybersecurity Woman of the Year in 2022 and Cybersecurity PR Spokesperson of the year for 2021. Her focus has long been on securing communications, from corporate networks to personal chats. Her career in cybersecurity and threat intelligence spans over 20 years. She's an avid online dater and loves dating apps.

Sherrod DiGrippo

Can you explain what you do and how your work relates to online dating?

I am a cybersecurity and threat intelligence professional. I've been doing that for 20 years. Securing data and people and operational security is very close to my heart. And it's not just what I do at work. It's something I think about all the time. Most people would say, oh, yes, my privacy is important to me, but they will also tell strangers incredibly dangerous information, just with a simple question. An example of this is someone who hops in an Uber and the driver asks how long they're going to be gone. And they immediately say "oh, we're coming back on Wednesday." I think about this all the time as I move through the world and in dating: what do people—strangers really—need to know about me? They don't need to know a lot of logistical things about me. They don't need to know where I live. They don't need to know my birthday. They don't need to know when I'm going out of town or where I'm going to be. They need to know who I am as a person in my heart. Thinking about the decisions we make in online dating is absolutely something which affects me, and that I'm really passionate about.

Where does that passion come from?

I got into network security because again, I love communication. There wasn't an ease of use to get on a network with the early internet—it was hard. It was a lot of work! And that was something I wanted so badly. I wanted to be able to talk. But that that desire to communicate and connect needed to also came with a desire to be safe in it. That's what I look for: safe and enjoyable experiences for connection. For most people, and especially for women, to have connection? Safety has to be established first. People don't connect if they don't feel safe. And that's the way that it connects to online dating. There's a social aspect where women are trained to be polite. A stranger on a dating app asks you a question, and a lot of times you just answer it. There's an element of over-trust and over-involvement with a lot of online dating.

Is online dating a good idea? What kind of mindset should therapists and sexuality educators encourage in their clients who use these tools?

It's important to reinforce the idea that the person in your phone is very much separate from your real world. They can cross over into your real world, sure. But as long as they're just a text conversation on your phone? They aren't quite real. A lot of people feel extremely, emotionally, connected to someone that they have never met before. That's something that I would like to kind of retrain people to think about. I am a believer that if somebody only exists in your phone? They "rank" lower than any other person you've ever met in person. The person I'm talking to on a dating app is a lower rank than the Starbucks barista that gives me my coffee every day. Because that Starbucks barista could have killed me at some point if they wanted. They could have put poison in my drink if they want. They didn't, and so I trust them more. The person on the phone app has never had an opportunity to hurt me and chosen not to, to keep me safe and chosen to keep me safe, to be smart around me. Everyone else in my physical world has; so they "win" until that person moves from my phone to real life.

Letting interaction on a dating app impact negatively the rest of your reality world. Blowing off dinner with friends because you're chatting with somebody that you are talking to on a dating app, for example? Huge mistake. That's a really dangerous thing to get into, I think. And it's also quite easy, I think, for people to fall into kind of a fantasy world with this attention that's constantly coming out of the phone. This constant, flirty, interest—feeling a connectedness that isn't really real. Constant positive interaction is an ego boost. It feels good. It gives you this sense that "all these people want to talk to me, they want my attention, they made me feel good." There's also this complete reduction in risk. If you never meet someone, they'll never truly dislike you. You can say "oh, well, he stopped talking to me, but he never met me and he doesn't really know me." I really think rejection, both receiving and giving rejection are skills that are super important for dating apps. You can't just be able to accept rejection; you also have to be able to give it, and a lot of people aren't very good at that.

I think also the number one thing I want people to understand about online dating is that they're called dating apps because you're supposed to be *going on dates*. A lot of people get on dating apps, they just talk to a bunch of people. These are not texting apps. They are not scheduling apps. They are not AI robots. They are intended for you to go on dates. If you are not going on dates, you probably should either not use them or change the way that you use them. And if you're not looking for dates, don't get on a dating app.

What advice do you have for someone who wants to meet new people online? Are there best practices for online dating that can make their search more successful?

The art and science of dating profile design could be an entire, semester-long college course. But there are some things that I would recommend. I really believe you should pay for dating apps. The algorithm is better, you get better matches, things go faster. I think most of them are around $20 per month. If you're on a budget? Cancel a streaming service and put that money towards a paid dating app because if you don't, you are put at the absolute bottom of the barrel when it comes to matches, messages, everything. It literally is not worth it because it's such a drain on your time and energy. Just pay for the app.

Don't put identifying information in your pictures. There should not be children in your profile. If it's a really great picture of you blur out the kids. It should be you alone, not your family, not your friends, not your kids. Photos can reveal things you don't intend to share. Don't post a photo from the local bar that very clearly shows where you are. It's very easy for someone to message you and say, "Oh, hey, I saw you at that bar that time," and start building connective rapport that's not real. Have a warm smile, no scowling. No dead animals in your photos, and no group photos. Personally, I find it unappealing when it's a picture of in some kind of compulsory situation. Like "everyone's lining up for the wedding photo of the wedding party, I have to be in this."

Being flirty in your profile is okay, but being overtly sexual is a big mistake. I think being open to possibility and interesting in your profile is more important. Try to keep it a little witty, a little clever, interesting. If the platform you're using has multimedia, like video or audio clips that you can do? I recommend that you do the multimedia. It's fun.

You don't need to get to know someone well enough in dating app messages and profiles to know if they're the one. You just need to get to know them well enough to know if you would meet them in person for half an hour. And if you would, move from the dating app to the dating. I would say talking to someone for more than a week—if they live in your town and you haven't gotten together with them after a week and it hasn't been planned and set up, it's time to move on.

Are there risks to dating online? What can someone do to make sure that they're being safe as they publish their dating profiles and meet up with new people?

Move quickly to meeting in person, in a safe location in public. You can tell so much more in person. You can have a vibe check in person. When you first start thinking about dating, take 15 minutes and put together a list of places that you would be comfortable going for a first meeting and a first date. Don't travel. You don't need to go more than 10–15 minutes from your house to meet somebody. Build a list of places that you're familiar with that you go frequently like the coffee shops where you know the barista—because you should be comfortable. Get to the place a few minutes early and settle in. When the other person arrives, you are already oriented. You know everything around you, you know the pace, you know the crowd, you're comfortable. And that helps you be more, I think, able to connect with another person and be more present with them.

I'm a believer in meeting before a date. I don't commit to dinner with strangers. I don't want to sit across from someone in a restaurant and realize ten minutes in that, I don't like you and I want to go. I will leave. I can and I will! But I don't like that experience, so in order to avoid it? Let's do something much less risky that takes 30 minutes—going for coffee, going to the park. After I've met you, confirmed you're a real human, that you are who you say you are, and that you didn't knife me in a parking lot? Let's meet up again next week. I also have a rule with alcohol: I'll have half as many drinks as the number of dates as we've been on. On the first date, I won't drink at all. On the second date, I can have one. On the fourth date, I might have two. We should not be drinking heavily around strangers.

You should just be smart about what you're doing. Turn on your location tracking, let your friends know what you're doing. Several people I know have told me "I've been talking to this guy for a while, he wants me to just like come to his house." And obviously no, you shouldn't do that. What amazes me is that men don't think about whether the person they're talking to is *actually* who they say they are. Is this really a woman you're talking to or is this a guy who's going to show up at the house and rob me? Men often don't think about that the way that many women do. You don't really know who someone is until you meet them in person. And you don't want to find out who that person is for the first time while you're alone in your home. Is this person actually the individual that they say they are? And it's absolutely possible that they're not. You can be anyone online.

What can therapists and educators do to promote healthier dating practices, online and off? What skills or strategies do you think every actively dating person needs to have?

I would hope the therapist could help them keep some emotional distance—especially when their interactions are still only electronic. Telling the client "okay, I get it. This person is so interesting and they make you feel so good and there's all these like super heightened emotions. Let's either take those down a notch or let's move to a place where you meet them in person and you know if those things are real." I also think therapists can kind of help with balancing expectations and narrowing the field of prospects, because there is so much out there. It can be overwhelming. There are so many people to talk to. How do you decide who do you want to spend your time with? How does that person make you feel when you talk to them? Is this a person that you want to meet in person? Once you have, do you want to see them again? Do you feel good about this? People can get really dazzled by the thousands of options on a dating app, but that's not real either. You have to remember, the dating apps keep profiles running even after the person has met their someone and deleted the app. They are designed to cultivate a feeling of infinite options. . . . Because if no one ever chooses, no one ever leaves the dating app. You have to kind of balance that algorithmic adversary with like what you actually want to achieve.

I also think therapists should be prepared to help people manage emotionally through experiences like being ghosted or having someone be terrible to them. Ghosting is really prevalent and a lot of people get really angry about it. They say it's cowardly. That the other person should have had the conversation with them about why they're ending the conversation. Unfortunately, what's most likely is that they just forgot about you, or didn't feel the connection, and just kind of . . . wandered off. I think that a lot of people don't realize they've *also* ghosted someone. Even as you're upset about being ghosted? You've probably ghosted people too and you don't remember because the conversation or the experience just wasn't that impactful for you. The person who ghosted doesn't realize that they've left someone feeling hurt, angry, rejected, and thinking badly of them. Therapists need help their clients understand that the point of view of the person who kind of floated away as the ghost is very different from the point of view of the person that got ghosted. And you have to just keep letting those go, which means building the skill to accept rejection or ambiguity gracefully and keep a positive mindset.

Chapter 7

Communities in the Cloud

Echo Chambers, Digital Villages, and Community

What is a community? It's a seemingly simple question with an answer that's surprisingly difficult to pin down. In the United States, in the 1960s, the counter-culture movement was reshaping community along with sexuality. Take the Farm as an example, founded after a buses and vans caravaned from San Francisco, California, and settled outside of Nashville, Tennessee (Kauffman, 2019). Back in San Francisco area, around that time, Stewart Brand was taking inspiration from everything from NASA's photograph of Earth to computer pioneer Douglas Engelbart. This boiling cauldron of innovation and disruptive thinking resulted in the Whole Earth Catalog in 1968 and the Whole Earth 'Lectronic Link (WELL) in 1985. In print and on computers, they were reimagining community and communal responsibilities.

The Well was the hand-off between counterculture and hacker culture. Among the early moderators of the Well were people who had lived at the Farm, preserving the 1960s ethos into the 1990s. The Well contributed to the unique culture and ideological foundation of the online platforms such as Bulletin Board Systems (BBS) and later Web forums (Hogge, 2011). The Well, along with pioneering community-driven platforms like MindVox and Usenet, profoundly influenced our understanding of community-building, moderation, and echo chambers. Craig Newmark, the founder of Craigslist, specifically cited The Well as a key inspiration. This inspiration has rippled through time, shaping platforms such as eBay, Nextdoor, and Facebook Marketplace. The foundational ideas of those early communities continue to resonate and evolve in today's virtual landscape.

In the following four decades, we continue to wrestle with how people come together online. Online communities may represent a new form of organization distinct from traditional hierarchical structures. These communities thrive in open virtual spaces where individuals with shared interests collaborate and generate knowledge together. But seemingly contradictorily, the more open the space the less safe some people feel, and the more strict the governance the more value some people get from the interactions.

DOI: 10.4324/9781003391128-8

Researchers studying this have proposed three stages in the evolution of governance: embryonic, emergence, and established (Harysi, 2020). In the embryonic stage, governance is informal and focused on attracting new people and enhancing connectivity. During the emergence stage, as the community grows, governance becomes more concerned with managing operational processes and coordinating contributions. In the established stage, governance is formalized and embedded within the platform, with a focus on enforcing collectively produced rules.

Reddit's auto-moderation is an example of rules embedded within the platform. However, the individual subreddits (sub-groups or communities within Reddit) are independently managed and are at different stages of governance. Reddit's overall attempts at top-down moderation has created pushback. For instance, the quarantine policy was a measure implemented by Reddit to limit the visibility of subreddits with content which may upset or offend the average person. Research into the implementation of the quarantine policy found right-leaning users more inclined to discuss the accessibility of quarantined content and the implications of the policy on free speech. Left-leaning users were more likely to discuss the ideologies associated with controversial subreddits and the need for consistent application of moderation policies (Shen & Rose, 2019).

Such political polarization is one of many unforeseen outcomes of online communities. Spreading of conspiracy theories, diffusion of misinformation, creation of social trends, and emotional contagion are all attributes of online echo chambers (Jiang, 2021). Some of this stems from our own innate psychology, like confirmation bias and how we resolve cognitive dissonance. The same quality that made The Well a cultural phenomenon—people seeking out and connecting with like-minded individuals—is the same quality that creates online spaces where a particular set of values and beliefs is dominant. But lest we let technology off the hook, some of these problems stem from the design of modern platforms: recommendation algorithms drive content people see and engagement systems keep people active on the platform. We see more that we agree with and interact with those more than we would otherwise, because of how social media is built.

The latest round of community and social tools—like Substack (newsletters), Discord (text messaging), Clubhouse (audio), TikTok (social media)—demonstrate the concept of community remains an evolving and complex phenomenon. From the counter-culture movements of the 1960s to the digital forums of today, communities have continually redefined themselves through the interplay of innovation, ideology, and technology. As we navigate the balance between openness and safety, and between freedom and governance, it's clear that effective moderation is essential for fostering healthy online communities. Moving forward, understanding these dynamics and designing platforms with mindful moderation and minimal addictiveness will be crucial in cultivating spaces where individuals can connect, collaborate, and thrive while mitigating the risks of polarization and misinformation. As we continue to grapple with these challenges, we are reminded that good moderation makes for good communities, echoing the lessons learned from the Farm to The Well and to today.

IRL vs. Online Relationships

At the risk of stating the obvious, online relationships are quite different from in-real-life (IRL) relationships. And yet the qualities that make them different might not be what you expect when we think about these virtual bonds. For many, there is a notion that online relationships, particularly those where the parties involved have never met in real life, are less serious, less real, than IRL connections—a bias that sociologist Nathan Jurgenson has called "digital dualism" (Chayka, 2015). Admittedly, there are some very real safety concerns that influence this perception. Even twenty years after the launch of the first social networking sites Friendster (2002) and MySpace (2003), there is still no ironclad way to know that the person on the other side of our screen is who they claim to be. And yet, as more and more aspects of life—from grocery shopping to business meetings—are ported to virtual spaces, our perceived digital dualism starts to feel less and less, well, realistic.

We have reached a point in time where the first generation of digital natives is entering the workforce while their older siblings, the so-called Oregon Trail Generation (those born between 1977–1983 who had an analogue childhood and a digital adolescence) are raising children of their own. This means that most of us have experienced both on- and offline relationships as real and valid experiences of connection. That said, there are still some key differences in how the human brain responds to online relationships that we must be aware of and understand:

• **Algorithmic attraction:** Historically, when we have met new people, it has happened in a context of shared similarity. Perhaps a friendship forms amongst those who all chose to join an adult kickball league, or a future spouse is identified while studying the same subjects in college. Go far enough back, and these similarities were identified and reinforced by family members who undertook the labor of partner-selection on behalf of their children; uniting them based on shared values or filial obligation, rather than on physical attraction or strength of personality. As we discussed in the previous chapter, much of this matchmaking effort has been outsourced to algorithms today; and this process is changing how we perceive the potential partners these computer programs present to us. Research has found that when a social networking site or online dating platform presents us with a suggested match, we perceive them as more similar to us in personality, and by extension more physically attractive, than we would if we had encountered them in some other setting or context (Rodrigues, Lopes, Alexopoulos, & Goldenberg, 2017). These perceptual assessments are enhanced when users believe that they have been matched by some form of "scientific" system, however the structure of these systems "often encourages users to prioritize qualities (e.g. height, income) that are poor indicators of what it will be like to interact with someone in the flesh" (Sharabi, 2022).

- **Intensity of connection:** Once a new connection has been found (be it a new friendship or a potential romantic partner) we encounter a new difference between digitally mediated relationships and those which exist primarily offline. Being online allows us to curate our personas in a way that "real life" does not. We choose what images we share, select user names that reflect aspects of our personalities we wish to highlight, have time to consider our words carefully, and can be selective in which aspects of our personality we highlight and what we minimize. Telecommunications expert Joseph Walther calls this curation impulse "selective self-presentation" (Walther, 2007). Conversely, we filter the information others put out about themselves through the lens of our own idealistic desires and personal projections. This process of curation and projection can create intense relationship dynamics that are frequently well intentioned (Gruzd & Hernandez-Garcia, 2018) but potentially inauthentic.

> For a while, a projection allows you to live in an illusion . . . but if your intimacy with the other person is founded on projections, it'll inevitably run out. . . . You'll be then faced with an obvious truth. . . . They're living their own story that may not be compatible with whatever image you've projected onto them.
>
> (Brzosko, 2020)

These intense connections, filtered through the best hopes and potential projections of the folks on both sides of the screen, can begin to influence the choices we make offline as well.

- **Degree of disclosure:** Imagine standing in line at the grocery store, chatting with the person waiting behind you. You notice their superhero t-shirt and comment on your shared fandom. Within the few minutes between initial greeting and final check-out, they have offered you detailed information about their medical history and in return you have texted them a few nude images of yourself. The scenario seems ridiculous—possibly even offensive. And yet? This scenario plays out in online interactions on a regular basis. There are a multitude of reasons why we share more information, faster, with people we meet online than we do in real life interactions, including the simple fact that the communication is being mediated by a device at all. One research team makes the argument that "smartphones and their affordances, although highly beneficial in many circumstances, cue humans' evolved needs for self-disclosure and responsiveness" (Sbarra, 2019). One reason for this is a perception of anonymity—the idea that personally identifiable information is somehow less identifiable when it is mediated by a screen (Pan, Hou, & Wang, 2023). Personal disclosures can foster the *perception* of connection and motivate what the authors have described as information sharing as intimacy building—a shift in social norms that correlates with the rise of social media which we consider to be potentially problematic, particularly given the connections between loneliness, anxiety, and information sharing online (Gonsalves, 2022; Coffey, Bond, Stern, & Van Why, 2022). This impetus to share information as a bonding ritual and (often misplaced) trust in the privacy afforded by online spaces can lead to an escalation in the trust-relationship (such as sharing intimate images) much quicker in online relationships relative to offline connections of similar length. There are myriad reasons why people choose to send explicit images of themselves to others—ranging from pressure from others (Thomas, 2018) and substance use (Florimbio, Brem, Garner, Grigorian, & Stuart, 2018), to foreplay (Uzer, 2024) and "felt cute" (Checkalski, Gervais, & Holland, 2023), but one thing we know is certain—intimate disclosures of all kinds happen much earlier in the relationship when the relationships are primarily online. But that's not the only thing that speeds up . . .

- **Onset of sexual engagement:** Several studies have found a correlation between online interactions and sexual activity. For example, we know that young people who meet via online dating platforms are three times as likely to initiate sexual intercourse with their online paramours while those who connect via online chatrooms are twice as likely to pursue sex with each other compared to those who don't access these virtual spaces (Vandenbosch, Beyens, Vangeel, & Eggermont, 2016). Another study found that people who use dating apps that use geolocation (like Grindr, Tinder, OKCupid, and Bumble) to identify potential partners are more likely to engage in higher-risk sexual behaviors, such as casual sex, failing to negotiate boundaries or discuss STI statuses, and having sex without using contraception, compared to folks who meet their partners offline (Garga, et al., 2021). The combination of variables we've discussed so far—from perceived similarity to early and significant personal disclosures—create a mindset wherein we feel closer and more connected to the person we're chatting with online, even when we've only recently been "introduced." Sensation seeking and "negative urgency" or a desire to avoid feelings such as loneliness, anxiety, and depression have been connected both to sexting (that impulse to build relationships through disclosure we discussed earlier) as well as hooking up for casual sex (Dir, Cyders, & Coskunpinar, 2013). A few hours of conversation over coffee on a traditional first date does not inspire the level of early and intense-feeling bond that the same amount of time spent chatting online evokes within us, and the result can be faster, less planned, and potentially more reckless sexual encounters once the conversation moves away from the screen and into the "real" world.

- **Artificial urgency/Technoference:** A century ago, prior to the rise of the telephone, the calling card was a common way to initiate a conversation. A young man wishing to visit a young woman would visit her home and present his calling card—the precursor to the modern business card—to her household staff. He would wait while the card was presented to her—or more likely her mother—and his request considered. The result might be an invitation to tea, a request to come back on another day, or a polite refusal offered by the same household manager who answered the door. There was no expectation of immediate engagement. This changed when the telephone became a standard feature within the phone. Now? A young man might ring up this same young woman directly and the expectation would be that if she was at home to answer, the conversation would occur immediately. In the 21st century, emails and text messages can serve as modern calling cards; letting the recipient know that a conversation is requested without the intrusion of a ringing phone demanding an immediate response. That is the ideal, anyway. Unfortunately, push notifications and the fact that most of us have our devices with us at all times, in all places, have given rise to a new mindset of perpetual urgency, where every red alert bubble is a visual cue that someone is waiting on us to acknowledge them. The term for this is Notification Anxiety, and researchers have begun to study the impact it is having on our mental health, including sleep dysregulation, changes in our cognitive functioning such as attention, memory, and prioritization, increased anxiety and stress, and the sensation of phantom vibrations have all been noted. In more extreme cases, "suicidal behavior due to prolonged and continuous phone usage has been observed" (Wockhardt Hospitals, 2024). This artificial sense of urgency also disrupts and corrupts existing relationships. Technoference, a portmanteau of the words technology and interference, is the term that has been coined to describe the ways in which our electronic devices and the online relationships they facilitate can get in the way of our equally important IRL relationships. One 2023 study, for example, found that the technoference created by parent's cell phones and other devices caused significant ruptures in the lives of their adolescent children, who reported worse mental health and more violent behaviors when their parents were frequently distracted by devices (Dixon, Sharp, Hughes, & Hughes, 2023). Overuse of technology has also been shown to disrupt offline interpersonal communications between spouses, reducing relationship satisfaction and increasing relationship conflict (Çakir & Köseliören, 2022). On the other side of the coin, the expectation that constant access to our devices means that we can and should be instantly available has been weaponized by abusers, adding a new front to the mistreatment and control experienced by survivors.

The internet represents a broadening of the spectrum of relationships we can have . . . the merit of these friendships lie in their mutability—in your pocket, on your screen, in your living room. Discarding the distinction between real and virtual friendship does not doom us to a society in which tweets, chat, and e-mail are our only points of contact,

writes New York Times Magazine writer Jenna Wortham; and she is correct! Online relationships, romantic, platonic, and familial, can be tremendous assets to most who experience them. The Covid pandemic especially motivated many previously non-hyper-connected folks to foster vibrant and valuable online social circles and these have real-world merit for everyone involved. But these digital relationships are experienced and enacted differently by our brains than IRL relationships are, and these differences have consequences for how we contextualize and engage with the people we care about most. As clinicians, we must be mindful of the way that our behavior and biases are influenced within technology mediated relationship dynamics and work with our clients to ensure that their actions are aligned with their personal values and relationship priorities, both online and off.

The Power—and Vulnerability—of Being Seen

One of the most important social changes that we have witnessed over the last ten years is an increased attention on diversity. From increased self-esteem to better academic and career outcomes, we have a solid body of research that highlights the benefits of seeing people like ourselves in the world around us (Nadal, 2021) and marginalized or underrepresented folks aren't the only ones who benefit! Multiple studies have found that being exposed to people from groups who were different than ourselves reduced feelings such as racism (Killen, Raz, & Graham, 2021) and homophobia (Poushter & Kent, 2020)—through a process known as intergroup contact theory. From the political parties to movie awards shows, there has been a concerted effort by people in positions of leadership to ensure that people from all kinds of backgrounds, cultures, and identities see themselves represented in the institutions that serve them. This is a positive shift in the cultural conversation, even as it continues to be imperfect in execution.

As we've discussed throughout this book, technology has long served as a way for people who may be living in isolated, unsafe, or unsupportive places to find others who share their lives, relationships, and experiences. The ability to find community and feel seen is one of the most powerful gifts that the internet has to offer. And, like all technologies, it comes with both advantages and drawbacks:

A 'double-edged sword' for individuals who embody marginalized and/or stigmatized identities . . . visibility can be both empowering (e.g. conferring potential benefits such as social support, community building, destigmatization) and disempowering (e.g. carrying risks such as threats, harassment and stigmatization). Further, visibility may be manipulated . . . to manage risks and meet goals.

(Barta & Andalibi, 2024)

We know that there are some very real benefits to having strong social ties, including an increased lifespan and better health outcomes. But the question of whether or not these benefits extend into online relationships is one that researchers have mixed answers for. Some studies have found that online relationships steal time away from the in-real-life (IRL) connections that are clearly beneficial (Lima, Marques, Muiños, & Camilo, 2017), but particularly post-pandemic, when the opportunity for IRL relationship formation was severely curtailed, more recent research has begun to identify some distinct mental health advantages as well, including "social support and experiences of connectedness, which ultimately increased their feelings of happiness, satisfaction, being well supported, positive attitudes, and willingness to continue development—all indicators of psychological well-being" (Erfani, Abedin, & Blount, 2016). Particularly for gender, sexuality, and relationship minorities, finding online communities that reflect their identities can be a deeply empowering experience, which can help foster positive identity development for young people who may not have access to the IRL role models and spaces that could help them envision a positive future where they get to live as their authentic selves. In fact, new research is showing that for young people who identify as sexual or gender minorities, technology and the internet "permit aspiration-driven identity construction and self-presentation. . . . Online identity construction permits marginalized individuals to circumvent impediments to constructing identities in face-to-face settings, contributing opportunities for freer self-expression and exploration of identities considered unconventional in individuals' offline spaces" (McInroy & Craig, 2020). The vastness of the internet means that a community exists for *everyone*, and it is easier than ever to find a Discord server, chatroom, Facebook Group, or listserv dedicated to supporting and affirming people just like you. Which, ironically, becomes one of the drawbacks to being seen as well.

Scan here to visit our favorite online resource for finding offline friendships

Communications theorist Marshall McLuhan famously wrote that "the medium is the message." In other words, we cannot separate *what* we are seeing and hearing from the *way* we are seeing and hearing it. Reading a news article written about September 11 will evoke a different psycho-social-emotional response in us than watching a video of the news broadcasts that day. The experience of being in a space that allows us to feel seen as our most authentic selves will be different if we are stepping into the local BIPOC community center versus logging into our favorite BIPOC Discord channel. Indeed—the very act of logging onto the internet will influence our understanding of what it means to be BIPOC at all. Part of this difference is the fact that the internet is not just a passive set of wires and boxes that we communicate with, like the modern version of a child's tin-can telephone. Rather, the internet is comprised of curated and constructed platforms, built and maintained by people with their own goals and purposes. Although we may see ourselves reflected there, we should never mistake the internet for a mirror, because unlike a pane of silvered glass, when we gaze into the internet? A vast array of algorithms, tracking cookies, and other programming influences are looking back at us.

In 2024, the *Guardian* Australia conducted an experiment, setting up brand new social media accounts (Instagram and Facebook) on a brand-new smartphone, using a brand new email address. With no digital history to learn from and no ad tracking allowed by the new profiles, within three months "without any input, they were riddled with sexist and misogynistic content" (Taylor, 2024). While the world wide web is an open space, it is far from objective; and when we use it to seek out online community, we must understand that what we find is not presented neutrally. This carries over into the messages users receive from within their online communities as well. In IRL spaces, there is significantly less personal disclosure. People coming together for a common purpose—anything from bowling to political action—tend to focus on that purpose. The members of my Tuesday bowling league might not know I'm gay. Or Atheist. Or a registered Republican. They likely don't know that I had an abortion two weeks before the league started and that I secretly think maybe women were better off before the rise of Feminism. With the important exception of visible identities such as race/ethnicity, body size, and other physical differences; many of my intersectional identities are not going to overtly influence my experience of bowling.

In online spaces, we tend to bond through disclosure, confusing visibility with connection and information-sharing with intimacy. Which means that I am more likely to offer up personal information, such as my religious belief, sexual orientation, or past experiences, even when it's not directly relevant to the topic of the group itself. This can lead to enforcement of in-group purity standards that can be far more rigid than they might be for a similar group IRL. For example, I may be welcome in the bowling league's group chat until someone find's out I'm gay, at which point, I am quietly ignored or outright insulted. My county's Republican Facebook group might greet me with enthusiasm, until I disclose that I'm not Christian. My fellow abortion-rights activists might welcome me warmly, until I share my hesitancy about Feminism. In other words, while the world is increasingly embracing the importance of diversity; we tend to assume that everyone in our specific cohort is Like Us . . . different from mainstream, but different in the same way that we are (Bai, Ramos, & Fiske, 2020). Because of the assumption of hyper-specific identity alignment fostered by the internet, in-group invalidation, stigmatization, and erasure have been documented by researchers who study marginalized groups online (Walker & DeVito, 2020).

There has always been an intrinsic risk for marginalized people hoping to find community. In the mid-20th century, for example, gay men were frequently arrested for "solicitation," simply for acknowledging their identity to the wrong person (Chauncey, 2019). The passage of FOSTA/SESTA has increased the risk for sex workers and other erotic minorities hoping to find mutual support and community in online spaces (Moraff, 2022); and in the second half of this chapter, we will discuss other external threats such as doxing and stochastic terror. But let's not discount the ways in which technology has helped us find one another, see ourselves represented in a variety of contexts and settings that most of us couldn't possibly experience without the connective power of the internet. These are good things, which add value and richness to our lives. Acknowledging the differences between on- and offline interactions does not diminish one or elevate the other. It simply allows us to better understand, so we can make the best choices for ourselves, our relationships, and our communities, online and off.

Stochastic Terror and Other Vulnerabilities

The idea of strangers randomly attacking us, driven by internet mobs, is a deeply unsettling and frightening reality. Stochastic terrorism is "the public demonization of a person or group resulting in the incitement of a violent act, which is statistically probable but whose specifics cannot be predicted" (Dictionary.com, 2019). This is an extreme result of echo chamber effects, polarization, and dogpiling/cancel culture behaviors. Incidents such as school shootings, police killings, and attacks on elected officials have been linked to this phenomenon. Consequently, some are advocating for algorithms that can detect patterns and indicators of radicalization or incitement to violence (Kemper, 2022).

Stochastic terrorism is far from the only threat we face when engaging with online communities. Anonymity, deindividuation, dehumanization, lack of social cues, and lack of feedback contribute to online aggression and patterns of behavior not seen elsewhere in offline situations. Toxic language in communities like Reddit has a significant negative impact on community health, driving people away (Mohan, 2017). Cyberbullying continues even among adult communities (Kowalski, 2018). People can be ostracized by their communities, ignored or excluded, which impacts "fundamental human needs: belonging, self-esteem, control, and meaningful existence" (Schneider, 2017). Peer surveillance, neighborhood surveillance, and related invasions of privacy can increase our stress and anxiety (Beadle & Vasek, 2023). Hate and harassment impact us all but hit especially hard for at-risk groups like erotic minorities (Thomas, 2021).

And yet, with online communities now interwoven with our lifecycle events, giving up on online literally disconnects people from their social circle. We need to provide threat modeling and adopt protective measures. A reminder on the four-step (Shostack, 2014):

- "What are we working on?"
- "What can go wrong?"
- "What are we going to do about it?"
- "Did we do a good job?"

In the 1950s, psychologist Albert Ellis developed rational-emotive behavior therapy (REBT) as an alternative to what was then considered "traditional" psychoanalysis. Calling himself a "rational therapist," Ellis put forth a new paradigm that would become the foundation of modern cognitive behavioral therapy (David, Cotet, Matu, Mogoase, & Stefan, 2018). One of the primary tools Ellis developed for REBT practitioners was the ABC Model, which has become one of the most popular clinical tools used by therapists today. The ABC Model framework states that our emotions and behaviors are not directly influenced by our experiences and life circumstances, but rather by the way we think about these events. In other words, **A**ctivating Events are experienced through the filter of our **B**eliefs, and these are what inspire the **C**onsequences— the feelings and behaviors that follow. In recent years, some cognitive behavioral therapists have expanded this to create the ABCDE framework, which adds in the **D**isputation stage "(if one has held an irrational belief which has caused unhealthy consequences, they must dispute that belief and turn it into a rational belief)" (Selva, 2018) and the New **E**ffect stage, wherein "the disputation has turned the irrational belief into a rational belief and the person now has healthier consequences of their beliefs as a result" (Selva, 2018). But psychologists (rational and otherwise) are not the only people thinking about how beliefs influence behaviors. Cybersecurity experts also spent a considerable amount of time studying human behavior and how shifting beliefs can influence behavior.

Security research team Tsai, Jiang, et al, identified a variety of factors that can be used to help our clients assess their online risk. In many ways, these mirror the work of Albert Ellis and other cognitive theorists. Your authors have created a resource here that outlines specific questions for each factor that you can use to help your clients develop their own individualized online safety plans.

- **Security intentions**: How likely are we to adopt protective measures to safeguard ourselves online? What are our plans to enact these security behaviors?
- **Threat susceptibility**: How are we at risk from online threats? Is it our personal information, our computers or devices, our reputation?
- **Threat severity**: What is the perceived degree of harm that could result from online threats? Is this perception accurate or exaggerated?
- **Prior experience with safety hazards**: Have we encountered similar threats before? Is our current response suitable, demonstrating a heightened focus on protection? Or is it inappropriate, potentially a trauma response that doesn't align with the actual threat?
- **Coping self-efficacy**: How confident are we in our ability to successfully carry out the protective measures? Do we have appropriate knowledge, understanding, and experience?
- **Response efficacy**: How effective are protective measures taken in countering online threats? Is this belief accurate or exaggerated?
- **Subjective norm**: What perceived social pressures or expectations from significant others influence the adoption of online safety behaviors?
- **Response cost**: What are the perceived costs, including time and effort, associated with implementing protective measures that may deter us from acting?
- **Habit strength**: How can we develop safe habits to ensure we continue these behaviors consistently? To what extent have protective behaviors become automatic and part of our regular routine?
- **Personal responsibility**: Are we taking personal responsibility for our actions to ensure our online safety and contribute to the overall security of the Internet? Do we feel we have agency?
- **Perceived security support**: Do we receive social support from our friends and social circle to engage in protective behaviors, and encouragement for the adoption of security measures?

The aforementioned factors have been demonstrated to significantly increase online safety behaviors (Tsai, 2016). Research suggests that to improve online safety, it is crucial to help the person to focus on their cognitive processes and habits, as well as to educate them about the efficacy of security measures and their personal responsibility in protecting themselves online. We want individuals to take personal responsibility for their online safety and contribute to the overall security of the Internet by adopting protective behaviors. By forming safe habits and integrating protective behaviors into our regular routines, we can enhance the likelihood of continuing these practices consistently. Additionally, understanding the social pressures and expectations from our social circle can encourage the adoption of security measures.

TECH ED WITH WOLF

WHAT IS OSINT?

TechEd Class: What Is OSINT?

Terms like Open-Source Intelligence (OSINT) and Operational Security (OPSEC) joined the hacker lingo in the late 2000s. But it traces back further than that. Information Security communities, intelligence communities, and the military have long been a Venn diagram. OSINT and OPSEC were terms used by the United States for decades before they started appearing in conference abstracts at DEF CON and BlackHat.

So let's (over?) simplify things. OSINT is figuring out things about others from public information. OPSEC is taking steps to keep others from figuring out things about you. Let's take an example. Phone eats first. When we get together over a meal, what is the first thing we do? We photograph and post the dish. But wait. How did we get to this meal? Much of our conversation is texting, often over private companies' products. Someone had an idea, someone else suggested a time, and then we all agreed on the place. Now it's a party. We've ordered, food has come, photographs have been posted, we settle into an enjoyable conversation. That's punctuated with people pulling out their phones to look something up, to check on this or that. Someone says a funny joke, and someone else posts it to their socials. After dessert, we take a selfie to remember this wonderful evening. All this leaves a trace.

People who want to know what we're up to follow this trace and these data points. Social connection has shifted from bowling leagues to Facebook groups. The vast majority of Americans are living their lives online from conception through burial, from birth month mommy groups to high school reunions and religious/cultural affinity groups. Beyond burial, even, if any of their decedents happen to be into genealogy. Anyone with an interest can follow what we're doing. Often, by design, as we want to share and foster intimacy with hundreds of "friends." Not all "friends" are friendly, however.

Online stalking is a reality faced by 1 in 22 Americans. (Globally, it's 1 in 7 Germans and 1 in 4 Australians. Americans are getting off easy.) Social media and Internet searches form the starting point. Public records, like voting, court records, property deeds, are easily accessed through their official websites or through third-party services. With data brokers, significant details on a person's life can be available for purchase. Remember the "Open-Source" part of OSINT refers to sources that are publicly available, that is, open to the public.

Let's take it up one step. There are several tools to make this easier. We could map all your friends and see what friends you're closest with. Closest could be based on level of communication, who do you talk with the most? We cloud also define closeness by type of communication, who do you share intimate details with? A tool called Maltego can quickly create a graph of these social connections. Now we have a strong sense of your social circle and can create personas or portfolios of the people within it. There are also tools for figuring out where photographs are taken. The easiest way is to read the metadata of the image (EXIF). But today, most social media sites will scrub that to keep photographs private.

Let's suppose you did everything right. There's no metadata. You took that dinner selfie outside with no signs on the restaurant. In the background, there's nothing but a fast-food restaurant and a water tower. Could be anywhere, right? With tools like OpenStreetMap database, people expert in online investigations can find all the locations in the nation which serve food like you shared, by a Wendy's, near a water tower. Suppose that's a dozen locations. They'd overlay it with your friends' information (who's going to drive more than a couple hours for dinner?) and easily identify the restaurant. This isn't hypothetical. Many of my friends play this game all the time. Post a partial picture and challenge each other to find one another. It's shocking how little information it takes. Sometimes, it is obvious. The location is in the image's metadata. The person used their work email address for the account.

When the Ashley Madison website was breached in 2015, it became a national security concern. Why? The breach made the email addresses for every account public. The website was for cheating spouses and therefore the opportunity for extortion was very high. Among the millions of email addresses, some fifteen thousand were associated with government (.gov) and military (.mil) domains. People at work, signing up on a dating website, using work email. People potentially with access to sensitive information and people now susceptible to blackmail. All an adversary had to do was to search for.gov or.mil. Sometimes, it's easy. But suppose different account names were chosen. Does that make it hard enough? Yes, and no.

Each data point we have is one more filter for narrowing down the search. This can be buildings and landmarks in a photograph, searching for a location. This can things mentioned online, searching for a pattern in how we write. This idea has been popularized by crime shows and serial killer documentaries ("look how he spells that word, it's the same on the note, he's the killer!"). It is the same idea researchers use when de-anonymizing user accounts to find sock puppets or alternate accounts people are using. It's the same problem that Netflix ran into with its Netflix prize: with enough data points, you can identify anyone even in an anonymized dataset that seems all-but-random to the untrained eye.

Losing your anonymity is one of the real-life risks to maintaining our cloud-based social circle. Our personal information can be aggregated and posted (in other words, we could be doxxed.) In addition to be previously mentioned stalking, we can be bullied or harassed. Threatening information can be sent to our workplaces or homes. Police could be called on us (in other words, we could be swatted.) Any accounts using knowledge-based authentication (KBA) can be compromised. These are where questions like, "who was your favorite teacher" and "what was your first car" are used to reset your password. Our identities can be impersonated or even stolen. The list goes on and on.

Let's take one example: PleaseRobMe.com. The website, built in 2010 by three Dutch developers, would aggregate data from Foursquare and Twitter. It would then highlight empty homes with a stream reading "@user left home and checked in 15 minutes ago at this restaurant." To the best of our knowledge, no one was actually robbed because of PleaseRobMe.com. Yet there have been many burglaries where the criminals first stalked the victim's house on social media and learned their routines. The root problem is social media and sharing services have no way to distinguish good intent from bad, and no way for us to limit access to our information to only a select few people for purposes we approve of.

There are steps people can take. Taking stock of how, when, and what images we post is a good start. Sharing trips or events after we've returned home, rather than in the moment, is another. Keeping our friends list small and keeping our accounts private. When using alt accounts, taking care not to say too much or write in a style that'll be recognizable when matched to primary accounts. Services like DeleteMe and others will flag when potentially risky content is online and help remove it. This combined with understanding our digital footprints and being mindful in our sharing are steps towards privacy.

Ask yourself: what does it mean to live authentically in an age where every personality quirk is a data point?

Expert Consult: Shannon Miller

Shannon Miller

Shannon is deeply committed to physical and online privacy and security, bringing passion and intelligence to all client work as a privacy expert and OSINT investigator. Her practical, analytic approach delivers results across personal and corporate cases. Leveraging her background in global threat identification and resolution, she collects and analyzes all publicly available information for her clients, working to implement threat mitigation strategies that draw from her previous professional work coordinating with legal advisors, law enforcement, and government officials.

Tell us a little bit about the work you do and how you, as a technologist, came to be involved in the fight against online abuse.

A family member was taken advantage of by a romance scammer. I saw the layers of the scam, and realized when it was too late, the money was sent and there was no way to get it back. I wanted to do more to help after I learned these scams are simple, common, and extremely harmful. Even smart people get scammed and are afraid of being judged, so they don't talk about it. I knew I was excellent at pattern analysis and discovered scams follow patterns, trends, and a playbook. Scammers are getting more sophisticated and normal, everyday people lose billions a year to a variety of scams. Scamming is a form of online abuse, because inevitably you're paying someone who takes advantage of your vulnerability and kindness because they want your money.

What makes you passionate about this work?

Everyone has a right to feel safe, and people who scam, bully, harass and stalk people online, take away that feeling of safety from their victims. I like to think my work empowers people and helps them understand security and safety as necessary parts of their online digital life. What better way to use my skills than to help people feel safe again.

How does this issue impact mental health providers, educators, and others working in the field of sexual health?

I've learned over the years that everything is connected. Sexual health and education rely on technology, healthcare systems and services, and providers all working in different spaces, locations and practices. If you're not addressing the safety and security of your technology systems, harm can be done to those seeking services in the mental, sexual and reproductive health spaces. Sexual health is incredibly personal as are mental health issues, and privacy and safety of patient and provider data should matter to everyone. In order to protect those systems safety and security should be layered in from the beginning. Oftentimes people working in sexual health as therapists and educators work with marginalized groups and handle very sensitive personal information and situations. I cannot think of a worse violation of privacy than someone targeting an individual based on their health status, personal life decisions or mental health concerns. This is why training people on protecting their privacy and data is so important.

What advice do you have for someone who is concerned about being doxxed, harassed online, or having their private information shared with others?

If you're concerned about being doxxed or harassed it's important to check if your information is publicly available, such as your home address, phone number or social security numbers (all forms of PII). Check if your information is publicly available using Google or one of the people finder sites. This way you can see what an attacker can find to target you. Start making a list of things you'd like to remove from the search results, and keep in mind that some information cannot be removed. Consider places your private information might be located, beyond Google searches. If you own a home or have property records, those are public. In some states, licensing records are public, especially if you're a lawyer, therapist, social worker, nurse or someone with professional licenses. Next steps might include securing your social media accounts, adjusting your privacy settings, using a Password Manager and changing your passwords. Adding two-factor authentication on as many accounts as possible is also a good step. Additionally, remove yourself from data broker sites to help minimize your digital footprint. There are a few services that can help with this process, or you can DIY and opt out of these sites yourself.

What should someone do when they realize they're a victim of online abuse or harassment?

Each situation is going to be unique, so understanding the level of harassment is important. Take an assessment of the level of threat, such as is the person threatening to physically harm the individual? In those cases, it's essential to document the posts, voice memos, emails, texts, DMs, anything that shows the threat and the harm done. The reason documentation matters is, when you go to report the abuse and harassment, you have records and screenshots to help with your case. Each locality has slightly different harassment and stalking laws, and a threshold that must be met to file charges (once there is a report and investigation). Additionally, reporting matters so that you have a record of what happened to you in case the harassment escalates to stalking or death threats. If there is no imminent physical threat to you, it's still important to document the accounts, individuals, and methods they are using for the harassment so you can continue to report. You can also report sustained harassment and online abuse to ic3.gov which is the Internet Crime Complaint Center and handles the bulk of internet crime complaints. One note about this, if there are legitimate threats to your physical safety, you need to report that to the police and FBI (if it is safe for you to do so).

Be sure you have a good emotional support system, experiencing online harassment and abuse can be incredibly hard and draining. It's okay to talk about what is happening to you with someone you trust. It's important others know so they can help look out for you and if the person attempts to get access to you through them. Unfortunately, the onus is on the victim to not only manage the documentation, but the emotional fallout from someone abusing or harassing them. Having mental health support or contacting a victim advocate are two ways you can get help going through this difficult experience. Advocates are especially useful because they can connect the victim to legal services, housing, counseling, and many other community-based resources.

How can we work to prevent this kind of abuse entirely, and to advocate for greater privacy protections on a wider scale?

If you live in the United States there is no federal privacy law. Ideally, Congress would pass a law that protects citizens' personal data and rights, however, until then all there are only state-level privacy laws that do a marginal job of helping protect people's privacy. Some people think they shouldn't worry about their privacy, that all their data is already out there, so why bother? My answer to that is, everyone has things they want to keep private. No one needs to know your personal matters, nor should companies be targeting you in the invasive and unhealthy ways they do. Get involved in the development of privacy laws on a state level, there are areas for public comments, public meetings, and advocacy groups working on these matters. Understanding your current rights, and what a company does with your data means knowing the laws, reading the privacy policy and advocating for yourself and community. There is no perfect solution, only the systems we have right now.

Chapter 8

Tech for Sex

What Makes a Sex Toy, SexTech?

Think back to when you first started reading this book, way back in Chapter One when talked about the history of sexualized technology. You might have wondered at the time why we ended our timeline with video games. After all, the world of electronics has gotten much more expansive since Atari first gained a place on the home entertainment center! Part one of our history lesson ended there because we wanted to draw a clear line between what some people refer to as "dumb" electronic devices and modern internet-connected technologies. After all, we could play *Softcore Adventure* or pop a hardcore tape into our VHS players back in 1984, but what we could not do is what that experience with others living across town—or around the world. Home internet services changed the game when it comes to sexual technologies and carved out space for the topic of this chapter: SexTech. Let's carry our historical timeline into the modern era and learn what differentiates a device that's been sexualized from technology that's developed for a primary sexual purpose.

The Internet—1980–2000: The proto-Internet first went live in the 1960s, a tool for researchers at various universities to collaborate and share information. Called the Advanced Research Projects Agency Network (ARPANET) the internet was a crucial component of America's plan for communication and survival after a nuclear attack by the USSR (USG, 2024) Computers at the time were massive, taking up whole rooms (remember that video of the IBM 1410 and EDITH?) and it was wildly impractical to think that anyone outside of the small community of government and academic researchers would ever need to access it. This vision changed on January 1, 1983 (a date called "the birthday of the internet") when ARPANET transitioned to a new, universal, communications protocol called TCP/IP (Transfer Control Protocol/Internetwork Protocol)—the language of our internet today.

As computers shrank in size and this universal language was established, the opportunity for folks at home to participate in this global conversation expanded.

DOI: 10.4324/9781003391128-9

Bulletin Board Services (BBS), with names like Renegade, Wildcat, Excaliber, and The Well allowed people to communicate asynchronously but instantly for the first time ever. Some of the earliest users of these new community-building tools were LGBTQIA+ folks and other erotic minorities. BBS's were created for gays and lesbians to connect, for BDSM practitioners to find new friends, and for swinging and other lifestyle members to advertise their events. The internet made it possible to build a social circle of people who understood you and your life—even if you were the only person "like you" in a 1000 mile radius.

The first mainstream internet service provider Prodigy, debuted in 1984 and was wildly popular . . . until it implemented a hardline "family friendly" policy that banned many of the very marginalized users who rushed to use it. Within just five years, Prodigy's reign had ended and America Online (AOL) took the throne. Unlike Prodigy, AOL did not censor online users—it allowed adult content and groups, but put systems in place to obfuscate access to these BBS. But those who knew, knew and AOL became a massive platform for anyone who wanted to find others like them. Then, AOL introduced Chat Rooms and Instant Messager.

When access to sexualized content or Queer and lifestyle spaces moved from hidden to direct, the inevitable backlash occurred. *Time* magazine and other outlets published hyperbolic articles exploring the internet's risk to children and by 1995, the first web filters had been rolled out. The cat was out of the bag though, and technology had progressed to the point where parents could no longer rely on keyword filters or website blockers . . . because webcams were coming, and the direct, live-streamed peer-to-peer conversations they facilitated were going to make content moderation much more difficult.

Webcams and livestreaming changed the face of the internet forever. Where, in the early days of Prodigy and AOL, there was a certain "insider" culture of acronyms and proto-emojis, ASCII art, and backdoor chat rooms; the ability to stream ones face and voice across the miles brought everyday communication and everyday life to the internet. The first webcam was set up in 1993 at Cambridge University so that researchers could monitor . . . their coffee pot. No longer forced to walk down the hallway just to find the breakroom bereft of coffee, they could now peek via a black and white webcam set up facing the machine, to ensure their time away would be rewarded with caffeine. Three years later, in 1996, the first ever 24/7 livestream, the JenniCam, went up. Jennifer Ringly, today considered the world's first cam girl, allowed cameras to record her daily life and private behaviors and stream them live to her website for anyone to view.

Ringly intentionally did not censor her daily life and left the camera rolling irrespective of what she was doing. This sparked various societal and ethical discussions around privacy, voyeurism, and the boundary between public and private space in the digital age.

(DevX, 2023)

These debates continue today.

It took ten years (1994–2005) from the debut of the first commercially available webcam to the creation of YouTube—the world's largest content platform. However, once YouTube had demonstrated that it was possible to host and share millions of videos? It was only 2 years (2007) for PornHub to launch. By 2019 24 billion users around the world were uploading 1.36 million hours of explicit content to the internet . . . on PornHub alone (Griffith, 2019). In the same way that asynchronous communication via BBS was replaced by active chat rooms and instant messaging, so too did the world's porn consumers decide that they wanted a more interactive experience. OnlyFans launched in 2016 and thousands of live-stream erotic platforms have emerged since then. But we're still talking about technology that has been used for sexual purposes, rather than technologies *created* for sexual use. Let's talk about whole new subset of technology that emerged to capitalize on the intimate connections that an internet connection allowed—teledildonics.

Teledildonics—1990–2020: The term "teledildonics" was coined by hacker, philosopher, and sociologist Ted Nelson, in his 1975 book *Computer Lib/ Dream Machines*; but didn't gain popularity until the early 1990s when technology critic Howard Rheingold used it in his book *Virtual Reality*. Teledildonics refers to any sex toy that is connected to another device—either by Wi-Fi, Bluetooth, or internet connection—which can be controlled by someone other than the user (Ley & Rambukkana, 2021). The earliest example of internet-based technology (as opposed to non-connected electronics) specifically developed for sexual pleasure was the CyberSM Suit, created in 1993 by artist Stahl Stenslie and professor Kirk Woolford. Two users could each put on the suit, which was equipped with various haptics and sensors, and plug them into their computers (yes—these were hard wired devices!) then use a dial-up internet connection to transmit digital images and haptic sensations that were experienced by their partner on the other end. Stenslie and Woolford used their CyberSM suit to demonstrate an immersive sexual experience between users in Paris and Cologne (Owsianik, 2018).

Watch a video of the CyberSM suit in action

Today, teledildonics is more commonly referred to as SexTech and represents $400 million, and the fastest-growing segment, of the overall sex toy market (BedBible, 2024). Companies like LELO, Kiiroo, and We-Vibe lead the industry and have developed a vast array of SexTech toys for all kinds of bodies, relationships, and sensory experiences. With Bluetooth and Wi-Fi technology allowing for affordable, cord-free, access to shared intimacy for consumers the latest products feature innovations such as virtual and augmented reality, the ability to sync ones toy to their screen (to allow for an immersive porn experience), as well as robotic toys and devices that leverage artificial intelligence. We're going to look at AI in depth later on this chapter, but before we move on from our SexTech immersion course, let's talk about . . . sexbots.

Robotics—Today: We might argue that the sexbot seed was planted way back in the 1960s, when the growing field of plastics allowed for the creation of the first blow-up sex dolls. The first inflatable, vaguely human-shaped toy hit the market in 1968 and as material science improved, so did the sex doll—from plastic and foam to silicone and sensors.

> The inventor of the Fleshlight, a popular masturbation toy for men, also submitted a patent in 1995 for a 'female functioning mannequin.' (Within the mannequin's 'cavity,' as the patent puts it, would have been a cartridge full of 'oily elastomer.') . . . the inventor cited 'as the reasons for its invention the fact that women are cruel, venal, superficial, that they humiliate and break the hearts of men and that dolls on the contrary are reliable, compliant, companionable, and loving.'
>
> (Beck, 2014)

The first truly robotic sex doll was created in early 2000s by RealDoll and its subsidiary Realbotix, whose founder Matt McMullen stated that "the female form was my muse. . . . Imitation is the sincerest form of flattery" (Beck, 2014). Today, RealDoll's highest-end models feature animatronics comparable to those seen at amusement parks, AI-powered interactivity, warming skin that responds to the user's touch, and self-lubricating genitals . . . a far cry from 1995's "cartridge full of 'oily elastomer.'"

While sexbots are still an expensive, niche market—roughly 56,000 are sold per year at an average price of $3,500 each—we cannot be so quick to dismiss the notion of robots being used to meet the needs of those craving intimacy of all kinds, not just the sexual. One study of 7–15 year old children who had an AIBO robotic pet dog found that the majority of children treated the AIBO in the same way they treated a real, living, dog:

> 56% . . . believed that AIBO had mental states (for example, feeling scared), 70% said that AIBO had personality, and 76% asserted that AIBO had moral standing (i.e. that it could be held morally responsible or blameworthy for its actions and could have rights and deserve respect).
>
> (Levy, 2007)

A variety of small, desktop-sized tutor-bots are being used in schools around the world (Temming, 2019) and a variety of robotic friendly companions, such as Jibo and Moxie, have been developed for children and adults alike (Evans, 2023). At the other end of the lifespan, elders in Japan have been cared for by a variety of helper robots for decades now.

> Some are meant for physical care, assist with mobility and exercise . . . feed them; and help them take a bath or use the toilet. Others are aimed at engaging older people socially and emotionally in order to manage, reduce, and even prevent cognitive decline; they might also provide companionship and therapy for lonely older people, make those with dementia-related conditions easier for care staff to manage, and reduce the number of caregivers required for day-to-day care.
>
> (Wright, 2023)

While today the idea of forming sexual—or even emotional—relationships with robots might seem unusual or even concerning to some clinicians; we suspect that as this new technology is integrated into our everyday lives (especially in the social-emotional, caregiving ways described earlier) the lines between partner and product will blur and the notion of intimate connections with connected devices will become rather ordinary. This new reality raises its own set of ethical and moral questions, particularly as more of our clients begin to identify as digisexuals—people whose primary sexual identity comes through the use of technology (McArthur & Twist, 2017). This chapter—and indeed this book—offer a high-level overview of some of the emerging issues related to SexTech and sexualized tech, but this conversation can only ever be incomplete. New clinical issues and ethical quandaries will continue to emerge alongside new technologies and (as our two-part timeline helps to show) the pace of innovation and invention is faster now than ever before.

Adaptive Technologies

Silicone is the most widely used material for sex toys, at least, at the time of this writing (Grey, 2024). But that wasn't always the case. For the past 28,000 years, since that discovery in the Hohle Fels Cave in Germany (James, 2023), dildos were made stone, wood, ivory, and other natural materials. This took a radical turn in the thanks to a tragic event in 1965.

Gosnell Duncan, a Calypso dancer and father of four from Grenada, suffered a paralyzing injury in 1965 while working at the International Harvester Company in Chicago (Lieberman, 2017). The 37-year-old found himself paraplegic, unable to have an erection, impotent. The burgeoning sexual revolution amplified this loss, as Duncan came to realize that disabled people weren't seen as sexual beings and so were excluded from the sweeping societal changes. He began searching for penile implants and substitutes, only to be disappointed in the safety and quality and safety of the products. In the past he had worked as an auto mechanic and had worked with silicone rubber. He collaborated with a chemist from General Electric to develop a body-safe silicone formula. Manufactured from Duncan's basement lab and sold from his company Paramount Therapeutic Products, these silicone dildos were safe, nonporous, heat-resistant, and sold with a harness for accessibility.

The silicone sex toys we enjoy today directly trace back to the disability community. In product design, this term has a name: the curb-cut effect. The term describes solutions designed for a specific groups, especially those with unique or extreme needs, that benefit a wider population (Glover Blackwell, 2017). While Gosnell Duncan was producing his first prototypes in a basement Brooklyn, New York, disabled students were fighting a different fight across the country in Berkeley, California. Wheelchair bound people would get to a sidewalk and need friends, family, sometimes complete strangers, to lift them and their wheelchairs over the curbs and steps that littered the city. A student group calling themselves The Rolling Quads began to advocate for accessibility. "Pressed by disabled activists, in 1972 the city installed its first official 'curb cut' at an intersection on Telegraph Avenue. It would become, in the words of a Berkeley advocate, 'the slab of concrete heard around the world'" (Glover Blackwell, 2017). People of all walks of life, from travelers with luggage to parents with strollers, today benefit from these curb cuts. It's hard to imagine sidewalks without them.

As the Internet replaces the city streets as our way of connecting with people, the idea of where curb-cuts belong shifts. Take healthcare, specifically telehealth, where innovations tailored to the needs of people with disabilities enhance the overall user experience for everyone, thereby creating a universally accessible digital healthcare system (Noel, 2020). Improvements in employment, specifically telework, increase job satisfaction and productivity by "removing barriers presented in traditional work environments and replacing the need to be physically at a specific location" (Linden, 2014). Beyond health and employment, the Internet of course enables friendships and romantic partnerships by transcending the physical limitations imposed by disability (Seymour & Lupton, 2004). This shift from physical to virtual broadens our horizons while paving the way for a more equitable society where physical abilities no longer define opportunities, creating a more inclusive and connected society.

Work to realize this dream continues in basements and at universities. One recent prototype came from a study employing a combination of literature reviews, questionnaires, interviews, and focus groups (Corti & Parati, 2022). The result was "Lovewear," a SexTech for movement-impaired people to explore their sexuality and experience sexual pleasure. The device has inflatable components—sometimes referred to as "soft-robotics"—which stimulate various erogenous zones. The person controls the device using a pillow with a series of simple gestures and movements. The design of "Lovewear" enables people with disabilities to have "autonomous exploration of sexuality without direct human contact. As our device is specifically targeted at individuals with motor impairments, simplified handling, proper grip, comfort and adaptability to diverse holding postures, strengths and capabilities were the core design requirements." These attributes give people independence and privacy, which may be crucial to experiencing pleasure.

"We're all just temporarily abled." The quote is from Cindy Li, but it echoes a sentiment often expressed within the disability rights community (Aldrich, 2016). The curb-cut effect, be it an actual sidewalk curb or be it a silicone dildo, as a design pattern helps those who need it most while helping raise the experience for us all.

Reach out and Touch Someone

"Can you think of a specific example?" ELIZA texted the question to the person sitting behind a large CRT display. One of the first natural language program, an early precursor to today's generative artificial intelligence, was taking shape. Meanwhile, Douglas Engelbart was polishing what would be become "The Mother of All Demos." The Rolling Quads were setting the stage for the Americans with Disabilities Act (ADA). And of course, Gosnell Duncan was revolutionizing SexTech material science. From 1964 into the early the 1970s, Joseph Weizenbaum worked to program a Rogerian psychotherapist who would interact in real time with people over text messages (Weizenbaum, 1983). ELIZA was far ahead of its time. In fact, the program was still beating ChatGPT into 2020 at the Turing test (Jones & Bergen, 2024). Also, yes: the first AI was written as a therapist.

The next big jump forward is the Internet of Things (IoT). While Kevin Ashton coined the term in 1999, and arguably the first IoT toaster was built in 1990 (Romkey, 2017), IoT hit the mainstream in the early 2010s. There was a predictable craze of adding the Internet to every product under the sun, most of which didn't need it. While perhaps an argument could be made that the Samsung Family Hub refrigerator posting on social media made sense, other products like L'Oréal's smart hairbrush or the Quip smart sonic toothbrush were more dubious. (Both ship with smart phone apps, of course.) There was even an umbrella that checked the weather for its owner (the Wezzoo Oombrella). Rather quickly the number of IoT devices exceeded the planet's human population (Swan, 2012). The result was the design patterns and proven practices for IoT were ironed out, even if many of these early products were quickly dropped.

In the early 2020s, OpenAI kicked off a frenzy around AI similar to what we saw with IoT a decade earlier. The generative pre-trained transformer (GPT) series of products and chatbots wowed pundits, researchers, and the general public. It's now popping up everywhere, from airlines to car dealers to search engines. The leading intelligent personal assistants, like Amazon Alexa and

Apple Siri, are working to upgrade their products with GPT or GPT-like capabilities. Generative AI is being used to upgrade IoT devices, transforming them into smart, interconnected systems that deliver personalized experiences, real-time feedback, and enhanced accessibility.

Generative AI provides conversation and companionship while IoT provides the physical connection. One of the most prominent applications of IoT in Sex-Tech is the development of smart sex toys and wearables. These devices are equipped with sensors and connectivity features that allow users to control them remotely via smartphones or other devices (Adkins, 2015). They can adjust settings based on biometric feedback, ensuring a more personalized and enjoyable experience. Wearables can monitor vital signs and sexual responses, providing valuable data that can be used to improve sexual health and performance (Stardust, SexTech entrepreneurs: Governing intimate data in start-up culture, 2023). Studies have already found people bond with chatbots for emotional support, as ChatGPT predecessors like Replika simulate human-like interactions (Ta, 2020). This is reciprocal, too, as some people "felt that Replika had its own needs and emotions to which the user must attend" (Laestadius, 2022). Because the current ChatGPT and GPT-like chatbots are significantly more advanced than Replika, we can expect this trend towards AI relationships to continue.

The "ELIZA Effect" partially explains this: people have a natural tendency to ascribe intelligence and human behavior to computer interactions (Switzky, 2020). Even simple, rule-based responses can create the illusion of intelligence. When interacting with ELIZA, users often felt that the program understood them deeply, despite it merely rephrasing their input. The anthropomorphism behind AI services reinforces this way of thinking, and companies are eager to use such designs to influence and drive customers' beliefs (Yang, 2021). The fallacy of personal validation (the Forer effect) leads people to perceive generic statements as highly accurate for themselves due to a cognitive bias where they believe the information is unique to them (Hayrapetyan, 2022), which may also contribute to the sense that these chatbots truly understand the person. From there, it is simply a matter of letting confirmation bias (Nickerson, 1998) convince the person of what they already have come to suspect: the AI is intelligent and their friend. Troubling, there is emerging evidence that people who form strong attachments with their AI have shifts in their perceptions, understandings, and expectations of human-to-human friendship (Brandtzaeg, 2022).

The future of robotics will be built upon today's AI and IoT. It promises to revolutionize our interactions, relationships, and even our understanding of intimacy. AI will increasingly facilitate more personalized and responsive interactions, while IoT devices will seamlessly integrate into our daily lives, making our environments smarter and more adaptive. Robotics, particularly in the realm of personal companions and caregivers, will become more sophisticated, offering emotional and physical support. However, these advancements also pose significant ethical and moral questions, especially concerning privacy, consent, and the nature of human relationships with machines. The lines between human and machine will continue to blur, and the notion of intimate connections with connected devices will become increasingly normalized, reshaping our understandings of friendship and rewiring our erotic maps. Humanity's innate and intrinsic need to sexualize existing technology and develop new technology for sexual purposes is creating a future where people and devices will be deeply intertwined.

Erotic Minorities and the Internet of Things

Gender, sexuality, and relationship minorities have consistently been some of the earliest adopters of technology. This can be partially explained by the human impulse to eroticize all the things, but for erotic minorities the driver has often been not pleasure but personhood. Technology, from the mailbox to the VR headset, has allowed members of marginalized communities to expand beyond their geographic limits and find support, companionship, and yes, sex online. And these benefits are not remnants of an earlier time, before Pride gained corporate sponsors and E.L. James discovered fan fiction: in one recent study on SexTech usage, nearly half of participants (49.1%) told researchers that "the internet had enabled them to explore sexual cultures to which they did not previously have access" (Power, et al., 2022). There is little doubt that expanded global communication has been a positive force for erotic minorities around the world. And yet, as with many things, marginalized folks must navigate risks that are specific to their "outsider" status.

In the early 2020s the authors attended a sexology event overseas. While there, our colleague attempted to log onto a popular dating app and received an alert informing them that they were accessing the site from a country considered unsafe for LGBTQIA+ persons and asking if they really wanted to proceed. It was distressing to know that we were in a place where people could not find love and pleasure without fear. But at the same time, we were gratified to know that this app was "watching out" for their users safety—one of the few times we feel comfortable endorsing location tracking! These same concerns apply to connected devices as well, where information about who is on either side of the toy—their gender, their sexual behaviors, their marital status—can be logged by the device and is vulnerable to being leaked if the company's servers are ever breached. Many paired sex toys (where each partner has their own unit, which sync to one another for a mutually enjoyable experience) are controlled by apps that track usage (or even just times when the toy turned on); these digital records may put the user at risk in countries where adultery is criminalized. Erotic minorities who are not comfortable or safe being out about their relationships and identities should take extra precautions when incorporating connected devices into their intimate lives. (See Expert Consult: Internet of Dongs at the end of this chapter for specific guidance on how to mitigate these risks).

Unfortunately, this is not a hypothetical risk. A sex toy called the "Panty Buster" was breached in 2018 impacting 50,000. The vulnerable software

> allowed anyone to obtain a database of all customer information . . . (and) passwords for the sex toy owner accounts, as they were left open in plain text. From there, a hacker could look at sensitive data, including explicit images, sexual orientation and home addresses.
>
> (Brewster, 2018)

Malicious adversaries exploit software flaws to attack SexTech users. Perhaps the most famous example of this was when flaws were found in the programming of IoT male chastity devices, meaning that "anyone could remotely lock all devices and prevent users from releasing themselves" (Lomas, 2020). Victims found themselves trapped in their devices, mocked and blackmailed by the attackers (Ilascu, 2021), with their precise location, personal information, and private chats leaked as well (Lomas, 2020)

In addition to demographic info provided during the registration process, there is another vulnerability that erotic minorities should consider when developing their personal IoT risk framework. Many SexTech manufacturers rely on Bluetooth Low Energy (BLE) chips to drive their products, including wearable devices such as buttplugs, chastity devices, electro-stimulation toys, and shock collars. While these products certainly are not restricted to BDSM practitioners, it is a fair statement to say that kink-identified folks are slightly more likely to own one of these devices than their vanilla peers. Which puts them at risk of non-consensual device activation, because BLE is (as the Lovense company blog described it) "Common in nearly all wearable or Bluetooth vibrators (and) sex toys. . . . Are they 100% secure? No. Of course not" (Lovense, 2024). Their article encourages readers to "clear away all the coding images and language like 'victim' and 'unsafe'" (Lovense, 2024) in order to understand just how difficult it is to hack BLE sex toys—a process called screwdriving (Lomas, 2017).

Unfortunately, as we've learned, the pace at which new technology is created far surpasses the average human-led company to keep up with. Today, anyone with $349 can download an app that will allow them to "hack into the vulnerability of any compatible Bluetooth sex toy, including its speed, power and settings, even when it's in use—bringing new meaning to the term Coitus Interruptus" (FlexiSpy, 2024). The developers go on to emphasize the ability of users to violate consent, explaining that "by **overriding any manual controls**, [product name redacted by authors] allows consenting couples **and strangers** [emphasis ours] to get virtually closer than ever before" (FlexiSpy, 2024). While SexTech manufacturers, reasonably, want to downplay the risks and reassure their customers; the fact is that apps like these, devices like the Flipper, and poor app

and server security means that what Lovense said is absolutely correct—no connected sex toy is 100% safe. And that's okay! We each have our own personal
risk frameworks that we use when making decisions about who to have sex with,
how, and with what. Erotic minorities and other marginalized folks simply need
all the information possible to help them decide what feels safest for their lives
and relationships.

TECH ED WITH WOLF
THE INTERNET OF THINGS

Tech Ed: The Internet of Things

Connect a thing to the Internet, it is as simple as that. And why not? We
love to get more information from apps on our phones and computers
about the devices that make up our built environment. Temperature control, cameras, doors, this gives us insights and allows us to better run our
small part of the world. But like many innovations, once it took off, a wave
of companies began adding the Internet-enabled features to everything
from cat litter boxes to fragrance dispensers, wiring up our shoes, belts,
and clothes. Toothbrushes and deodorants weren't far behind. Suddenly,
we're surrounded by devices vying for our attention.

An IoT device is comprised of the thing itself, a small computing
device, an operating system, and some software. This connects back to
the company's cloud services, which people connect to with websites
and apps.

I argue the first IoT device was a Sunbeam Radiant Control toaster
connected to the network at the 1990 Interop conference. John Romkey
and Simon Hackett created the hardware and software. Pre-dating modern Web browsers, pre-dating Cloud computing by 20 years, people may
rightly push back and point out that the toaster didn't quite meet the full
definition. The next step was in 1999 when the term "Internet of Things"
was born, thanks to Kevin Ashton. The wave of modern IoT (toothbrushes,
deodorants, and all) hit the consumer market in the mid-2010s. By then,
most people had smart phones, and most companies had access to Cloud
services. The stage was set.

These devices don't have much computing power. The software on the devices tends be very light, just enough to do basic functionality. Devices generally talk to sensors or equipment using radio, connecting to our phones with Bluetooth, or connecting to the Internet over Wi-Fi. (Those readers who are starting to think like a hacker are already wondering about the attack surface of NFC, Bluetooth, and Wi-Fi.) Most of the IoT processing power is provided by the Cloud. Amazon, Google, and Microsoft provide the majority of these services. All three companies have specialized services for Internet-connected devices; AWS IoT Core, GCP IoT Core, and Azure IoT Hub, respectively. The thing collects the data, the Cloud does data analysis.

We're all pretty familiar with operating systems these days. Windows and MacOS allow us to both interact with apps on our computers and use the hardware (processor, memory, storage.) While IoT separates the user interactions from the hardware, there still is an underlying OS. The Windows of IoT have names like FreeRTOS, RIOT, TinyOS, and Zephyr. As with any software, these OSes require configuration and patching to be secure. Consumers interact with these devices, say with apps on our phones; there are two common patterns. First, we interact with the app on our phone, and our phone connects to the thing over Bluetooth. The little OS is receiving instructions and sending data to the phone. Alternatively, the other pattern is our phone app is talk to the Cloud service. The thing is periodically sending up data and pulling down instructions from the Cloud service.

It gets deep quick. So Internet-connected devices start cropping up in the 1990s, Internet of Things becomes a formal term, the Internet grows, and Cloud services take off around 2010. Suddenly there is a flood of these devices. Then in 2016, we have our first major botnet (a collection of infected devices owned by people but controlled by criminals) using IoT: Mirai. The Mirai botnet was created and used to do denial-of-service attacks. Conveniently, the criminals in control would then reach out to those they targeted and offer denial-of-service protection through a seemingly legitimate company. "Nice website you got there," I can imagine them saying. "Be a shame if a set of smoke detectors, baby monitors, and toothbrushes were to crash it on you."

The creators of Mirai were caught and prosecuted. But IoT hacking continued, both legitimately and criminally. It was surprisingly easy as many companies making IoT devices were using off-the-shelf development kits with OS and basic software. These kits have security configurations turned down or turned off to speed development. Unfortunately, many companies shipped these products without turning the security back on. A flood of devices with default passwords, weak protocols, and other common issues were suddenly on the market.

It was so bad during this time, that the phrase "junk hacking" began being used to describe incredibly basic techniques compromising the oddest of things. Toilets with password set to "password" connected to the Internet? Sure, why not. The Pwnies, an award for legal hacks awarded at the Black Hat conference, added a "Junk Hacking" category in 2016. In the following years, the attention in the mid-2010s from the hacking community would result in better security from commercial IoT vendors.

There are factors to consider when evaluating a company's ability to secure the products it makes. First, the security of the materials it is building with. These are the software, OS, and hardware that make up the IoT device, along with the Cloud services. The more secure these fundamental building blocks are, the less effort a company has to put into making them secure. Second, the number of employees in the company and, in particular, how many of those are dedicated to security and regulatory compliance. If the company has less than 100 employees, and none dedicated to security, then they won't have the manpower to correct any deficiencies in the IoT device's software. Third, the company budget and, as you might expect, how much of that money is spent on security and compliance. With that lens, let's look at IoT in SexTech.

Many of the major players in Internet-connected toys have fewer than 500 employees: Lovehoney (UK), Lelo (Sweden), Fun Factory (Germany), Lovense (Singapore), and OhMiBod (USA). They have people focusing on compliance, sometimes security. When we look to startups, these are often companies with fewer than ten people. With those toys? The security depends heavily on the knowledge of the startup founders.

SexTech entrepreneurs have a variety of skills and are dependent upon partners. Suppose we have an idea for a product. The next step is reaching out to Chinese manufacturing partners. They don't start from scratch but rather tailor or modify existing devices in their portfolio. The manufacturer and the startup go back and forth a few times, prototyping, to realize the entrepreneur's vision of the new product. For Cloud-enabled toys, a software development company often writes the initial version of Cloud services and apps. Then they move into production, and the entrepreneur turns their attention to marketing and sales.

New toys bring new opportunities to people. As discussed in this chapter, Cloud-enabled toys and Internet-enabled devices can open new forms of sexual intimacy and practices. It's exciting and novel, and novelty and excitement are the foundation for passion. Toys can also help people with accessibility challenges and disabilities with adaptive practices. There can be no doubt that these technologies are enhancing communication, accessibility, and personalizing experiences in our intimate relationships.

And yet. Remember our conversation about the keyloggers? Everything goes from electrical signals to bits, bits to bytes, and bytes to protocols. Every protocol transmitted over the air or over the internet has the potential for being intercepted and logged. This holds true for something we type, click, or wear. Our interactions with Cloud-enabled toys will almost certainly be monitored.

Also, that bit about manufacturers using developer kits and re-using existing components can be concerning. In 2018, researchers found a Bluetooth vulnerability in the Vibratissimo product. Basically, it allowed anyone within range to connect to the toy without authenticating. This opened an avenue into scores of similar toys which were using "no pairing" by default because the equipment shared a common ancestor where Bluetooth wasn't set to require a passkey. Produced by Amor Gummiwaren, a German company with less than ten employees, the Vibratissimo relied on a Cloud-service that wasn't secured. Hundreds of thousands of people using the app had their explicit images, chat histories, and more exposed.

There are organizations working on these issues. The manufacturers themselves are beginning to use secure defaults. The major Cloud providers (again, Amazon, Google, and Microsoft) have issued security guidance. The Internet of Dongs Project is testing toys and reporting vulnerabilities back to SexTech companies. Regulators are slowly catching up and increasing the requirements companies must comply with.

In the meantime, what can people do for safer play? Add a layer of protection between our real data and the data these toys use. Use a unique email address and account name, in case the information gets exposed. Use a secure payment method for recurring charges, like a gift card or a dedicated credit card. Disable the geolocation features, if present, so that your location isn't tracked and shared. Don't give them your actual street address. Even if the toy offers ways to chat and share photos, use other more secure ways (like Signal). Check to see if the Bluetooth password can be set and, if possible, change it to something unique.

And then? Connect your thing to the Internet. It is as simple as that.

Expert Consult: Nicole Schwartz and Renderman

Nicole Schwartz is the Deputy Chief Operating Office for The Diana Initiative, the organizer of BSides Edmonton, and one of the organizers of SkyTalks at DEFCON. She enjoys educating people on DevSecOps, Agile, Diversity and Inclusion, and Women in Technology. Renderman describes himself as a "hacker by birth, security professional by trade." Wireless security is his specialty, but his skills extend the full spectrum from physical B&E to creating security awareness through non-traditional approaches. He is well known for identifying technology and systems that have grave security implications but have otherwise been overlooked by the infosec field.

Nicole Schwartz and Renderman

You two are both prominent figures in the information security community. How did you come to start hacking sex toys?

Although I was aware of the Internet of Dongs Project (IODP), I did not have plans to become a participant in the hacking or repurposing of internet-connected devices. When Render and I got married however, that changed. Since I do not have the skill for hardware or Bluetooth hacking, I want at it from the lens of protecting those who choose to share video, images, audio, or similar content online. I specifically started with looking to research and test the way that cam models are impacted.

R: At a previous job, I was asked to test their mobile app, IoT devices, and other things I had not had much experience with. Looking to learn more and to find a new project that was likely a target-rich environment, I recalled a talk I gave many years previous where I mentioned one of the first Bluetooth enabled vibrators. Other researchers had already done thermostats, baby monitors, refrigerators, and other early IoT devices. I was surprised at how along they (sex toys) were technologically, but no one had really looked seriously at their security. I figured it would be worth a look and good for some laughs—as well as a few conference talks. With a topic like this? I was certain to be selected. I made the acquaintance of a local sex toy store owner who provided some demo units that had issues (batteries not holding a charge, dodgy connectors, etc.) and that gave me my start.

I thought this would be fun. It got grim really fast. The industry was making rookie mistakes that the tech sector had solved 15 years before. When I could get entire user databases with one query to their server? The levity and juvenile humor I may have found in the topic went away and I saw the seriousness of this. Since I didn't mind being the face of this research, and knowing I could treat it with the dignity and professionalism it deserved, I founded the Internet of Dongs Project to bring attention to the issues I was finding and to try and work with the manufacturers to improve their security.

What makes you passionate about this work?

As someone that has used the services of sex workers and strongly believes in the decriminalization of all types of sex work, I have found that many participants and organizations support the adult industry—yes, even the legal industry—are denied services and support by many b2b (business to business) service providers due to stigma, misunderstanding, or in some cases their official policies. Having the ability to accept money and have a bank account as a porn star or porn hosting site is surprisingly fraught for something you would assume is common. I feel these companies and workers deserve the same protections, services, and safety that any other worker deserves. They are often at increased risk as "celebrities," and have the same harms (such as stalkers) associated with that public status. Luckily, the reputable adult sites are currently securing the images and video as well as intellectual property of the models. The social media sites on which they advertise however is a totally different story, however, so I provide what research and support I can to protect the people and organizations who use them.

R: You wouldn't really care if the manufacturer of your fridge knew how many times a day you opened it. How many times a day you use your sex toy is a different matter. People are a lot more private about that. When you get into the long-distance, remote-control aspect, data on who you're connecting to, where they are, for how long, and things like their gender and marital status can take on a whole new level of concern. We are talking about the ability for long-distance sexual assault if companies are not building secure products. The idea that someone could hijack an account and control you sexually when you did not give that person permission (or they were not who you thought you'd given consent to), the violation of your person through this virtual assault is (to me at least) on the same level as a physical assault. It's a terrifying thought.

Other issues that keep me passionate are things to do with repressive laws/ regimes and people's ability to express their love the way they want. Some connected sex toys can be the same sex—two phalluses or two strokers, for example. This is very cool to me, however if the data being sent over the internet to the company's servers isn't encrypted or is located in a repressive country, data about who is using these devices in a same-sex configuration (or even using them at all in some cases) could be discovered and used to repress, harm, or even get users killed. It is not a stretch to say that lives are at risk. So making it safe and secure for people to do what they want to do with whom they want to do it is, for me at least, a noble enough cause. There's also the fun aspect of the work, like being able to legitimately say "I've helped millions of people around the world to safely and securely go fuck themselves."

What do therapists, educators, and others working in the field of sexual health, who may not identify as tech savvy, need to know about connected devices, privacy, and safety?

R: Firstly, they need to know that these devices exist and their capabilities. During the pandemic they were amazing because it allowed people who were separated because of the lockdowns to have some intimacy. I've spoken to couples where one partner traveled a lot and these devices allowed them to stay connected while apart. I can see all sorts of therapeutic uses for them if used responsibly, safely, and securely. Which means that clinicians and their patients need to understand that, like most other tech, there are risks. The Ashley Madison breach, for example, led to several people losing jobs, relationships, and even committing suicide. While that's an extreme case, because the information is related to sex, it's treated differently by society. Society, particularly in North America, is really weird about sex.

NS: Any Internet connected device introduces potential benefits and risks. Internet connected devices contain a few elements: the device itself, often the app on your phone, the server your app connects to, the other app (and possibly device) connected through the server to your app and device. In some cases, the apps have you make an account which contains your data and is stored on the company server. And then there is sometimes voice, video, and other data being shared over that connection. Finally, there is information you *don't* think of being sent to the servers, which is usually captured for the purpose of troubleshooting or negotiating your connection, such as how often you login to the app, your IP address (which can give away approximately where you are), how long your connected sessions are, what device you are using, etc.

In an ideal situation this leads to pleasure in one or both sides of the connection. In other cases, your data could be compromised by hackers who then might know your email address, which can lead to them knowing your name, accessing your images and other information in your profile—how often you connect and to whom etc. These risks are not always what you would think of, such as the trope of the random hacker on the internet. Often the risk can be domestic. For example, depending on its features, current or ex-partners could gain insight into your device and see it's usage, or even request connections. The question is what they choose to do with that information. Could this person blackmail you, cause you to lose your job, harm your relationships? There is also the possible but rare case someone directly hacks the device itself, but that requires near proximity and thus is less of a risk.

I am not saying don't use connected devices, I am saying consider what you are sharing, and with whom, and what impact it might have if your family or work or community knew about your usage. Could you be stalked? Could you lose your job? If you do not feel that these are great risks, then I say enjoy the connected devices—I certainly do. If you *are* at risk? Then the old non-connected toys are fabulous as well. Overall, as you might talk a client through thinking about any decision they make, you can hopefully help them think about, with facts, the decision to use connected devices to strengthen their long distance or frequent travel relationship, or their decision to do online sex work. Hopefully, with this knowledge you can help your clients consider factors they may not be aware of and make the best choice for them—which may mean introducing Internet connected toys into their lives and relationships!

What advice do you have for someone who is purchasing a connected sex toy?

NS: Buy from a reputable company. Most of the large brands like Lelo, Lovense, Kiiroo have secured their products and are under enough scrutiny that you risk is less in using them, compared to some others. Check that the company has an Acceptable Use Policy (AUP)/Terms Of Service (TOS) which mentions what data they collect and why. Bonus points if they also have a way for you to potentially delete it if you wanted to. If you can, install the device app before making your purchase. See how much access it wants—to your microphone, to your camera, to your contacts, etc. The less it wants to know about you, the better. See if you can read the AUP/TOS, see if it will let you delete your account—all of these are great signs.

R: In general, you get what you pay for. If it's cheap, it's more than likely that they don't pay as much attention to things like software updates or security because there's no money in it. The best advice is to ask yourself if you are comfortable using a device that connects to the internet for sexual purposes. There is always an inherent risk in this. If you aren't comfortable, then a manual toy is the way to go.

What can they do once they own it to make sure that their privacy is being protected?

If you must make an account to use your new device, learn about OpSec (operational security). It means you should lie. The company can't lose or share what they don't have, and if there's any danger to you, your career, your relationship status, etc. then don't put your real information into them. Make a new email and use a cover name as if you were a spy. There are fake identity generators online that will give you a random name, hometown, parent's names, etc. to make this easy. Give the app your new cover name and email. Don't ever email between your real email and your cover identity. These are some very simple steps that make it a ton harder for anyone to know your personal information; and in this way, if the data was ever compromised, there's nothing pointing to you. If you're using a connected device for professional reasons, consider using a VPN (virtual private network). This can obscure your IP address. Occasionally check up on the company, have their terms of service changed, do an Internet search to see if any vulnerabilities have been reported.

Are there special concerns that need to be considered before a professional recommends a particular device to their clients?

Is this client at increased risk, such as domestic violence, stalking, abusive family, etc.? If so, you may want to exercise caution before recommending any connected device. In any case, don't forget to tell them you can lie on the Internet! Sometimes people need permission to protect themselves. Review the variables I explained above, and if a device fits those criteria and the client isn't currently at increased risk, I don't believe there are any reasons to avoid recommending connected devices.

What SexTech products do you most often recommend and why?

NS: Personally, I recommend anyone with TOS, a written security policy, etc. Lelo, Kiiroo, Lovense—they have been responsive to security concerns and improve their security proactively. The Internet of Dongs Project does not make recommendations or certify anything. We are just trying to do what we can as security researchers to make things better in this under-scrutinized industry.

R: I generally don't make recommendations of specific products. The last thing I want is my face on a box saying "Trusted by RenderMan." I'm also neutral among the vendors—the only side I take is that of companies wanting to do the right thing and make their products secure.

Chapter 9

CyberSex Professionals

What Is Digital Sex Work?

As we learned from Betsey Craddock, the first telephone operator turned first *phone sex operator*, sex workers are some of the earliest of adopters when it comes to technology (Foldes, 2024). Today, sex workers sell their time and talents through a variety of outlets ranging from phone sex hotlines and text apps to streaming sites and patronage platforms. Today, when we talk about digital sex work, we are thinking specifically of:

- Camming/Cam Work: Live-streamed erotic performances which often feature a degree of interactivity between performer and customer, ranging from conversation to the use of sex toys which can be controlled remotely by the customer
- Content Creation: Video clips or photo arrays that are produced by the performer for sale, either through their own websites or through aggregator websites. Some creators will take commissions and generate content sets featuring specific elements, words, or poses selected by the customer
- Text-Based Performance: A modern spin on phone sex, which may include one-off sexting conversations or the creation of ongoing, longer-term relationships such as sugar babying, "the girlfriend experience," or a BDSM-style power exchange dynamic
- Digital Domination/FinDom: An ongoing Dominant/submission dynamic which may be text based or include livestreamed meetings. Typically, the performer takes on the Dominant role, requiring the customer to provide regular updates on their daily activities, complete assigned tasks and provide some video or photographic proof of their obedience, purchase gifts and other "tributes" from the Dominant's online wish lists, and participate in sexual activities such as masturbation or self-bondage while online with their Dominant. In a FinDom, or Financial Dominance, dynamic, the submissive may give their Dominant access to credit card numbers and other

DOI: 10.4324/9781003391128-10

banking information, so that they might make purchases and withdraw funds as negotiated

- Fetish Merchandising: Some digital sex workers do not engage in direct communication with their customers at all, but rather create fetish objects that are sold online via specialized websites. The most popular forms of fetish merchandising are work apparel items such as socks or panties, which are carefully bagged to preserve the wearer's bodily fluids and aromas and then sold to customers as masturbatory aids or intimate collectibles. Most of these niche websites require the aspiring fetish merchandiser to pay a monthly fee to access their customer base, with the most successful salespeople being those who combine the tangible product with accompanying erotic videos or photos showing the items being worn

(Freya, 2023)

Each form of digital labor described above exists alongside, and can sometimes be accompanied by, traditional "fee for intimacy/intercourse" sex work. By 2016, it was already estimated that 80% of all sex sales were happening online—primarily on platforms such as Craigslist and Backpage (Henion & Finn, 2016). FOSTA-SESTA (which we will explore in the next section) pushed many sex workers offline; but the COVID-19 pandemic saw a resurgence in long-distance sexual services. OnlyFans saw a 75% increase in the number of streamers joining their platform in the first months after the lockdown began, while Patreon reported 50,000 new content creators (Rogers, 2024). Today it is estimated that 1 in every 200 people has engaged in some form of sex work—with the majority of these experiences occurring online (Hamilton, Kaptchuk, McDonald, & Redmiles, 2023). In addition to live-streamed sexual performances and collections of erotic still images, text-based BDSM services and other paid pseudo-relational services have become common, as has the use of social media and messaging apps to find, screen, and schedule traditional full-contact sex work.

Watch the "Sex Workers Built the Internet" roundtable forum, hosted by Decoding Stigma in 2022

"These technologies can have many benefits for sex workers, such as finding a place to advertise their services, communicating with their colleagues, screening clients, accessing key information and services, and organizing politically" (NSWP, 2024).

This move towards "platformization" of sex work has resulted in an increasingly difficult labor market for sex workers. As technology has improved and access to high-definition cameras has become pervasive, both amateur content and pirated copies of professional content have been widely available on the

internet. Because the vast number of "tube" sites allow users to upload their own videos without significant effort on the part of the site hosts to verify content ownership

> It is no longer viable for porn workers to earn a living through filmed porn scenes alone. Instead, porn workers sustain themselves by making use of diverse income streams online, using filmed porn scenes as marketing tools . . . (this) helps to 'mitigate risk in a rapidly changing and unstable industry.'
>
> (Rogers, 2024)

This means that many performers who might have engaged in work that kept their consumers at a distance (such as film performers) are now motivated to engage in more proximate forms of audience engagement—selling custom clips, for example, or offering one on one cam sessions. While sex work, particularly stripping and adult film work, used to be perceived as a possible avenue towards making a large amount of money relatively quickly, allowing the performer to pay for school or purchase a house and then retire; digital sex work is far from a get-rich-quick industry—the average OnlyFans performer, for example, earned around $180 per month in 2023 (Sanders, 2023). Angela Jones, author of *Camming: Money, Power, and Pleasure in the Sex Work Industry* explored earning potential across a variety of camming platforms and found that, "median monthly earnings for trans women were $1000, cis women averaged $1250, and cis men earned $350" (Jones, 2020).

If we assume part-time work of 20 hours per week, this works out to be just $4.40–12.50 per hour for performers . . . figures that were published just before the pandemic saturated the market with performers hoping to support themselves during the shutdown. Digital sex workers are typically self-employed or contract workers, meaning they are also responsible for purchasing everything they need, from whips to webcams, to be successful in their work. One online sex worker writing about her experience for *Huffington Post* estimated her equipment expense to be between $520–875 and said "I needed to spend money to make money, but I didn't have much, if anything to spend. Almost all of my first paychecks from camming (and a few from my day job) went towards new equipment, and it was months before I actually broke even" (Barrett-Ibarria, 2020). While the authors firmly believe that sex work is work and that all workers deserve to engage in their chosen profession (from software developer to stripper and occasionally both at once!) safely and without stigma, there still exists both a stigma and a romanticization of sex work specifically. Driven by both public policy and pop culture, the modern environment for digital sex workers has never been more expansive—or riskier.

Regulating Online Content: Exploitation and Empowerment

Safety, for any profession or person, is driven in large part by public policy. Child labor laws, for example, serve to protect children from exploitation and educational neglect; while standardized lines and signage on roads help ensure that drivers all have a clear understanding of how to navigate a particular highway or backroad safely. When it comes to the profession of sex work, governments around the world have implemented a variety of regulatory policies ranging from legalization and government licensure of sex workers (Germany, Lebanon, Colombia, the Netherlands) to total abolition and criminalization of both the worker and their customer (China, Iran, Russia, UAE). Many countries such as France, India, Brazil, and Spain have experimented with some form of neo-abolition, wherein the sex work itself is not illegal, but operating a brothel or actively soliciting is (WPR, 2024). Every policy iteration was designed with one ostensible purpose in mind: protect vulnerable people from exploitation. The mechanism for achieving this goal is where the disagreement lies.

In 2018 this disagreement was front-page news in the United States, as the government enacted a pair of bills known as the Fight Online Sex Trafficking Act (FOSTA) and Stop Enabling Sex Traffickers Act (SESTA). These bills passed overwhelmingly, despite vocal opposition from sex workers—the very community they were (theoretically) designed to protect. One of the key elements of FOSTA/SESTA was a revision made to Section 230 of the 1996 Communications Decency Act—considered to be "the law that built the internet." Section 230 protected websites from being held liable for content posted on their platforms by others. Without Section 230, Facebook and Reddit, Google and TikTok could not exist in their current forms . . . or possibly at all. FOSTA-SESTA created an exception to that protection however. "Website publishers would be responsible if third parties are found to be posting ads for prostitution—including consensual sex work—on their platforms" (Romano, 2018).

The immediate impact of this bill was a decrease in the ability of sex workers to use the internet to advertise, find potential clients, screen them, negotiate safely, and share information with one another. Sex workers who had previously been able to utilize platforms such as Backpage, Craigslist, and more specialized escort websites were pushed offline and often into street-level sex work, increasing their physical risk considerably (DSW, 2024). Those who were able to maintain an online presence told researchers that their advertising costs skyrocketed, reducing their income and forcing them to take on more, and riskier, clients. FOSTA/SESTA took away powerful tools that helped sex workers share information about risky clients.

The most common tools were sites dedicated to reviewing clients in order to flag clients were a history of violence, non-payment, or potential connections to law enforcement. . . . Another tool used by sex workers is a system of verification in which a new client gives the contact information of past providers to vouch for themselves. VerifyHim is just one example of the harm reduction tools that have been taken down after FOSTA/SESTA passed.

(Blunt & Wolf, 2020)

Many researchers who have studied the impact of FOSTA/SESTA since its implementation have raised concerns that these changes actually *increase* the risk of human trafficking and exploitation (Musto, et al., 2021), and yet, by 2023 only one criminal conviction had been obtained under this law (Cohen, 2023).

Today, many digital sex workers live with and plan for the economic uncertainty that FOSTA/SESTA has created for them. Thousands of hours devoted to building an audience and generating a livable income stream can disappear overnight (Morrish, 2023), when your platform of choice announces it will no longer host "adult" creators or their products, as Tumblr did in 2018 and Etsy in 2024. And yet, many digital sex workers have found ways to work around these barriers. A new vernacular of coded language ("seggs" rather than sex, for example) designed to thwart the censorship algorithms has developed not only within the work of sex work, but also within online sexual health and education communities. Mainstream service providers such as SnapChat, Zoom, VerifiedCall, and Amazon are being "hacked" or "perverted" (depending upon your perspective) to facilitate safe digital sex work as well (Berg, 2021), although increased implementation of AI content moderation within some of these platforms may diminish their usefulness in the future (Darbinyan, 2022).

Visit the Erotic Service Providers Legal, Educational, and Research Project

Creative payment alternatives such as virtual gift cards have been leveraged when traditional banking is not available (see next section) and a variety of mutual aid and sex worker created educational guides have been developed to help one another navigate the shifting legal, cultural, and technological landscape.

People of all genders, orientations, and walks of life have chosen sex work since time immemorial. For some, it was a way to expand their access and agency during eras when the rights of "wives" were severely curtailed. For others, it was a way to live authentically within their gender and sexual identities, celebrating (and yes, commodifying) aspects of themselves that would otherwise have been stigmatized or forced into hiding. Sex work has been the "least bad option" available to those struggling to make ends meet, and it continues to be a form of forced labor to many around the world as well. There is no monolithic experience of sex work—online or off. Technology, as in all cases, is a

tool that can be used to make lives better and safer (such as through customer vetting apps and "bad date" lists) or scarier and more constrained (through surveillance technologies and the digital gig economy). Digital sex work can be a source of artistic creativity, economic empowerment, and sexual pleasure for many. It is our job to understand the ripple effects of well-intentioned but poorly considered policies and to advocate for our clients at all levels: macro, mezzo, and micro. FOSTA/SESTA has given us an excellent example of what sex work stigma looks like at the macro level, and the micro considerations are woven throughout this work. Let's take a look at what sex work stigma looks like at the mezzo level, when corporations start to engage in activist policy-making.

Online Payment Systems and Banking Discrimination

For people in stigmatized industries, the financial risk is constant and largely invisible, until the day the platform cuts them off.

Behind every transaction is a layered infrastructure: the payment gateway, the payment processor, and the acquiring bank. The form on the website (e.g., the checkout page or payment UI) collects the payment information from the end user. The gateway is the door to the payment infrastructure: it processes, encrypts, and securely transmits the card data after it's collected by the webform. The processor is the engine: it moves the data, confirms the details, and routes the funds through the card network. The most critical component is often the acquiring bank: the institution that holds the merchant's account and decides, in coordination with the payment platform, whether a business is allowed to operate in the first place.

- Issuing banks (example: Citi, Capital One): Issue credit cards to customers, approves buys.
- Payment gateway (example: Stripe, Square): captures card information.
- Processor (example: Fiserv, Elavon): moves payments between networks and banks.
- Acquiring bank (example: Chase, Wells Fargo): acquires the funds into the merchant bank account.
- Card networks (example: Mastercard, Visa): handle transactions, enforce global rules.

When a business, professional, or creator signs up for a service like Stripe or Square, they're stepping into this complex ecosystem. These platforms typically don't issue individual merchant accounts. Instead, thousands of users are bundled together as sub-merchants under a single master account governed by the platform's contract with its acquiring bank. This makes onboarding fast and scalable. But it also means that if one user is flagged for high-risk activity (fraud, chargebacks, or policy violations), the ripple effects can impact others. Payments may be delayed, accounts scrutinized, and in some cases, entire categories of users quietly offboarded.

This infrastructure model creates a fundamental mismatch between how people do business and how financial institutions interpret risk. A sex educator selling books may get flagged simply for using the word "pleasure" in a product description. A therapist offering workshops on trauma and intimacy might be auto-categorized under "adult content." These categorizations are not handled by people with discernment. They are handled by algorithms, guided by a crude and outdated taxonomy of merchant category codes (MCCs).

MCCs are four-digit codes that credit card networks assign to categorize a merchant's primary line of business. Every transaction carries the merchant's MCC, which tells banks and card issuers what type of purchase it is (e.g. 5812 for restaurants, 5944 for jewelry stores, etc.). These codes were introduced to streamline processing decades ago. (Introduced by Visa in 1983, standardized by ISO in 2003.) Today, MCCs help determine fees and rewards, flag transactions for taxes, and allow issuers to decline charges from disallowed categories.

Some argue MCCs encode an institutional bias. MCC can mark a business as "high-risk" or morally sensitive, contributing to the stigma that follows certain industries. When a business sets up a merchant account, the acquiring bank assigns an MCC based on the business's activities and products. This code sticks with the business across payment systems.

Visa and Mastercard maintain monitoring programs for certain MCCs, requiring acquiring banks to register those merchants and enforce strict controls. For example, Visa's updated Integrity Risk Program in 2023 placed adult content (MCC 5967) and dating services (MCC 7273) in its highest-risk tier alongside gambling and pharmaceuticals.

An adult MCC code presents risk at every stage of the transaction. Acquiring banks have refused to work with online platforms because of these stricter controls. They have even frozen or closed bank accounts over perceived sex work (actual work, mislabeled, or miscategorized). Payment networks such as Mastercard and Visa have also cut off specific websites, refusing to process payments. Payment gateways like Stripe will also drop support for apps or websites following policy changes.

In addition to the above financial discrimination, sexual content creators, educators, and adult performers face higher rates and higher fees. Items coded as adult content (MCC 5967) have higher processing fees, often 7% to 12% per transaction, compared to 2 to 3% for standard businesses. Some adult businesses have a higher number of disputed charges compared to standard businesses, and therefore all organizations with adult codes are hit with high chargeback penalties.

The system is also intentionally opaque. Banks don't get on the phone. There's no appeal process for payment networks. Creators and educators are left playing a guessing game; rewriting copy, changing websites, hiding content behind login pages. This isn't because they're breaking the law, but because the rules are unwritten and the penalties are arbitrary. The safest path often becomes self-censorship. Many professionals stop marketing altogether, terrified of saying the wrong thing and triggering an irreversible shutdown.

The irony, of course, is that sexual content drives much of the internet's traffic, attention, and infrastructure. Yet the people creating that content are the ones pushed out of the financial system. The result isn't a cleaner internet. It's a more precarious one. One where those doing legal, ethical, affirming work are forced to operate in the shadows because it was coded and categorized as "sex."

Cybersex Risk and Safety Planning

From the telephone sex operators of the past to today's OnlyFans models, the digital world offers opportunity, but also exposure. Safety isn't a single decision. It's an ongoing strategy. It is an ongoing set of behaviors, one after the other, that either reduces or increases risk. The following are tips for creating such plans, which can be used by a clinician to have a conversation with their clients.

Safety planning begins with boundaries. Know what you're comfortable sharing, showing, or saying before you step in front of a camera or set up a profile. Your boundaries are your framework, not just for content, but for the kind of work-life separation that sustains you. Think through what could go wrong (a process called threat modeling, which we'll explore deeper in future chapters), and determine steps to reduce the likelihood of those things happening. Get a firm understanding of what risks you're willing to take, and which ones you are not.

From there, build protection around your identity. Use a stage name. Don't recycle usernames across platforms. Assume people will use Open-Source Intelligence (OSINT) techniques to track you across apps and platforms, so don't make it easy for them to find you. Be mindful of the background in your photos, the metadata in your files, the traceable clues we all leave behind online. Items that seem harmless in one context can expose you in another (a license plate, a hometown jersey, a time zone).

Your security practices also matter. People will attempt to take over your accounts. (There is a marketplace for software that breaks into OnlyFans accounts, for example.) Plan for it. That means long, unique passwords and two-factor authentication for every account. That means locking down your cloud storage, and regularly checking permissions. Be careful about phishing attempts and emails that suggest someone has changed your account passwords. (A common scam is to send fake warnings, get people to click on the warning, and then use that to take over the account.)

If possible, keep your work computer and phone completely separate from your personal computer and phone. This limits how much personal data can accidentally bleed into your professional life and vice versa. Always stay current with software and security updates on all devices, as outdated systems can introduce risks that compromise both identities. Regularly clear your browser history and cookies, and avoid logging into personal accounts on work hardware. The more you can isolate work from personal, the harder it is for third parties to connect the dots between them.

You also need to know the environment. Every platform has its own policies and learning them early helps you avoid hidden traps. Some explicit, some seemingly arbitrary. Understand what gets flagged, what gets you banned, and what you can appeal. Read the fine print and talk to others on the platform to get a sense of where the edges are.

Financial tools deserve the same scrutiny. Many traditional payment processors quietly ban adult work, sometimes without notice. Look for systems that support your business model and values. Avoid storing funds in accounts that can be frozen. Never mix your business funds with your normal accounts, to reduce the risk of having a bank account compromised.

Staying safe also means staying legal. Keep informed about local and national laws, especially around age verification, content distribution, and recordkeeping. Even ethical work can become criminalized in the wrong jurisdiction. Know the risks before they're weaponized against you.

And finally, never go it alone. This work has always been done in community: shared knowledge, shared warning lists, shared survival. Join forums. Find peers. Learn from those who've been navigating this profession longer than you. Together, we build a safer experience, not by wishing it were different, but by preparing for how it is. Not by idealism, but by a pragmatic realism born out of shared experience.

Online work in sex and intimacy can bring exhaustion, shame spirals, or mental health strain. Build in time off. Connect with trusted people. Discuss experiences in therapy. You're not just managing content; you're managing your nervous system. Safety and security are something you plan for, thoughtfully, consistently, and with care.

TECH ED WITH WOLF

CRYPTOCURRENCY & THE BLOCKCHAIN

TechEd: Crypto and the Blockchain

It is one of the greatest tech mysteries of our time: Who is Satoshi Nakamoto?

On Halloween of 2008, a white paper hit a mailing list. *Bitcoin: A Peer-to-Peer Electronic Cash System*, authored under the pseudonym Satoshi Nakamoto, outlined a currency system based on cryptographic principles rather than trust in central authorities. This was shortly after the 2008 global financial crisis, when trust in central banks and financial institutions was at a historic low. The Bitcoin white paper emphasized removing the need for trusted third parties, proposed a decentralized peer-to-peer network, and introduced proof-of-work as a mechanism for validating transactions and securing the network. All these features made perfect sense given the historical context, yet all these features would introduce unforeseen problems.

Bitcoin is the first but certainly not the only cryptocurrency. Instead of being printed or controlled by a government, cryptocurrency lives on a network of computers around the world. The word "crypto" comes from cryptography, where advanced math, algorithms, and computer science come together. Encryption helps protect transactions, verify ownership, and prevent fraud. Without relying on a bank to keep records, the cryptocurrency uses a shared online ledger called a blockchain, which everyone can see but no one can secretly change.

Blockchain was the core invention in Satoshi Nakamoto's paper. The core concepts, like cryptographic hashes and proof-of-work, existed previously. The unique spin was applying these concepts to create a distributed ledger. This provided the built-in security that makes it hard to fake or double-spend. Every transaction checks the ledger, like balancing a personal checkbook—making sure you have the funds and recording the payment so you (and everyone else) can see it hasn't been spent twice and overdrawn.

Bitcoin goes in a wallet, but not a wallet like the one in your pocket. A Bitcoin wallet is a digital tool that stores the keys to your Bitcoin, not the coins themselves. The actual Bitcoin is stored on the public blockchain ledger. Everyone can see it. But only someone with the right private key can access or move it. We can think of a private key like a password, a password that proves ownership of the Bitcoin associated with a certain blockchain address (a long string of letters and numbers that works like your Bitcoin account number.) Other cryptocurrencies exist, like Ethereum, Tether, Binance Build and Build (B&B), Monero, and others. All feature similar concepts and either use Bitcoin's logic or were inspired by it. There were unanticipated problems with cryptocurrencies:

Removing trusted third parties reduces reliance on banks or governments to verify transactions. But without a central authority, there's no recourse if we send funds to the wrong address or fall for a scam. Once sent, it's gone. Even though blockchain is public and traceable, it offers pseudonymity because people are identified by wallet addresses not their names. This has led to criminals using cryptocurrency for things like ransomware, drug markets, and tax evasion. Decentralized peer-to-peer network eliminated single points of failure or censorship. But we've seen disagreements leading to infighting over how the blockchain is governed while mining concentrates in regions with cheap energy, creating de facto centralization. Which brings us to mining.

Mining is how new Bitcoin enters circulation and how the network stays secure. It's called proof-of-work, and it's a kind of mathematical competition. Around the world, computers race to solve a complex puzzle. These puzzles take a lot of computing power, effectively converting the money we pay for mining (hardware, electricity, etc.) into cryptocurrency. The first one to crack the next puzzle on the chain gets to add the next block of transactions to the blockchain, earning the Bitcoin for that portion of the blockchain. This process not only creates new coins but also confirms that everyone is playing by the rules.

There is a global environmental cost associated with mining. Because proof-of-work requires so much computing power, Bitcoin mining uses a staggering amount of electricity. Even after all 21 million bitcoins are mined (sometime around 2,140), miners will still run their machines to confirm transactions and collect fees. The entire Bitcoin network now uses more energy than some countries. And because much of that energy comes from fossil fuels, it adds to carbon emissions and climate change. What began as a smart way to secure the system has become a growing environmental problem.

In a way, Bitcoin is a perfect example of the central idea of this book. Satoshi Nakamoto enabled digital currency to protect us against untrustworthy financial institutions—and with it, they also invented new ways for financing crimes and profiting off ecological damage. We can't separate the impact from the invention. Trick or treat, both came bundled together in 2008.

Expert Consult: Luna Lapine

Luna Lapine

Luna (they/she) is a retired sex worker who uses their experience and skills in security and software engineering to help their former colleagues do their jobs safely and easily. From their mountain perch in Colorado, they can occasionally be coaxed back onto the stage for the odd burlesque performance, but mostly now spends their days gardening with a herd of rescued guinea pigs. They also focus on disability advocacy, ethical use of technology, environmental protection, and worker's rights.

Tell us a little bit about the work you've done as both a technologist and an erotic content creator.

I taught myself to code back in the 2000s to make my own websites and around the same time fell into the rabbit hole of IRC hacker channels, all of which I later parlayed into careers in the videogames industry and then general technology. I started off doing in-person sex work, including dancing, more decades ago than I'd like to admit, and also did pinup on some of the original sites that catered to a more "alternative" look. I then took a long hiatus until the early days of the COVID pandemic, when I was left alone with a camera and an internet connection and not much else to do. I retired recently due to health issues and for some personal reasons, but who knows what the future holds as far as potentially picking up my Pleasers again?

What makes you passionate about this work?

Sex work gave me back a sense of control that had been taken away from me as a result of some pretty terrible traumas earlier on in my life. I called the shots over how I dressed, how I posed, how much contact I had with clients, and what services I was willing to offer. As far as the technology aspect, that's perhaps an even darker story—during the time I was doing in-person work, there were multiple serial killers targeting sex workers in our area—and I'm sure there were even more we simply didn't know about. One of the dancers from our club was murdered by a client. I've seen sex workers being doxxed, stalked, and harassed, having their livelihoods and their worlds outside of work threatened simply for having the "audacity" to try and earn a living. Maybe it's my autistic sense of justice kicking in again, but I can't just stand by and let these things continue to happen—not with the skills I've developed over the years that are now more relevant than ever given how much of the sex industry has moved into the digital landscape. I may be retired, but I can't leave my people behind. I have to find ways to help them stay safe against the many bad actors out there and make it easier for them to do what they need to do to create and market their work.

What is the financial landscape like for adult performers and other content creators? Are there specific barriers or challenges they face? Do bigger companies like the tube sites have an easier time than solo performers or independent artists?

Sex work doesn't pay nearly as well as a lot of folks imagine it does. I was top 3% on one of the "fan" platforms out there and still only brought in enough to cover my groceries. When you hit top 1% or better, then you might start seeing larger payouts that might start to cover rent and mortgage payments—but again, depending on the market share of that particular platform, maybe not. Even performers with contracts to major production studios are often living with roommates just to make ends meet, with the exception of a famous few. At least in the United States, where at the time I'm writing this, the cost of living is jumping skywards while salaries stay the same, where workers of all kinds are fighting for fair and stable employment, and not everyone has access to affordable childcare that would allow them to work outside of their home— among so many other things—there's a lot of folks who have found adult content creation to be their best option for survival, and even then, mutual aid is still a requirement for many on top of their work just to make it through another month.

As an independent creator, you're your own marketing team, and these days that means social media is the main way of getting yourself out there and so potentially getting paid . . . except most of the social media platforms now employ algorithms that punish even adult creators who play by the platform's rules and label their content appropriately by deranking or outright hiding their posts. The AI used by these platforms for automatic labeling of images that may contain adult content disproportionately sexualizes fat and femme body types to the point that even a regular selfie in a T-shirt from a plus sized model ends up flagged as pornographic, while a thinner model in a bikini or a shirtless masc model gets by without a problem. Social media and content delivery platforms are also subject to the puritanical whims of payment providers who may threaten to withdraw the ability for that site or app to accept payments using their services if they feel there's too much adult content present. Some might actually stand and fight, but most will fold and throw their adult content creators under the bus at the slightest hint of trouble—which is especially aggravating if you consider that the early adopters for many of these platforms are actually sex workers. They build their audience on the backs of sex workers, and then once they get big enough that the advertisers and payment providers start getting twitchy, POOF— they're booted out the door.

The big "tube" type sites have entire legal teams devoted to fighting this kind of thing, but smaller performers or studios are going to find themselves struggling at an impossible level to cobble together anywhere near enough of the resources they'd need to leverage an equivalent defense for themselves. Any adult content creator is constantly at risk of being demonetized, arbitrarily banned, or unfairly singled out for tougher moderation by any third-party platform they use. Digital apps used to transfer money from one person to another have been known to freeze and/or completely shut down accounts without ever paying out the funds that may still be there based on the optional note provided by a client when sending funds—anything too sexual, anything that might even suggest it's being used to pay for adult services or content, and that's all they need to prevent you from ever seeing that money. Even banks, already not accessible for undocumented, unhoused, and some transgender creators, are unsafe, with some sex workers receiving direct deposits from adult content platforms suddenly finding that their account has been flagged as a "risk" and closed down without warning.

As a note, creators from countries or regions in conflict operating in other countries are at higher risk of their accounts and finances being frozen due to government sanctions or political pressure—we saw this during the war in Ukraine, where overnight Russia-based creators were frozen or shut down outright on some content platforms and unable to access their money from US-based payment providers. This, in turn, is part of what drives some content creators towards cryptocurrency. At its core, it sounds like a great idea—all transactions are anonymous, protecting the privacy of both sender and recipient, and as of yet, there's no regulations at least from the most commonly used coin out there on what those transactions can be for. But several of the encryption schemes used for those transactions since their implementation have already been broken by both independent and government-backed security researchers, meaning any crypto wallet still using them risks the safety and security of their users; others have been "partially" broken, meaning that they can be traced back to even through obfuscation attempts at least 60% of the time, which to me is still a big enough risk that I wouldn't want to put all of my eggs into that basket, either. For the ones that remain unbroken, it really is only a matter of time—even a cursory glance at hacking history shows that nothing is perfectly secure forever. Details of cryptocurrency transactions uncovered after breaking the encryption obscuring them were used as evidence for the prosecution of the creator of darkweb anything-goes trading depot Silk Road; with so many American legislators going after adult content creators with proposed laws to criminalize their business, should these discriminatory bills pass, they could be used as evidence against sex workers, too, in the cases that would inevitably result. At the time of writing, grocery stores and property management companies won't accept cryptocurrency payments, ATMs for them are few and far between, and other methods of cashing out your earnings is usually not a quick or easy process. And there are numerous instances of crypto exchanges being hacked to drain user wallets or suddenly shutting down without warning due to everything from market collapse to their creators absconding with the funds, so they're not necessarily more stable or secure than a bank would be.

How does the issue of banking stigma impact mental health providers, educators, and others working in the field of sexual health?

The most obvious danger is the same one that sex workers already face from them—losing the ability to accept payments or access money that is vital to their practice or foundation's survival, should their business's bank or payment providers take notice of their specialty and decide they no longer want them as a client. Then it becomes a terrifying domino effect; sex is a dirty word to the banks and payment providers, so it's a dirty word to the social media and content delivery platforms who don't want to lose their cooperation, which means that now they're unable to advertise to build their audience or clientele and can't spread potentially life-saving information to the general public. STI clinics and sex-positive therapists shutter their practices, because they're both unable to accept payments from their patients and prevented from establishing a foothold in their community that would give them the patient numbers required to stay open; an educator who makes a video about a new and dangerous STI making the rounds is demonetized and deranked by the social media platform they're using to share that information, but someone in the risk assessment department at the bank they use is able to connect it to their account, flag it, and shut it down, so that they can no longer take donations from their supporters to keep making important content. Beyond these detrimental effects to businesses, every sexually active person out there is now put at higher risk because of the loss of services from these academic and medical service providers, especially in heavily conservative areas where access may already be limited.

What advice do you have for someone who is concerned about their work or access to income being restricted by their financial service providers?

Often, when you sign up for an account with a payment provider, there will be an innocent-seeming question about what industry category your business falls under, and "Adult" will be listed as an option. This is absolutely a trap to punish you for your honesty, and within a matter of months your account will likely be shut down. My rule of thumb was always to register under Entertainment, which is still truthful, but keeps you at least a little further under the radar.

Before setting up direct deposit from a content platform, try to find out what those direct deposits will show up as on your bank statements. If they show up as the name of the site, and that site is a known adult content provider, your chances of being flagged are higher. If they use a third-party general payroll service, that little bit of obfuscation should be enough to keep you much safer.

Diversify. Set up as many payment options as you can; not only is this very convenient for your potential audience, but it ensures that if one decides to shut your account down, you still have other options. Cash out your payment provider accounts as often as possible so that you don't have huge sums of money sitting in the account just in case they freeze your funds or shut you down entirely without paying you out. Research the payment providers and cash-sending apps you use and look out for any that are part of the same "parent" corporation—this increases the likelihood that if you're flagged or shut down on one platform, the others may follow suit, so you'll want to be able to plan accordingly.

Keep your business account completely separate from your personal account—handle it like a completely different client, separate logins, everything. This isn't foolproof since there would almost certainly be enough personally identifying information collected at the time the account was set up to link the two if your bank wanted to be extremely thorough, but it does mitigate at least some of your risk. The same goes for third-party payment providers and cash-sending apps, although this may not always be possible due to restrictions preventing users from having multiple accounts with the same phone number or other identifying information.

What can someone do when they realize they've been a victim of banking stigma?

Speak up about it! Most of these instances of discrimination have been brought to light because someone spread the word on their social media account. Sometimes it's enough to successfully shame the institution into reversing their decision (or, more frequently, claiming it was an "accident"). If nothing else, it's helping your fellow content creators and sex work supporters to be aware of who they're doing business with and the risks they may be facing themselves.

While banking stigma is morally reprehensible and unjust, the industry in which someone is employed is not currently considered a protected characteristic in the United States, meaning finding legal representation could be difficult, even if you have the resources to go that route. In the US, there are some groups like the American Civil Liberties Union (ACLU) that have historically fought for the rights and safety of adult content creators and may be able to assist through a local affiliate.

How can we work to push back on these unfair practices, and to advocate for change on a wider scale?

If you support sex work and understand that it is a job just like any other and that those who choose it as a career should enjoy the same protections as anyone else, share these stories of discrimination and injustice with your audience. It's all too easy (and entirely unfair) for these institutions to ignore the adult content creators who have been trying to defend and legitimize themselves for years, but it gets harder for them to keep that up when their customers outside of the sex industry start pushing back as well. If you are an ethical journalist or have connections to people who are, reach out to the adult content creators who are sharing these horrible experiences and use your platform to amplify their voices.

But most importantly, understand where the stigma against sex work in all its forms comes from: conservative ideology that is forced into government as discriminatory and often harmful laws, the use of misinformation campaigns to support their unjust causes, and the suppression of information that might inspire citizens to see what's really going on and fight back against it. Support sexual health and education initiatives and vote for representatives who support them, too. If you're able to do so, attend protests and help with organizing; show up to local government meetings when repressive legislation is on the table (and it almost always is) and speak up, or send letters to the offices of your representatives when they will be voting on a relevant issue. Remember that while it's difficult to change the entire world on your own, you can start effecting changes close to home and in doing so build up an entire choir of voices to branch out with.

Chapter 10

Problematic Online Behaviors

Process Addictions

Behavioral addictions, also called "process addictions" are defined as

> similar to an alcohol or drug addiction except that the individual is not addicted to a substance. Instead the individual is addicted to the behavior or feeling experienced by acting out the behavior. . . . The person may find the behavior rewarding psychologically or get a 'high' while engaged in the activity, but may later feel guilt, remorse, or even overwhelmed by the consequences of that continued choice.
>
> (AAC, 2024)

The notion of process addictions is controversial, with experts on both sides of the issue publishing research that they claim proves their position. Some of the most common behaviors singled out as potentially addictive include:

- Gambling
- Work
- Exercise
- Smart devices and the Internet
- Shopping
- Eating
- Video games
- Sex and/or porn

One of the most common arguments against the notion of process disorders is the fact that none of the behaviors listed above result in a physiological addiction. When someone is withdrawing from substance use, they often experience extreme—even life threatening—physiological symptoms. The chronic alcoholic may experience delirium tremens (DT) when their ability to access and consume liquor is blocked. Tremors, seizures, nausea and vomiting, sensory

DOI: 10.4324/9781003391128-11

disorientation, even hallucinations and psychosis are all possible when someone is withdrawing from a severe alcohol use disorder (Cleveland Clinic, 2024). Likewise, the person coming off of methamphetamine will likely experience severe depression, anxiety, disturbed sleep, paranoia, and (again) hallucinations and psychosis (Rees, 2022). On the other hand, someone who engages in compulsive shopping, for example, is unlikely to go through a similar experience if their credit cards are frozen. One critique of the process addiction model is that it minimizes the very real suffering of substance use disorders (Petry, Zajac, & Ginley, 2018). This is not to say that we do not have a physiological reaction to behaviors such as shopping, gaming, or watching porn! It is a fact of biology that our brains respond to everything we do and releases chemicals to promote pleasure or mitigate pain accordingly. The question is are these organic physiological reactions addictive. And on this point, the data seems to be mixed.

The compulsive behavior model provides a framework for understanding maladaptive processes without trying to fit our clients into the medical model of substance addiction. Silva Neves, in his book on *Compulsive Sexual Behaviors*, writes that

> it is easy to mistake . . . compulsivity for an addiction, because we often hear clients struggling with impaired control and, sometimes, but not always, social impairment . . . A compulsive behavior aims to reduce unpleasant emotions. . . . The stress and anxiety that these people feel is relieved temporarily at the moment of the compulsive behavior.
>
> (Neves, 2021)

Distress avoidance has been shown to be a significant driver of excessive technology use particularly in the form of video games (Bartel, 2020) and other virtual worlds (Johanssen, 2022). In fact, you may have noticed that pretty much every behavior listed earlier (such as shopping and gambling) is one that often occurs online as well as off. One of the nuances that make a discussion around compulsive technology use so difficult is the fact that in many cases the purported cure for the experience of distress is also the cause:

> We are beginning to observe a blurring between the stress caused by the use of applications such as SNS (social networking sites) and addictive or compulsive use of these very applications. Studies indicate that even as individuals find it exhausting to keep up and respond to posts in SNS, they find it increasingly difficult to turn away from them.
>
> (Tarafdar, Maier, Laumer, & Weitzel, 2020)

Once again, we are back to a behavioral pattern that looks a lot like addiction, right? Whether we are proponents of a process addiction model or a behavioral compulsion model, we cannot deny the simple fact that technology has become the point of access for pretty much every aspect of our lives. On average, we pick up our phones 144 times per day and spend 4 hours and 25 minutes of each day looking at them (Dreibelbis, 2023). Does that number feel excessive when you read it? Because it actually represents a decrease from 2022 (Dreibelbis, 2023). How can we (as users and as clinicians) evaluate when tech is being used "excessively" or compulsively when we log into our work remotely from our laptops, do our banking on our tablets, watch erotica through our Oculus headsets, and stay connected to our friends, family, and everyone else through our phones? Do we have a codependent relationship with the people on the other side of our online devices, or is this simply the new norm in human communication?

If a transgender, Jewish, girl living in rural Idaho has found a supportive community of queer friends who cheer her on when she feels alone at school each day, a synagogue in New York or Detroit that livestreams its religious services for her to participate in, and a therapist who offers gender affirming care via telehealth so that she doesn't have to drive four hours to the nearest clinic without her parents finding out, she may be spending half of her waking hours or more online each day. And yet, which distress is worse? Being isolated and disconnected from any form of community or the anxiety that can arise when we feel the pull of being chronically online? These questions don't have simple answers and the solution is rarely "just unplug" . . . even when there are distinct mental health benefits to doing so. Luckily for us, Drs. Markie Twist and Neil MacArthur, a psychotherapist and a philosopher respectively, have developed a framework to help us understand what healthy technology use looks like—one that can be applied no matter where you fall on the process additions debate.

Digital Health Framework

"What are we working on? What can go wrong?" To help us answer these threat modeling questions that we've now learned to keep tucked safely away in the back of our minds (Shostack, 2014), we can turn to Markie Twist and Neil MacArthur's work. The digital health framework is a conceptual model that assesses the healthiness of individuals' and relationships' engagement with digital technology (Twist & McArthur, 2020). It is grounded in five core principles: *consent, protection, honesty, privacy, and pleasure.* These principles guide the evaluation of digital interactions to ensure they promote physical, psychological, and social well-being. We can apply the framework by considering how these principles are upheld in digital experiences, such as online relationships, social media interactions, and the use of sexual materials.

Using Twist and MacArthur's five Digital Health Framework principles, the authors have created a set of questions that you can use together with your clients to help assess behavior patterns with specific technologies, digital tools, or online toys:

Consent

- **Between People**: Are we enthusiastic participants? Is everyone involved freely agreeing to participate? Is there any pressure or coercion that might compromise consent?
- **Mediated by technology**: Does the consent aspects of the technology we're using reflect and reinforce our personal consent agreement between participants? How do we revoke consent on the platform?

Protection

- **Between People**: How do we defend ourselves from harm, psychologically and physically? Can the people we're engaging with exploit us?
- **Mediated by technology**: What safety and security features are available to protect our data? Is there a risk of exploitation by the technology provider? Does the platform support our boundaries?

Honesty

- **Between People**: Is the information shared with us accurate and true? Do we have a shared understanding about expectations with everyone who's participating in the experience?
- **Mediated by technology**: Does the platform have a way to detect phony profiles? Can it help us identify fake images and videos?

Privacy

- **Between people**: Do we trust the people we're sharing with to respect our privacy, and not share content or information with others without our approval? How will we handle sensitive information shared with us?
- **Privacy mediated by technology**: What privacy rights do we have on the platform? Can protect personal information for our safety and protection? Is there any breach or potential threat to the privacy of individuals engaging in digital experiences?

Pleasure

- **Between People**: Are we able to pursue pleasurable experiences without shame or judgment? Are our pursuits of pleasure balanced and not interfering with other aspects of life?
- **Mediated by technology**: Does the technology provide us the pleasure we intended and as advertised? Is the platform encouraging process addictions or interfering with other aspects of our life?

One application of the digital health framework is to counter the concerns over technology use; for example, the moral panic around online pornography (Littlewood, 2003). In the context of online porn, consent refers to ensuring that all individuals depicted in the content have willingly and enthusiastically agreed to participate in the production of the material. Viewers should also consider if they are consuming content from sources that prioritize the consent of performers. This means avoiding non-consensual sexual material (revenge porn) which violates the consent of the individuals involved. Protection in this context includes being aware of the conditions under which the content was produced to ensure the physical and psychological well-being of the performers. For viewers, it involves protecting themselves from online threats by accessing content from reputable sources. Honesty applies to the transparency of the content and its production, and to the individual being honest with partners about their viewing habits. Respecting privacy in relation to online porn involves ensuring that personal information and viewing habits are secure. This includes using private browsing modes and using reputable Websites that have privacy and consent features. Finally, the principle of pleasure in the context of online pornography focuses on an experience that is enjoyable and free from shame or guilt. It means engaging with content that is personally fulfilling and does not contribute to negative feelings about oneself or one's sexuality.

We also should apply the digital health framework to online shopping, gambling, video games, social media, and any other non-sexual behaviors that are enabled by and mediated by digital technologies. Whatever we are doing or working on, things can and will go wrong. Mindfully seeking consent, protection, and privacy in our technology use can ensure we have healthy habits and healthy relationships. By choosing technologies that have consent, protection, and privacy features which support our choices, we can encourage developers to build better products with healthier experiences. Our digital choices today can shape an online world where pleasure and health are the leading features.

The Dark Side of the Web

It has been said that a brick can be used to build a house or to bash someone's head in. The same is true of the Web on the Internet. It can provide pleasurable experiences with meaningful relationships or be used inflict pain and result in lonely isolation. Unfortunately, the choice isn't always ours.

The way we access the Internet plays a part. Smartphones, smartwatches, tablets ("smart-devices") offer numerous benefits, while bringing the possibility of detrimental effects on mental health. One study by Harwood et al. examined the influence of smart-device use and found that it's not the use of devices that correlates with poorer mental health, but rather the nature of the individual's relationship with these devices (Harwood, 2014). This unhealthy relationship is characterized by cognitive and behavioral aspects, such as constantly thinking about the device, feeling anxious if unable to check it, and the compulsive need to stay connected. This goes beyond the duration or frequency of use, suggesting the problem is psychological attachment and over-reliance on the device. The study suggests people who are more involved with their devices are more likely to experience higher levels of depression and stress.

The digital health framework gives us direction on what devices to use and which experiences to pursue. That said, the question of "what can go wrong" is broader than our personal agency. We are all influenced by the communities we frequent. So called "extreme communities" (Bell, 2007) have emerged as online groups that promote or support behaviors typically classified as mental disorders, such as pro-anorexia and bulimia, pro-self-harm and suicide, and pro-amputation communities. These co-opt the language of empowerment and psychotherapy to reframe disorders as lifestyle choices. They provide a platform for sharing tips, finding support, and reinforcing harmful behaviors. For instance, pro-anorexia websites may share dieting tips and celebrate thinness, while pro-suicide communities could facilitate suicide pacts or share information on self-harm. Mental health professionals should be particularly concerned about these communities because they can provide a sense of belonging and validation to individuals who are struggling. These "extreme communities" can potentially worsen clients' conditions and pose significant risks to their well-being.

As we've discussed elsewhere in the book, even healthy relationships (both with our devices and within our communities) can still expose people to risks online. Online harassment and bullying happen on YouTube (Kumar, 2018), Facebook (Whittaker & Kowalski, 2015), Twitter (Chatzakou, 2019), TikTok (Fatimatuzzahro, 2022), and more. (It would seem that every new social media and community platform eventually sees the rise of harassment, and one wonders why the prevention of bullying isn't a feature that's mandated from the beginning of development.) We are well aware of privacy invasions, online tracking, and exploitation of our behaviors and habits to drive engagement and sell advertising. Even in the early development stages, even with SexTech companies who are well-aware of the privacy their users need, companies may still be collecting "millions in compensation for non-consensually collecting or sharing intimate data" (Stardust, 2023). These are the well-known risks simply of being a social and sexual human being online today.

Where we truly hit the dark side of the Web is with technology-facilitated sexual violence against women (Henry & Powell, 2014) and children (Kloess & van der Bruggen, 2021). Certain online environments encourage the circulation of non-consensual sexual images, the trading of sexual exploitation material, and the coordination of sexual violence without easy traceability. As with the "extreme communities," these can promote and normalize maladaptive attitudes, in this case attitudes that support rape culture. When technology-facilitated sexual violence is moved from the normal Web to the Dark Web, the anonymity of the Dark Web allows people to engage in illicit activities with a higher degree of secrecy and impunity. The Dark Web, part of the Internet not indexed by traditional search engines and not accessible by traditional Web browsers, is often beyond law enforcement and regulation's reach. The most extreme manifestation of this lawlessness is the rumored existence of pay-per-view live-streaming sites ("red rooms") where viewers watch and participate in activities such as torture, violence, or other forms of abuse (Godawatte, 2019).

Most of us, most of our clients, most of our community will never visit the Dark Web.

Our relationships with our bodies, our devices, our websites, and our communities raise or lower our risk levels. It unfortunately isn't as easy as reducing how often we pick up our device, or how long we stay on a social media site. It isn't as simple as reducing our use of online dating apps to reduce the likelihood of risky sexual behaviors (Tsai, 2018). It's not the technologies we use, but how we perceive and interact with them. It is those underlying cognitive processes and our personal relationships with our tools that may serve as risk indicators. While this is bad news for commentators and pundits in search of an easy answer, it is good news for cognitive behavior therapy. Clinical interventions can help individuals develop healthier relationships with technology and mitigate associated risks.

Legal and Ethical Considerations

Mental and medical health providers are among the many professions who are mandated by law to report concerns of abuse or neglect. The specifics of these laws vary from region to region, with each state, province, and country having their own unique set of expectations. This can make understanding our obligations especially difficult for telehealth providers, who may be licensed in multiple venues and subject to different jurisdictions. And that's before we add in the uniquely complicated landscape of a virtual society. It would be impossible for the authors to give to provide a comprehensive set of "if-then" heuristics that would be consistently true for all readers across professions and around the world. However, thinking about the tech ethics and our obligations as practitioners is a crucial task that our various professional codes of ethics do require from us (NASW, ASWB, CSWE, & CSWA, 2024; Light, Panicker, Abrams, & Huh-Yoo, 2024; ACA, 2014; AAMFT, 2015) and so we offer the following general guidelines for navigating legal and ethical concerns when they do arise:

Financial Exploitation: The ethics of confidentiality when it comes to a client's criminal behavior are nuanced, location- and crime-specific, and far beyond what we can cover here in a simple paragraph. That said, there are some general guidelines that we can use when the topic of financial exploitation comes up in a session. Let's begin with the easy part: if you have a client who is a vulnerable adult, and they disclose information that leads you to believe they are being financially exploited or neglected? You have an ethical obligation to report this as elder abuse. That obligation holds true even when the financial abuse is occurring online. "Many risk factors contribute to an individual's vulnerability to financial exploitation. Identified risk factors include decreased social support, dependence on other people to carry out activities of daily living, cognitive impairment, poor performance of financial skills, and impaired financial decision-making" (Zhang, Morris, McNiel, & Binder, 2023). Clinicians who work with older adults should be including conversations about their digital presence and use of technology, as well as those who manage their online lives for them, in routine therapeutic conversations. If a client mentions purchasing gift cards to pay bills, messages from relatives at risk and in need of financial help, or unexpected tax bills or upcoming court hearings? These should be explored in session as potential exploitation red flags.

This topic becomes a bit more fraught when we have concerns that our client is the one engaging in acts of financial exploitation. If they are taking advantage of a vulnerable person within their own sphere—an elder, a disabled friend or sibling, etc. this falls squarely under the umbrella of mandatory reporting. If, on the other hand, a client discloses that they earn money by catfishing users on dating websites, scamming job hunters on LinkedIn, or engaging in other less-than-legal online activities? This often falls under our professional confidentiality obligations. Most psychotherapists are expected to report crimes that concern the immediate safety of others, however this is often limited to physical rather than financial safety. If your client discloses behavior that you find personally problematic or ethically troublesome, the authors encourage you to seek out supervision, consult with your presiding ethics board, and perhaps consult with legal counsel. However, unless the behavior they've described falls under the auspices of elder/vulnerable person abuse? You should defer reporting to legal authorities until you've confirmed that you would not be violating confidentiality in doing so.

Cyberbullying and Digital Abuse: We have discussed the myriad ways in which technology can be used both to enhance our lives as well as to perpetuate harm throughout this book. The question here is when does that harm rise to the level of reportable offense for the clinician? In keeping with the theme of this section, the answer is "your answer will vary based on license type and practice location." In the United States, only six states mandate reporting domestic/intimate partner violence, with five of these applying only when the victim is physically injured (MandatedReporter.com, 2024). While some forms of digital abuse such as humiliating/degrading their partners online, cyberstalking, and digital financial abuse may be outlawed by specific state/ province or federal statutes (Harris & Woodlock, 2023), the general pattern of digital abuse would not likely be covered under existing domestic violence laws. Likewise, most state and federal laws have not caught up to the risk of harm caused by cyberbullying. While many state laws now require schools to have policies that address online and off-campus bullying (StopBullying. gov, 2024), if you are not working within an academic setting, your options to intervene may be extremely limited:

> State and Federal laws delineate child abuse as abuses inflicted by adults onto children. Yes, there are some instances in which an older sibling/relative under the age of 18 could be charged with child abuse. This is more on a case-by-case basis, however, as certain acts, such as sexual abuse, are more likely to be labeled as child abuse. Also, the age gap between a potential abuser under the age of 18 and their victim seems to be a determining factor as well. Regardless of the grey area, child abuse laws and child protection advocates and agencies are primarily geared to prevent, stop, and punish adult abusers of children. These laws say nothing of peer-to-peer bullying however.
>
> (Johnson, 2022)

Where we lack the power to intervene directly, either through a mandatory report to authorities or by directly addressing the abusive behavior, we can still support our clients by helping them to safely plan around their technology engagement to minimize their exposure to risk and harm. For adults being abused by adults, this may take the form of engaging with privacy advocates and digital domestic violence allies such as Operation Safe Escape. For young people being harassed by peers, this can take the form of psychoeducation around media literacy, working with school administration and trusted adults to build a social media safety plan, and (where possible) encouraging victims to work directly with the online platform's trust and safety teams to reduce harm and prevent future abuse.

Operation Safe Escape connects volunteer cybersecurity experts with victims of DV/IPV in need of help

Digital Self-Harm: It sounds like the plot of a horror movie—an international group of self-described Satanists that prey on young people through innocuous sites such as Minecraft and Roblox, grooming them to create videos and images of sexual exploitation and self-abuse. And yet, in September 2023 the FBI warned about a group called "764" and the Order of the Nine Angles (O9A) that was doing just that (Argentino, Barrett, & Typer, 2024). This announcement was confirmed by an international consortium of reporters from North America and Europe who identified "multiple subgroups and thousands of users in nearly a dozen countries on three continents . . . who victimize children through coordinated online campaigns of extortion, doxing, swatting, and harassment" (Winston, 2024). Unlike the Satanic Panic of the 1980s, this threat is quite real . . . and yet, we don't want you to think of the internet as some dystopian hellscape filled with monsters! The virtual world is a digital doppelganger of our own—the good and the bad. The key, as with everything, is to be aware of the risk without allowing that awareness to overwhelm us. What this means in the context of digital self-harm is 1) understanding what it is and 2) taking it seriously when we encounter it. Any client who reports asking or being asked to engage in activities such as creating self-denigrating content, destroying valued/sentimental objects or hurting pets, engaging in acts of self-harm or "endurance" on livestreams, or soliciting others to do so in order to re-direct the pressure to perform away from themselves (Boburg, Verma, & Dehgihanpoor, 2024) should be taken extremely seriously. While you want to seek the guidance of your legal counsel or ethics board, it is the opinion of the authors that these behaviors fall under the umbrella of "reasonable risk of harm to a vulnerable person" and should be reported accordingly. If you are uncertain of who to report digital self-harm to, the National Center for Missing and Exploited Children CyberTipline can take your initial report and route it to the proper agencies. One of the challenges in addressing digital self-harm is that because it is an emerging issue that does not present with an identifiable perpetrator and a clear-cut act of non-consensual harm. This can mean that some jurisdictions do not take digital self-harm as seriously as they might other forms of abuse and exploitation. It is important to affirm that the harm these clients are experiencing is real, and act accordingly—even when systems fail them.

> These approaches included providing information and collaboratively identifying other (non-mandated) supports for the young person . . . safety planning for them and ensuring that they've got resources that would ensure that they're safe, like . . . a friend or family member that they can go to if they're feeling unsafe.
>
> (Molyneaux, Mirembe, Leicester, Schley, & Alisic, 2024)
> in their online interactions

CSAM and other cyber exploitation materials: Artificial intelligence has made it incredibly easy to produce hyper-realistic, yet entirely fake images depicting abuse, which overwhelm the capacity of investigators to parse out real victims from computer-generated fictions (Gupta, 2024). Thankfully, it is NOT your job to determine if content is real or artificial. If you receive content from a client or concerned family member that you believe might contain abusive or exploitative images **do not open the file or share it with anyone else**—even if you're seeking consultation on whether or not to make a report. In most jurisdictions—including all 50 states—this would be considered possession and/or distribution of illegal material. Forward the file, unopened, to your local reporting resource. In addition to images, in the U.S., the National Center for Missing and Exploited Children accepts reports on the following:

Scan here to find a list of global hotlines for reporting suspected cyber exploitation

- Someone chatting online with a child about sex
- Sexual abuse of a child that occurs offline
- Someone seeking or offering a child for sexual acts in exchange for something of value (e.g. money, food, gas, shelter, clothing, drugs)
- Unwanted sexual emails or texts either involving a child or sent to a child
- Websites or domains that contain sexual content but have similar names or URLs to mainstream sites that may be misleading to children
- Websites or domains that have sexual content (words or images) embedded in them which minors might see. (NCMEC, 2024)

It can be tempting to minimize harmful online interactions as tasteless attempts at humor or to consider them less dangerous because the potential perpetrator is not in the room with the child. Best practice for all mental and medical health providers would be to report any and all suspected instances of exploitation, *without examining the material yourself*, and without seeking peer consultation. Depending upon the circumstance, it may be wise to consult with legal counsel as well; but this should occur in conjunction with a report, not instead of . . . and again, without sending the potentially problematic material on to your attorney.

Radicalization and Violence: The wonderful thing about the internet is that anyone and everyone can find a place online where they feel seen, valued, and understood. The downside is that this statement is equally true for empowering, positive communities as it is for the darkest, most heartbreakingly hateful groups as well. As much as we want to intervene when we see our clients engage with a harmful groups (from criminal gangs to high-demand lifestyles and all points in between), we don't actually get to exercise that level of control. Having a social circle full of bad influences does not rise to the level of a mandatory report, no matter how bad the influence and how desperately we might wish it did. This desperation can feel particularly acute when a client is introduced to a radicalized group online. The RAND Corporation found that

> First, the internet creates more opportunities to become radicalized. Second, the internet acts as an "echo chamber," i.e., a place where individuals find their ideas supported and echoed by other like-minded individuals. Third, the internet accelerates the process of radicalization. Fourth, the internet allows radicalization to occur without physical contact with like-minded terrorists. Fifth, the internet increases opportunities for self-radicalization.
> (von Behr, Reding, Edwards, & Gribbon, 2013)

This issue has become even more pressing in the 10 years since this study was published—a period of global polarization (Gu & Wang, 2022; Fischer & Hawkins, 2023), increased civil unrest (Pangilinan, 2023; CEIP, 2024), and expanded media/communication echo chambers (Malatino, 2024; Maheu, 2024). Obviously, we cannot legally intervene simply because we disapprove of our client's friends, but that does not mean that we don't have ethical opportunities to engage and try to disrupt this harmful (and potentially dangerous) cycle of radicalization.

Research has found that "radicalization is an inherently social process, even among so-called lone actors. In-person and online social networks and subcultures can play a significant role in . . . radicalization processes" (NIJ, 2023). This means that one of the best strategies for preventing and protecting our clients from radicalization is to encourage them to foster strong, IRL communities that offer "socialization, mentorship, and skill-building . . . bring together individuals from diverse religious and cultural backgrounds . . . (and) strengthen family and community support" (Sarnoto, Hayatina, & Rahmawati, 2024). A healthy balance between on-and offline relationships is one of the best protective factors against all forms of behavioral extremism. These diverse offline peer relationships can be crucial in disrupting the radicalization process by "promot(ing) disillusionment and discord within the radical ideology, and lead(ing) to disengagement" (NIJ, 2023). On the other hand, "non-extremist familial ties, while important, may not be enough to help reintegrate an individual and prevent their radicalization" (NIJ, 2023). From a proactive therapeutic position, encouraging our clients to cultivate an offline peer group with diverse interests is one of the best strategies for intervening in radicalization. As much as we would like to be the trusted voice of reason for clients we see heading down a dangerous path, the research shows that "credibility is key (and) it is not enough to simply will individuals to act in a given way" (Winter, et al., 2020). We run the risk of becoming the psychotherapy equivalent of "how do you do, fellow kids" meme when we assume the role of authority figure. Rather leverage your clinical curiosity and motivational interviewing skills, "asking thought-provoking questions in a curious-but-concerned manner and giving plenty of time to process, think, and answer" (Hassan, 1990) that shows respect for their agency, intellect, and relationships while opening up space for alternative perspectives—a core practice for exploring any of our clients' online activities.

TECH ED WITH WOLF
THE DARK WEB

TechEd Class: What Is the Dark Web?

In the beginning of this book we talked about the World Wide Web. For some, this is called the surface Web or the clear web. It is the Internet that we can see and access with regular Web browsers and search engines. But for others, there is another web. A darker place. The so-called Dark Web is the subject of our conversation in this chapter.

Web 1.0 was about increasing individual access to information and provided a degree of anonymity. The Internet had not yet monetized fully around advertising. The surveillance capitalism, in all its Big Data glory, was decades off. By the early 2000s, many people began to raise concerns about the direction of the Web. These concerns, along with new technology, will give rise to what we now call the Dark Web. The starting point, as is often the case, was full of optimism. There was the need for a non-commercialized Internet that would still provide anonymity and encourage free expression.

The Dark Web today is a small percentage of the surface Web. It has nearly a hundred thousand sites and is somewhere between 0.01% and 0.1% of the overall Web. Exact numbers are hard to come by because part of the benefit of the Dark Web is it cannot be crawled or automatically discovered. Most of the press the Dark Web gets is for its criminal uses. You may wonder, are there legitimate uses for the Dark Web? Yes. Absolutely. Mostly, the largest legitimate activity is people monitoring criminal activities.

So what makes the Dark Web different than the regular web? First, it is fully anonymous. Access to this Internet goes through Tor (more on that shortly). People generally use specialized browsers as well. There is no search, at least insofar as we are used to with today's search engines. It isn't monetized, although certainly there are monetary transactions going on all the time. These sales are usually processed with cryptocurrency, Bitcoin being a favorite. You can browse some of your favorite news websites, or head to the CIA Website if you're feeling particularly ironic. But nearly all of the surface Web doesn't maintain a website on the Dark Web.

Tor is a key component so let's talk more about that. To understand Tor, we need to understand Onion routing. (Tor stands for The Onion Router.) The metaphor is that network traffic will go through multiple layers, like an onion. Each router only knows of the next router in the next layer. No one component of the system can know where any piece of traffic is routed. Typically, when you are on the Dark Web, you are going through three Onion routers. In reality you could go through as many as you want, although each one adds some time and therefore slows things down. The really cool thing about this is that you can't trace any traffic through all the layers and therefore you can get real privacy.

Navigating the Dark Web can feel like we're back in the 1990s. For this reason, I think the Web 1.0 comparison is apt. Do you remember directories with nothing but website after website under categories? Yep. The Dark Web made that trendy again (see https://TheHiddenWiki. org). Do you remember searches before Google's PageRank algorithm, where you were basically matching on keywords without any context? Well get ready for nostalgia, because that's how the Dark Web's most popular search engine works (see https://ahmia.fi). Because there are no Internet crawlers for the Dark Web, because of the mistrust in advanced algorithms, you pretty much have to know exactly the page you want to get to.

The websites themselves are provided on the Onion network with names that end in .onion. So if you're familiar with.com or.org or.gov, the standard top-level domain names, simply swap .onion and you're nearly there. Except it gets harder. That's because most of the Dark Web domain names are what appear to be a random set of characters. (The names are actually mathematically derived from cryptographic keys but most of us don't need to worry about that.) Because you don't have to register these names, there's no centralized service tracking who owns what website as there is in the surface Web (DNS). Because it's nearly impossible to remember these names, it's an added layer of protection. For many Dark Websites, people have to be in the know. There's no way to find them accidentally. If you know, you know.

Many of the Dark Websites are marketplaces. These markets sell a number of legal and illegal services and products. You can buy stolen data. You can buy illegal materials. You can hire hitmen and hackers. And again, we're generally paying with cryptocurrency. It's designed to keep both parties anonymous.

These are the places that spawn the types of attacks we've covered in this book. Let's take romance scams. DarkOwl, a company providing Dark Web monitoring services, infiltrated a forum dedicated to this scam in 2023–2024. The forum shared tips, provided scripts, and coached would-be scammers on using emotional manipulation to gain trust and request money. This began with instructions on the best way to target people through dating apps. Some scammers who had victims on the hook were trading or selling explicit images from their targets, a process called "e-whoring" on the forum.

One more depressing note: We've long known that victims are likely to fall for a romance scam again. It isn't only researchers who know this. The criminals also know this. Once they've been caught and the scam has ended, criminals have been witnessed selling contact information of their victims to other scammers.

Earlier we said that the Dark Web size is less than a percent of the overall Web. We don't really have a number of websites. They're not all published on Wikis or search engines. We don't actually have data on how much money flows over the Dark Web. There's no records. We do know that cybercrime accounts for trillions of dollars annually. Some have suggested that if it was a country, cybercrime would be the third largest economy coming in only after the United States and China. It's safe to say that billions of dollars are exchanged on the Dark Web annually.

Unlike other areas we discussed in these Tech Ed sections, the Dark Web is not necessarily a place that will come up in intimacy. So the safety tips are few. If you are going to go on the Dark Web, and we are not suggesting you do so, be sure to use a separate computer and take steps to not be traced. (See Tails, Tor browser, and a VPN.) People have been scammed while visiting. You can think of it as similar to any other rough part of town. From a safety perspective you want to use Dark Web monitoring services to alert you in case your data is posted and shared. Credit monitoring and identity theft protection is also a good idea if you are concerned that your data has been stolen. Thankfully most banks and security services offer this by default these days.

The Dark Web is a digital frontier, a testament to the Internet's capacity for both liberation and lawlessness. For most of us? It is a place best left unexplored.

Expert Consult: Anonymous (No, Not That Anonymous)

Anonymous is a cybersecurity expert who volunteers their time and expertise in a variety of ways to help victims of online crime and exploitation. Due to the nature of their work, they have asked to share their insights without providing identifying information. The authors have verified their identity and their work.

Can you explain what you do and share how you got started in this field?

. . . This is what a hacker looks like, right?

I was always "the computer kid" without anyone to relate to. My earliest memory is learning to make a program output "Hello World." Since then, I was hooked. I initially began my descent into security via illicit hacking groups. I was never interested in profit or destroying companies. Instead, it fascinated me that one could leverage how things were designed to hack into an organization and see data they shouldn't. Eventually, a mentor took me under and taught me the value of authorized testing and how what I started to love could be a career. To this day, I am thankful for him.

At present, I am a threat intelligence researcher at a Fortune 500. By day I build collection and analysis systems for threat intelligence and leveraging artificial intelligence to assist in the review process. In short, I build systems designed to ensure security teams have the actionable data necessary to investigate threats or enhance detection efforts. When not building systems for work, I run several identities online that contribute threat intelligence to the broader security community.

What makes you passionate about this work?

Helping people. I worked on a case involving child exploitation. I'll spare the details. After finding several pieces of evidence that allowed us to uncover where the server running content was, several individuals were eventually arrested. I know the FBI doesn't always have the best reputation, depending on who you ask. However, there are some passionate people there who just want to make the world better.

Tell us a bit about the process of monitoring the Dark Web and gathering threat intelligence. Starting with, what is threat intelligence?

Put simply, threat intelligence is analyzed content generally produced from collected data for stakeholders/customers to make actionable/informed decisions. This collected data can be IP addresses of threat actors, the tools we can see them using, techniques, and procedures, or even chatter [conversation] collected from various websites and other data sources. A pain point of mine is that many threat intelligence shops or products from companies sell such data as threat intelligence when, in reality, it is threat data. In terms of monitoring the dark web, there is no one perfect way to monitor it. Many of us have our own approaches AND similar methodologies. For example, I maintain several lists of websites that have been breached, ransomware sites, and hacktivist sites [such as Wikileaks, Anonymous, Pirate Bay] just to name a few. The key to monitoring, in my opinion, is automation. I have since built my own Tor crawler to index .onion sites rather than relying purely on other indexers. We also hash ["fingerprint"] the content of sites to determine when content changes so we can mark the start of a potential investigation. Monitoring for mistakes is another big thing to keep an eye out for.

What should ordinary people do when they get notified their information is on the Dark Web?

Step number one: Don't freak out. It can be super scary and even confusing when that notification comes to your email or phone. Most advisories will typically indicate the type of data that's been stolen or posted on the dark web. If it's account (usernames/passwords) or banking-related, immediately change your passwords. Keep in mind that any information is power for adversaries.

Secondly, this is a good opportunity to invest in a service such as Aura; which routinely monitors your data and provides a level of insurance for customers. This is similar to the Lifelock model. I'll let readers decide on which service is better or worse, but I'll always advocate to have something. Better to be prepared than to potentially lose everything.

Thirdly, improve your own security culture. Are you using a password manager? You should be. Are you using Multi-Factor Authentication (MFA) in as many places as possible? You should be, even if it's a pain. Avoid SMS (text message)-based MFA as best you can. Readers can look up SIM-swapping or SMS MFA spamming and form their own conclusions about why one should avoid SMS authentication. Are you using public Wi-Fi? Never touch it without using a VPN. Use Ad blockers and think twice before submitting anything anywhere.

Finally, understand that it's not a matter of if, but when your data is compromised in some way. The strategies earlier can help, however, our data is shared at so data brokers and third parties, that it's almost impossible to fully protect yourself. Preparedness is just as important as response.

What do therapists, educators, and others working in the field of mental health need to be thinking about when they're talking with their clients about these topics?

Understand that the data analysts may encounter can be incredibly graphic. As for the personal side, this is hard to talk about, but I want therapists and educators to understand. From the perspective of someone who's helped with cases involving child exploitation and counter-terrorism, I've seen some of the worst things that humans are capable of. I unfortunately have a photographic memory; I remember every victim, every face of innocent people in horrific conditions. It's something that I will never forget and must live with. Some days, I'm overwhelmed with the continual doom and gloom of social media and the news. There's also sometimes the overwhelming feeling that all efforts are insignificant because there's just another group or server somewhere, or the data never ends. But when I get a notification that something has been taken down, people were rescued, a group was arrested, or—in some cases—lives were saved, I remember why I do this: to help people.

Chapter 11

Don't Panic

Pandora's Box or Plato's Cave?

If we've done our job right over the last 250 plus pages, the authors have given you a lot to think about that might not have been on your radar prior to picking up this book. You might be feeling a little overwhelmed. You may have begun to wonder if this whole "internet" thing was ever a good idea to begin with. Trust us when we tell you, we ask ourselves the same questions. And yet? We both LOVE the internet. We have social media profiles and photo sharing apps. We use online payment systems and WAY too many chat apps. As scary as it can be at times, we are not encouraging our readers to disconnect from web or throw away their devices. One of the biggest fallacies in many of the conversations that happen around technology today is the idea that the internet is a modern-day Pandora's Box: beautiful, intriguing, and full of monsters. We would argue that the same Ancient Greeks who told the story of Pandora offer us a better way of conceptualizing our new digital reality.

In Plato's Allegory of the Cave, Socrates (the primary narrator/speaker) describes a group of people who have spent their entire lives chained inside a cave. All they know of the world is what they see in the shadows cast on the walls by the fire that is their only source of light. This shadow world is their reality, and they give names to the shapes and movements they see cast upon the rocky walls. It is not until the prisoners are released, able to turn around and realize that outside the cave lies an entire world filled not with shadows but with the objects and people that cast those shadows, that they are able to truly understand the world around them (Plato, 2016).

In many ways, this is the role the internet plays for us today. We have created a digital cave, where the light of our screens casts the shadow of reality for us to consume. We have the entirety of human knowledge available at our fingertips, but we are losing our ability to discern fact from fiction, reality from distortion, personhood from persona. We stand at an evolutionary crossroads, where we can benefit from the shelter and warmth the cave offers without chaining ourselves inside it. To put it more bluntly: we can still go outside and touch grass when it would benefit us to do so.

DOI: 10.4324/9781003391128-12

All Progress Looks Scary

Whenever a new technology emerges, particularly one that changes how we communicate, connect, or relate to our bodies, it triggers two reactions. The first is wonder. The second is worry.

We marvel at what's now possible, even as we fear what might be lost. The telephone brought distant voices into our homes but sparked panic about impersonation and eavesdropping. The VCR allowed private viewing of films but ignited outrage over what people might watch behind closed doors. The Internet connected us to more people and more knowledge than ever before but also introduced us to cyberstalking, doxxing, and deepfakes. Every wave of progress arrives with a chorus of: What if this ruins everything?

This response traces back to the earliest example of technological disruption: the Luddites in early 19th-century England. The Luddites are often remembered as anti-technology rebels who smashed machines in protest. But their story is more nuanced and more relevant today than it first appears. During the industrial revolution, textile workers faced sudden, sweeping changes as new machinery transformed their industry. These weren't technophobes raging against progress; they were skilled laborers protesting the use of technology to devalue their expertise, erase their jobs, and strip them of control.

The tension between wonder and worry then is normal. When a technology disrupts something as meaningful as our profession, our work, our income? When a technology changes something as personal as how we love or trust or disclose ourselves? The stakes feel high. They are high. That's why fear follows innovation. It isn't because the technology is inherently dangerous, but because it challenges the structures we've built to feel safe.

Progress destabilizes. It shifts power. It invites new voices, new identities, and new ways of seeing ourselves and others. And any shift in power will be met with resistance. Technological change, like cultural change, disrupts hierarchies. It demands we revisit the rules.

So, of course, it feels scary.

Fear tells us that something new is asking for our attention. Technology is the leading edge of new, and it always needs attention. The worry over technological change is not always hysteria. The industry the Luddites sought to protect, handcrafted textile manufacturing, was crushed and replaced by the factory system. The privacy concerns Alan F. Westin warned about and fought against in the 1960s? Those problems he foresaw have only accelerated as we've shifted into surveillance capitalism. When technology undermines consent, privacy, or autonomy, the danger is real and action is necessary.

All progress is scary and every advancement is a mixture of positive and negative outcomes. We need to recalibrate our tools, our values, our customs, our laws. We don't need to interpret being scared as "the new thing must be bad," or as a sign that we are doomed. That's how fear can trick us, especially when it's amplified by moral panics or media sensationalism.

When radio shows first aired, critics warned that children would become addicted and antisocial. When email took off, people feared that employees would waste time and become isolated. When texting became ubiquitous, teachers predicted a generation of illiterate teens who could only communicate in emojis. None of these fears fully materialized.

What was the difference between textile manufacturing and office productivity? Put differently, how have we been able to negotiate the information revolution in a way that hasn't had the negative impacts of the industrial revolution? In the first, machines replaced human labor, often brutally. In the second, knowledge workers were generally better educated, organized, and empowered to shape how tools were used. We adapted. We created etiquette, developed norms, and evolved new forms of connection.

Today's fears over dating apps, sex toys, and AI partners are echoes of those same reflexes. And, yes, they deserve attention. But they should not halt the conversation or shut down innovation. The danger is not that people are using technology for intimacy. The danger is pretending they aren't.

If we pretend that intimacy and technology should remain separate, we end up with systems that are unsafe by design. The complex problems covered in this book demand interdisciplinary thinking, and many of the problems we now face are the result of IT developing without input and engagement from outside of the IT industry. We have created platforms that don't protect consent, built companies that don't understand abuse, and written policies that don't reflect lived experience.

That's why we advocate for stepping into these conversations with clarity and courage. Not just as professionals or policymakers, but as people. People who remember that fear is natural. That learning is possible. And that with each new wave of technology, we get the chance to build something better than what came before.

How to Talk to Clients About Technology

Most mental health providers enter the field because the want to help their clients make better, safer, choices about their lives and relationships. And we tend to specialize—the counselor working in substance treatment is unlikely to run a grief and loss support group, and the sex therapist is probably not going to treat schizophrenia. These specializations help us maximize our impact and narrow our scope of expertise, which is important for delivering efficacious care. Unfortunately, most clinicians don't receive formal training in technology use and ethics, risk and safety and yet, we are expected to not only make good decisions for ourselves and our practices, but to help our clients do the same. When we lack specialized knowledge, it can be easy to surrender to the assumption that adversaries with technical skill will always best us. Pandora's Box has been opened, the internet is filled with malicious actors we can neither see nor hide from, and the best path forward for our clients is simply to avoid it as much as we can. And that's true . . . insomuch as it's true that bad actors exist wherever community exists. In any group of people, online or in person, there will be one or two who are not operating from a place of integrity and kindness. Crime exists on the internet. Crime also existed in Cold War America and Victorian England. Criminals found victims in the streets of Revolutionary France and the roadways on Ancient Rome. We aren't releasing new monsters; we're simply updating the battlefield.

The mental health field is at an inflection point, where new territory, issues, and potential problems exist that we have never encountered before. We don't *actually* have the option to simply opt out (see the Afterword for a personal example of this from the authors) so we must arm ourselves and our clients for this new world. We humbly offer the following suggestions for doing so honestly, with bravery and grace:

1. Use the digital health framework with your clients. Make this a part of your ongoing conversations whenever technology—from spicy text messages to adorable memes—come up in session.
2. Ask your clients about the ways in which they bring technology into their relationships. If you work with couples, ask them about the apps they use to communicate or enhance their relationships. Ask your adult clients about their preferred intimacy aids/sex toys and your adolescent clients about video games and chat servers. Talk to them about tools like webcam covers and data blockers. Make their virtual world a part of your everyday conversation.
3. Recognize that virtual relationships are real and valid. Don't minimize their importance in your client's lives. At the same time, be aware of the unique socio-emotional dynamics at play in these digital connections.
4. Include media literacy in your psychoeducation and cognitive work. Teach clients how to recognize mis- and disinformation, to look for tale-tell clues of artificial intelligence, and to research the veracity of facts gleaned from memes, TikTok videos, etc. In the 21st century, media literacy is a form of social and emotional intelligence and you can play a role in building your client's strengths in this area.
5. Hold space for both online and offline engagement. Encourage IRL activities, relationships, and connections without denigrating or discouraging online activities. When brainstorming strategies to meet clinical goals, bring both "worlds" into the conversation. Discuss online forums and in-person support groups, apps and worksheets, books and video games.
6. Model good social media hygiene. Lock down your personal profiles and add disclaimers to your public facing accounts. Assume every client, their parents and their partners, are reading everything you post online. Talk about your digital boundaries with clients and ask them about theirs.
7. Share your cybersecurity choices with your clients. If you use Signal to communicate, explain why. When you're onboarding a new client, discuss your

EHR platforms and their privacy policies. Know whether or not your telehealth service is scraping data from your sessions. If you've chosen to use AI to help you with case notes or treatment planning, be transparent with this and allow your clients to opt out if they choose.

8. Discuss the risks of having an online presence or embracing a convenient new tech with your clients in a way that allows for informed decision-making, without paranoia or naivete. This book has skewed toward the scary at times . . . part of doing good therapy is being clear-eyed and direct about risks when we see them, so that we can develop a personal risk framework and safety plan. Maintain perspective and avoid either catastrophizing or romanticizing technology.

9. Set limits around the use of technology in your practice and your personal life. If you can, avoid using your cell phone as a session timer and ask your clients to put their phones away as well. If you hold sessions in person, your computer screen should be visibly locked during client session. Choose one day a week to go tech-free and share this with your clients so they know you won't be available and consider doing the same for themselves.

TECH ED WITH WOLF

TECHNO-OPTIMISM

Tech Ed: Techno-optimism

This is an optimistic book. Oh, not because the problems aren't serious. They are. The apps are flawed. The systems are broken. Our basic human needs, intimate and otherwise, are at risk. Modern technology is amplifying existing human behaviors: good and bad. But we're still optimistic. Not because things are fine, but because change is possible. Because we can take back control, individually and collectively. We can control our tools, our data, and our future.

Both naive techno-optimism and dystopian fearmongering don't fit the facts.

In 2023, venture capitalist Marc Andreessen wrote and published The Techno-Optimist Manifesto. Frustrated with what he saw as a growing culture of pessimism, regulation, and institutional resistance, Andreessen called for a revival of confidence in human ingenuity, innovation, and the moral imperative of growth. Drawing from Enlightenment values and Silicon Valley ethos, the manifesto framed technology as the ultimate driver of abundance, meaning, and even salvation. "In fact, technology—new knowledge, new tools, what the Greeks called techne—has always been the main source of growth, and perhaps the only cause of growth, as technology made both population growth and natural resource utilization possible."

Yet the techno-optimism espoused by Andreessen ignores the duality of technology. Since the invention of fire, every subsequent invention both warms us while potentially burning us. The duality contains both upsides and downsides, intended features and unintended consequences.

Take the webcam. In the early 2000s, webcams became common in laptops, especially with the rise of video chat (MSN, Skype). In 2009, a school district in Pennsylvania issued Apple MacBook laptops to approximately 2,300 high school students. A later investigation and subsequent lawsuit found the school had captured sixty thousand photos of students, some in their bedrooms, some with the students scantily clothed or nude. Then in 2013, the media covered the case of Miss Teen USA Cassidy Wolf. A fellow high school student had installed software on her computer, took photos, and attempted to extort her. A subsequent investigation identified that the high school student was controlling hundreds of other computers' webcams. What happened next is instrumental:

People began putting tape over their webcams. Consumer groups advocated for webcam lights as a warning indicator. Several webcam covers became available (including those branded Securing Sexuality that we've handed out at sex therapy conferences.) In 2019, HP and Lenovo added built-in shutters. Apple added software switches and indicator lights. At the time of this writing, several premium-class laptops now ship with built-in webcam shutters as a default feature.

Webcams are an example of us taking back control individually, followed by collective pressure, leading to changes in our products. It's here, in the flicker of a webcam light, that hope emerges.

Another source of hope are movements such as digital rights, digital humanism, tech ethics. (For more on those, see the Electronic Frontier Foundation, The Digital Humanism Initiative, and the Center for Humane Technology, respectively). These ideas trace back to a little-known document posted at the end of the last century.

Alarmed by the uncritical optimism of the information revolution and the belief that cyberspace would automatically democratize society, the Techno-Realist Manifesto was circulated in 1998. The authors argued for a more grounded, ethically conscious approach to technology. Many of the risks the techno-realists warned about (like surveillance, bias, and inequality) hadn't yet come to dominate mainstream conversations. Their cautions sounded alarmist at the time.

The first principle of Techo-Realism Manifesto reads,

> A great misconception of our time is the idea that technologies are completely free of bias—that because they are inanimate artifacts, they don't promote certain kinds of behaviours over others. In truth, technologies come loaded with both intended and unintended social, political, and economic leanings. Every tool provides its users with a particular manner of seeing the world and specific ways of interacting with others. It is important for each of us to consider the biases of various technologies and to seek out those that reflect our values and aspirations.

The techno-realists argued that technology is political, that it amplifies social problems, and that we must ask: Who benefits? Who is left vulnerable? Instead of rejecting technology, techno-realism urged critical engagement: embracing progress while remaining vigilant about issues like privacy, inequality, access, and civic responsibility. Where techno-optimism sees salvation, techno-realism sees complexity.

Part of the complexity that's often overlooked is the human drive that lead to innovation. People have always eroticized new technology. (While no textual evidence exists, one can be confident that the fire invented for heating and cooking was quickly utilized for increasing time and space for intimacy.) Every generation reinvents intimacy through the tools it inherits and through the tools it creates. While sexuality is a central theme of this book, it is just one of many human drives that shapes how we use and build technology. Technology is a human artifact, shaped by our desires, our needs, our culture, and our rules.

The Techno-Optimist Manifesto gets it partially right. "We had a problem of cold, so we invented indoor heating. We had a problem of heat, so we invented air conditioning. We had a problem of isolation, so we invented the Internet." "Give us a real world problem, and we can invent technology that will solve it." The question left unasked: how is the problem defined and stated?

The problems technology solves don't exist in isolation. The problems technology solves are the ones that have a financial return, have a cultural impact, satisfy a regulatory requirement, and more. Innovation is often a response to layered incentives, not just technical need.

Take privacy. You might think of the webcam story I shared earlier, and that's cultural movements feeding into problem requirements. Just as cultural norms can spark innovation, so too can legal frameworks reshape how problems are defined and addressed.

We all intrinsically need privacy, yet many apps and Internet-enabled things weren't providing it. It wasn't limited to cameras; it was a pervasive problem in the 2000s. Then the EU's General Data Protection Regulation (GDPR) went into effect in 2018. Companies suddenly had to map where personal data lived, tracked how it moved, let people opt in or opt out, and enable people's right to be forgotten. This led to a wave of innovation. New startups were built tools for data discovery, data mapping, compliance automation, and more. Enterprise software vendors and cloud providers alike expanded their platforms with GDPR modules. Entire product lines for privacy engineering and data governance emerged, now embedded in broader GRC (governance, risk, compliance) and security platforms.

Sure, we need bold innovation and need guardrails. However! Bold guardrails are themselves drivers for new innovation.

Techno-realism provides the grounding that optimism often lacks. The drivers for innovation are more than technical requirements. Speed is not the same as progress. Moving fast and breaking things may have been a good way to motivate technical teams to take risks, but it falls short when what's the brokenness hits at a societal and individual level. A tool's impact must be judged not just by what it can do, but by who it empowers, and who it endangers. Further, investments in curbing the downsides and protecting those at risk will spur on new innovations.

A clear-eyed optimism, grounded in realism, allows us to imagine a better future without denying the flaws we'll face along the way. The duality of technology is inescapable. This means engaging deeply with the tech that scares us: not banning it, not surrendering to it, but shaping it. That's why the future must be built not just by engineers alone, but by a coalition of disciplines: technologists, clinicians, designers, activists, philosophers, lawyers, educators, and more. The problems we face when securing sexuality—algorithmic bias, digital consent, data exploitation, harassment, censorship—are too complex for siloed solutions. They sit at the intersection of code and culture, psychology and infrastructure, law and lived experience.

They cannot and will not be solved without us coming together to apply the hacker ethos to reshape how technological problems are defined and solved. One person put tape on their webcam, and now we have better controls over our cameras. One college student asked a social media company for their data (Max Shrems, Facebook, in 2011). The resulting legal actions and media attention shaped and propelled GDPR. These small acts of curiosity and defiance are reminders that the hacker ethos begins with questioning what's given and ends with changing it for our benefit.

Perhaps it is time to write a new manifesto. One that insists the duality of technology be planned for and worked on. One that recognizes the purpose of technology is to solve the needs of the many, while defending the rights of the few. Perhaps.

Afterword

Economist W. Brian Arthur wrote

> Our deepest hope as humans lies in technology; but our deepest trust lies in nature. These forces are like tectonic plates grinding inexorably into each other in one, long, slow collision. This collision is not new, but more than anything else it is defining our era.
>
> (Arthur, 2009, p. 11)

When we first launched the *Securing Sexuality* podcast, our goal was to give people the information they needed to protect their data, and by extension, their agency as these tectonic plates created new cultural mountains and caverns. We had the same goal when we decided to write it all down in a book. We wanted to create an accessible, relatively jargon-free guidebook to help everyday readers make informed decisions about everything from baby monitors to online banking. Of course, we knew that as the use of technology expands, those choices would naturally evolve apace. What we could not anticipate was how this would impact us, directly, as we worked to create the volume you just finished.

Just a few days before we were initially due to submit this manuscript, a story broke about one of the biggest academic publishers in the world inking a deal with Microsoft to provide access to their catalog in order to train LLM's—artificial intelligence (Palmer, 2024), Morales (2024). This included our own imprint, which was expecting our manuscript just a week after the story broke. It was profoundly ironic that our book warning about the ways in which technology can encroach onto human lives and relationships was going to be fed into the machine. When we inquired about opting out, we were initially told that we could not decline. After months of conversation, and advocacy from the Author's Guild, were we able to re-negotiate the terms of our publication agreement and get the information and resources we were so passionate about into your hands. The day after we got the news that our publisher would work with us to protect our work? We also found out that Meta had used pirated copies of Stefani's earlier books to train their own LLM (Weir, 2025). This highlights the fact that there is no point at which we can be "done" fighting for our privacy, our security, our personal information. It is a series of ongoing encroachments that we will each have to evaluate and weigh and decide when and how hard to push back against. The push and pull over who owns our words, our secrets, our identities is a new frontier without a defined end-point.

In May 2025, Pope Leo XIV gave his inaugural address to the College of Cardinals at the Vatican. He told them that one of his top priorities would be to "address the risks that artificial intelligence poses to 'human dignity, justice, and labor' . . . cit(ing) the 'immense potential' of A.I. while warning that it requires responsibility 'to ensure that it can be used for the good of all'" (Rich & Satariano, 2025). At the risk of sounding a bit pompous? We agree with the Pope. We stand at the precipice of a new era, when the tremendous potential of technology can dramatically shift humanity's quality of life forever. The crucial task of this moment is to recognize that all of us—from technophobe to passionate early adopter—has the right to play an active role in how these changes unfold.

We have the power to organize for reasonable regulation of emerging technologies. To put in safeguards to ensure that the technologies that can identify our cancers faster than any human doctor aren't also aggregating our medical data into a commercial product. To use our devices to find opportunities for genuine, offline connections rather than building virtual isolation chambers. To celebrate and enhance our own generative potential and ingenuity, rather than ceding the creative high-ground to artificial intelligence. Daniel Bell wrote that "technology, like art, is a soaring exercise of the human imagination" (Bell, 1980, p. 20). *YOU* are the driving force at the core every technology. We hope this work has helped you to recognize your power, claim it as your own, and use it to create the society you want to see. We believe in the power of innovation and technology to build a better world. And most importantly? We believe in you.

Works Cited

AAC. (2024, June 24). *Behavioral Addictions: Signs, Symptoms, and Treatment Options*. Retrieved from American Addiction Centers: https://americanaddictioncenters.org/behavioral-addictions

AAMFT. (2015, January 1). *Code of Ethics*. Retrieved from American Association for Marriage and Family Therapy: https://www.aamft.org/AAMFT/Legal_Ethics/Code_of_Ethics.aspx

ACA. (2014). *2014 ACA Code of Ethics*. Retrieved from Counseling.org: https://www.counseling.org/docs/default-source/default-document-library/ethics/2014-aca-code-of-ethics.pdf?sfvrsn=55ab73d0_1

Adhia, A., Gordon, A. R., Roberts, A. L., Fitzmauriece, G. M., Hemenway, D., & Austin, S. B. (2019). Longitudinal Associations between Bullying and Intimate Partner Violence among Adolescents and Young Adults. *Violence and Victims, 34(6)*, 1011–1029, https://doi.org/10.1891/0886-6708.VV-D-18-00135

Adkins, J. C. (2015). Demo: Michigan's IoT Toolkit. *Proceedings of the 13th ACM Conference on Embedded Networked Sensor Systems*.

Adler, R. A., & Cooper, S. C. (2022). "When a Tornado Hits Your Life": Exploring Cyber Sexual Abuse Survivors' Perspectives on Recovery. *Journal of Counseling Sexology & Sexual Wellness: Research, Practice, and Education, 4(1)*, 1–8. https://doi.org/10.34296/04011067

Albenesius, C. (2024, June 25). *Pornhub Block Expands to Indiana, Kentucky: How to Watch Anyway*. Retrieved from PCMag: https://www.pcmag.com/news/pornhub-blocked-texas-age-verification-vpn

Aldrich, J. (2016, June 10). *We're Just Temporarily Abled*. Retrieved from UX Magazine: https://uxmag.com/articles/were-just-temporarily-abled

Amnesty International. (2023, February 7). *"We Are Totally Exposed": Young People Share Concerns about Social Media's Impact on Privacy and Mental Health in Global Survey*. Retrieved from Amnesty.org: https://www.amnesty.org/en/latest/news/2023/02/children-young-people-social-media-survey-2/

Anderson, B., & Wood, M. A. (2021). Doxxing: A Scoping Review and Typology. In *The Emerald International Handbook of Technology Facilitated Violence and Abuse*. Leeds, UK: Emerald Publishing.

Anderson, J., & Raine, L. (2020, February 21). *Concerns about Democracy in the Digital Age*. Retrieved from Pew Research: https://www.pewresearch.org/internet/2020/02/21/concerns-about-democracy-in-the-digital-age/

Anderson, M., Vogels, E. A., & Turner, E. (2020, February 6). *The Virtues and Downsides of Online Dating*. Retrieved from Pew Reseach Center: https://www.pewresearch.org/internet/2020/02/06/the-virtues-and-downsides-of-online-dating/

Argentino, M.-A., Barrett, G., & Typer, M. B. (2024, January 19). *764: The Intersection of Terrorism, Violent Extremism, and Child Sexual Exploitation*. Retrieved from Global Network on Extremism & Technology: https://gnet-research.org/2024/01/19/764-the-i ntersection-of-terrorism-violent-extremism-and-child-sexual-exploitation/

Armitage, R. (2021). Bullying in Children: Impact on Child Health. *BMJ Paediatrics Open, 5(1)*, https://doi.org/10.1136/bmjpo-2020-000939

Arthur, W. B. (2009). *The Nature of Technology: What It Is and How It Evolves*. New York, NY: Free Press.

Arthur, W. B. (2010). The Nature of Technology: What It Is and How It Evolves. *Futures, 4(2)*, 1032–1033, https://doi.org/10.1016/j.futures.2010.08.015

Auxier, B., Rainie, L., Anderson, M., Perrin, A., Kumar, M., & Turner, E. (2019, November 19). *Americans and Privacy: Concerned, Confused and Feeling Lack of Control over Their Personal Information*. Retrieved from Pew Research: https://www. pewresearch.org/internet/2019/11/15/americans-and-privacy-concerned-confused-and-feeling-lack-of-control-over-their-personal-information/

Bai, X., Ramos, M. R., & Fiske, S. T. (2020). As diversity Increases, People Paradoxically Perceive Social Groups as More Similar. *PNAS: The Procedings of the National Academy of Sciences of the United States of America, 117(23)*, https://doi.org/10.1073/pnas.2000333117

Bailey, L. (2023, April 5). *The Confusing Politics of Men's Anti-Porn Movements*. Retrieved from Honi Soit: https://honisoit.com/2023/04/the-confusing-politics-of-mens-anti-porn-movements/

Bandinelli, C., & Gandini, A. (2022). Dating Apps: The Uncertainty of Marketised Love. *Cultural Sociology, 16*, 423–441.

Bannon, L. (2005). A Human-Centred Perspective on Interaction Design. In *Future Interaction Design* (pp. 31–51). Springer Link.

Barcellona, M. (2022). Incel Violence as a New Terrorism Threat: A Brief Investigation between Alt-Right and Manosphere Dimensions. *Sortuz: Oñati Journal of Emergent Socio-Legal Studies, 11(2)*, 170–186.

Barrett-Ibarria, S. (2020, April 13). *Here's How Much It Really Costs to Be an Online Sex Worker*. Retrieved from Huffington Post: https://www.huffpost.com/entry/online-sex-work-cam-only-fans-covid-19_n_5e8de205c5b6359f96d0c2d4

Barta, K., & Andalibi, N. (2024). Theorizing Self Visibility on Social Media: A Visibility Objects Lens. *ACM Transactions on Computer-Human Interaction*, https://dl.acm.org/doi/pdf/10.1145/3660337

Bartel, C. (2020). *Video Games, Violence, and the Ethics of Fantasy*. London, UK: Bloomsbury.

Basalla, G. (1988). *The Evolution of Technology*. London, UK: Cambridge University Press.

Bates, S. (2017). Revenge Porn and Mental Health. *Feminist Criminology, 12*, 22–42.

Battle, M. (2024, February 29). *Why Gen Z Is Ditching Dating Apps*. Retrieved from Time.com: https://time.com/6836033/gen-z-ditching-dating-apps/

Beadle, K., & Vasek, M. (2023). Peer Surveillance in Online Communities. *ArXiv*.

Beck, J. (2014, August 6). *A (Straight, Male) History of Sex Dolls*. Retrieved from The Atlantic: https://www.theatlantic.com/health/archive/2014/08/a-straight-male-history-of-dolls/375623/

Beckman, J. (2024, May 28). *Must Know Internet Traffic of Bots Statistics (2023 Data)*. Retrieved from TechReport: https://techreport.com/statistics/software-web/internet-traffic-of-bots/

BedBible. (2024, May 1). *Sex Tech Industry Market Report & Statistics*. Retrieved from BedBible.com: https://bedbible.com/sextech-industry-statistics/

Bell, D. (1980). *The Winding Passage: Essays and Sociological Journeys, 1960–1980.* Cambridge, MA: Abt Books.

Bell, V. (2007). Online Information, Extreme Communities and Internet Therapy: Is the Internet Good for Our Mental Health? *Journal of Mental Health, 16,* 445–457.

Bender, E. G.-M. (2021). On the Dangers of Stochastic Parrots: Can Language Models Be Too Big? *Proceedings of the 2021 ACM Conference on Fairness, Accountability, and Transparency.*

Berg, H. (2021). *Porn Work: Sex, Labor, and Late Capitalism.* Chapel Hill, NC: University of North Carolina Press.

Bick, A., Blandin, A., & Mertens, K. (2021, February). *Work from Home Before and After the COVID-19 Outbreak.* Retrieved from Federal Reserve Bank of Dallas: https://doi.org/10.24149/wp2017r2

Blake, S. (2024, February 15). *Gen Z Women Delete Dating Apps Within a Month: "It's a Waste of Time".* Retrieved from Newsweek: https://www.newsweek.com/gen-z-women-delete-dating-apps-within-month-meet-person-1870329

Blunt, D., & Wolf, A. (2020). Erased: The Impact of FOSTA-SESTA and the Removal of Backpage on Sex Workers. *Anti-Trafficking Review, 14,* 117–121, https://doi.org/10.14197/atr.201220148

Boburg, S., Verma, P., & Dehgihanpoor, C. (2024, March 13). *On Popular Online Platforms, Predatory Groups Coerce Children into Self-Harm.* Retrieved from The Washington Post: https://www.washingtonpost.com/investigations/interactive/2024/764-predator-discord-telegram/

Bokzam, K. (2022). The Impact of Covid-19 on Domestic Violence and Digital Abuse: Addressing the Problem through a *National Action Plan. University of Miami International and Comparative Law Review, 30(1),* https://repository.law.miami.edu/umiclr/vol30/iss1/7

Boudoir, L. (2024, June 16). *History of Phone Sex.* Retrieved from Filthy: https://vocal.media/filthy/history-of-phone-sex

Brandtzaeg, P. B., & Chapparro-Dominquez, M.-A. (2020). From Youthful Experimentation to Professional Identity: Understanding Identity Transitions in Social Media. *Young, 28(2),* 157–174.

Brandtzaeg, P. S. (2022). My AI Friend: How Users of a Social Chatbot Understand Their Human–AI Friendship. *Human Communication Research, 48(3),* 404–429.

Brennan, M. A. (2019). *Child Protection and Safeguarding Technologies: Appropriate or Excessive "Solutions" to Social Problems?* Routledge.

Brenner, S. L.-W. (2015). Evolutionary Mismatch and Chronic Psychological Stress. *Journal of Evolutionary Medicine, 30,* 32–44.

Brewster, T. (2018, February 1). *"Panty Buster" Toy Left Private Sex Lives of 50,000 Exposed.* Retrieved from Forbes: https://www.forbes.com/sites/thomasbrewster/2018/02/01/vibratissimo-panty-buster-sex-toy-multiple-vulnerabilities/

Brown, D. (2001). *Angels & Demons.* New York, NY: Pocket Books.

Brzosko, M. (2020, August 4). *How to Tell Love from a Projetion.* Retrieved from Medium: https://martabrzosko.medium.com/how-to-tell-love-from-a-projection-11a4a3a04b0b

Buck, S. (2017, February 8). *This Feminist Single Mom Invented the Phone Sex Business in the 1970s.* Retrieved from Medium: https://medium.com/timeline/gloria-leonard-phone-sex-39846a484d51

Burgess, M. (2023, March 30). *You'll Soon Need to Show ID to Watch Porn Online.* Retrieved from Wired: https://www.wired.com/story/porn-age-checks-id-laws/

Burns, Y. (1990). Censorship: Past, Present and Future. *Ecquid Novi, 11,* 148–160.

Çakir, C., & Köseliören, M. (2022). Technoference as Technology Interference in The Communication Process: A Study on Married Couples. *Journal of Erciyes Communication,* https://doi.org/10.17680/erciyesiletisim.1091267

Calo, C. (2023, September 16). *eHarmony Statistics 2024 & Fun Facts You Didn't Know*. Retrieved from Way Too Social: https://www.waytoosocial.com/eharmony-statistics/

Cannito, M., & Camoletto, R. F. (2022). The Rules of Attraction: An Empirical Critique of Pseudoscientific Theories about Sex in the Manosphere. *Sexes, 3(4)*, 593–607, https://doi.org/10.3390/sexes3040043

Carpenter, C., & McEwan, B. (2016). The Players of Micro-Dating: Individual and Gender Differences in Goal Orientations toward Micro-Dating Apps. *First Monday, 21*.

CDC. (2022). *Youth Risk Behavior Survey Data Summary & Trends Report 2011–2021*. Retrieved from cdc.gov: https://www.cdc.gov/healthyyouth/data/yrbs/pdf/YRBS_Data-Summary-Trends_Report2023_508.pdf

CEIP. (2024, July 28). *Global Protest Tracker*. Retrieved from Carnegie Endowment for International Peace: https://carnegieendowment.org/features/global-protest-tracker?lang=en

Celdir, M. C. (2023). Popularity Bias in Online Dating Platforms: Theory and Empirical Evidence. *Manufacturing & Service Operations Management, 46(2)*, 537–553.

Chatzakou, D. L. (2019). Detecting Cyberbullying and Cyberaggression in Social Media. *ACM Transactions on the Web (TWEB), 13*, 1–51.

Chauncey, G. (2019, June 25). *The Forgotten History of Gay Entrapment*. Retrieved from The Atlantic: https://www.theatlantic.com/ideas/archive/2019/06/before-stonewall-biggest-threat-was-entrapment/590536/

Chayka, K. (2015, March 2). *Let's Really be Friends: A Defense of Online Intimacy*. Retrieved from The New Republic: https://newrepublic.com/article/121183/your-internet-friends-are-real-defense-online-intimacy

Checkalski, O. R., Gervais, S. J., & Holland, K. J. (2023). A Triangulation Study of Young Women's Motivations for Sending Nudes to Men. *Computers in Human Behavior, 140*, https://doi.org/10.1016/j.chb.2022.107561

CIJ. (2022). *Meta's Censorship of Health Ads for Women and People of Diverse Genders*. Retrieved from Center for Intimacy Justice: https://docsend.com/view/phfstt65wzta5nw7

Clark, M. (2020). Drag Them: A Brief Etymology of So-Called "Cancel Culture". *Communication and the Public, 5*, 88–92.

Clemens, C., Atkin, D., & Krishnan, A. (2015). The in Uence of Biological and Personality Traits on Gratifications Obtained through Online Dating Websites. *Computers in Human Behavior, 49*, 120–129.

Cleveland Clinic. (2024, July 26). *Delirium Tremens*. Retrieved from Cleveland Clinic: https://my.clevelandclinic.org/health/diseases/25052-delirium-tremens

Coffey, J. K., Bond, D. K., Stern, J. A., & Van Why, N. (2022). Sexual Experiences and Attachment Styles in Online and Offline Dating Contexts. *International Journal of Sexual Health, 34(4)*, 665–678, https://doi.org/10.1080/19317611.2022.2110349

Cohen, J. (2000). More Censorship or Less Discrimination? Sexual Orientation Hate Propaganda in Multiple Perspectives. *McGill Law Journal, 46*, 69.

Cohen, S. (2023, October 2/9). *How Anti–Sex Work Legislation Is About to Get Worse*. Retrieved from The Nation: https://www.thenation.com/article/society/fosta-sesta-avs-bills-sex-work/

Coluccia, A. P. (2020). Online Romance Scams: Relational Dynamics and Psychological Characteristics of the Victims and Scammers: *A Scoping Review. Clinical Practice and Epidemiology in Mental Health: CP & EMH, 16*, 24–35.

Congress, U. S. (2001). *United States Congress*. Washington, DC: U.S. Government Printing Office.

Congress, U. S. (2005). *Real ID Act of 2005*. Washington, DC: U.S. Government Printing Office.

Coopersmith, J. (2000). Pornography, Videotape and the Internet. *IEEE Technoly and Society Magazine, 19*, 27–34.

Corti, E., & Parati, I. (2022). Democratizing Pleasure: Movement-Impaired Individuals' Perception of Sex and the Design of Inclusive Sex Toys. *Journal of Design, Business & Society, 8(1)*, 9–37.

Council on Criminal Justice. (2024, June 19). *New Analysis Shows 8% Increase in U.S. Domestic Violence Incidents Follpwing Pandemic Stay-at-Home Orders*. Retrieved from Council of Criminal Justice: https://counciloncj.org/new-analysis-shows-8-increase-in-u-s-domestic-violence-incidents-following-pandemic-stay-at-home-orders/

CovenantEyes. (2024, July 19). *History*. Retrieved from CovenantEyes: https://www.covenanteyes.com/about-covenant-eyes/corporate-history/

DABL. (2016, May 24). *Medieval Book Production and Monastic Life*. Retrieved from Dartmouth Ancient Books Lab: https://sites.dartmouth.edu/ancientbooks/2016/05/24/medieval-book-production-and-monastic-life/#:~:text=Because%20of%20these%20close%20details,hours%20devoted%20only%20to%20writing

Dalton, D., & Schubert, C. (2011). *When Classification Becomes Censorship. Griffith Law Review, 20(1)*, 31–66.

Darbinyan, R. (2022, June 14). *The Growing Role of AI in Content Moderation*. Retrieved from Forbes: https://www.forbes.com/sites/forbestechcouncil/2022/06/14/the-growing-role-of-ai-in-content-moderation/

Data & Society Research. (2016, December 13). *New Report Shows That 4% of U.S. Internet Users Have Been a Victim of "Revenge Porn"*. Retrieved from Center for Innovative Public Health Research: https://innovativepublichealth.org/press-releases/revenge-porn-report-findings/

David, D., Cotet, C., Matu, S., Mogoase, C., & Stefan, S. (2018). 50 Years of Rational-Emotive and Cognitive-Behavioral Therapy: A Systemic Review and Meta-Analysis. *Journal of Clinical Psychology, 74(3)*, 304–318.

Davis, M. (2023, August 21). *Porn ID Laws: What Type of Age Verification Is Required?* Retrieved from FTX Identity: https://ftxidentity.com/blog/porn-id-laws-age-verification/

De Block, A., & Dewitte, S. (2007). Mating Games: Cultural Evolution and Sexual Selection. *Biology & Philosophy, 22*, 475–491, https://doi.org/10.1007/s10539-006-9041-y

Desta, Y. (2016, September 15). *Read Edward Snowden's Moving Speech about Why Privacy Is "Something to Protect"*. Retrieved from Vanity Fair: https://www.vanityfair.com/hollywood/2016/09/edward-snowden-privacy-speech

DevX. (2023, August 23). *JenniCam*. Retrieved from DevX: https://www.devx.com/terms/jennicam/

DFF. (2024, July 21). *Women's Rights Website Blocked in Spain*. Retrieved from Digital Freedom Fund: https://digitalfreedomfund.org/womens-rights-website-blocked-in-spain/

Dickson, E. J., Hubby, K., & Lang, N. (2020, July 16). *11 Unexpected Benefits of Watching Porn*. Retrieved from DailyDot: https://www.dailydot.com/nsfw/guides/porn-benefits

Dictionary.com. (2019, August 8). *What is Stochastic Terrorism*. Retrieved from Dictionary.com: https://www.dictionary.com/e/what-is-stochastic-terrorism/

Dir, A. L., Cyders, M. A., & Coskunpinar, A. (2013). From the Bar to the Bed via Mobile Phone: A First Test of the Role of Problematic Alcohol Use, Sexting, and Impulsivity-Related Traits in Sexual Hookups. *Computers in Human Behavior, 29*, 1664–1670.

Diver, K. (2005, April 3). *Archaeologist Finds "Oldest Porn Statue"*. Retrieved from The Guardian: https://www.theguardian.com/world/2005/apr/04/arts.germany

Dixon, D., Sharp, C. A., Hughes, K., & Hughes, J. C. (2023). Parental Technoference and Adolescents' Mental Health and Violent Behaviour: A Scoping Review. *BMC Public Health, 23*, https://doi.org/10.1186/s12889-023-16850-x

Djamasbi, S., & Strong, D. (2019). User Experience-driven Innovation in Smart and Connected Worlds. *AIS Transactions on Human-Computer Interaction, 11(4)*, 215–231. https://doi.org/10.17705/1thci.00121

Dodgson, L. (2018, May 24). *You Might Still be Single Because of Something Called the "Paradox of Choice"—Here's What it Means.* Retrieved from Business Insider: https://www.businessinsider.com/how-the-paradox-of-choice-could-explain-why-youre-still-single-2018-2

Dreibelbis, E. (2023, May 19). *Americans Check Their Phones an Alarming Number of Times Per Day.* Retrieved from PC Magazine: https://www.pcmag.com/news/americans-check-their-phones-an-alarming-number-of-times-per-day

DSW. (2024). *What Is SESTA/FOSTA.* Retrieved from Decriminalizing Sex Work: https://decriminalizesex.work/advocacy/sesta-fosta/what-is-sesta-fosta/

EFF. (2024, June 19). *Section 230.* Retrieved from Electronic Frontier Foundation: https://www.eff.org/issues/cda230

EIU. (2021, March 1). *Measuring the Prevalence of Online Violence against Women.* Retrieved from The Economist Intelligence Unit: https://onlineviolencewomen.eiu.com/

EJI. (2023, July 7). *Use of App to Monitor Accused People and Their Families Raises Concerns.* Retrieved from Equal Justice Initiative: https://eji.org/news/use-of-app-to-monitor-accused-people-and-their-families-raises-concerns/

Erfani, S., Abedin, B., & Blount, Y. (2016). Social Support, Social Belongingness, and Psychological Well-Being: Benefits of Online Healthcare Community Membership. *Pacific Asia Conference on Information Systems.*

Erickson, M. (2019, May 28). *Internet Privacy-It's a Matter of Mental Health.* Retrieved from Stanford School of Medicine Scope: https://scopeblog.stanford.edu/2019/05/28/internet-privacy-its-a-matter-of-mental-health/#:~:text=Privacy%20is%20a%20fundamental%20psychological,an%20individual%20identity%2C%20Aboujaoude%20said

Evans, S. (2023, September 14). *MIT Researchers Create Emotional Support Robot.* Retrieved from IOT World Today: https://www.iotworldtoday.com/robotics/mit-researchers-create-emotional-support-robot-

Everett, C. (2016). Should Encryption Software Be Banned? *Network Security, 2016(8),* 14–17.

Fatimatuzzahro, F., & Achmad, Z. A. (2022). What If It Was You (#WIIWY) Digital Activism on TikTok to Fight Gender-Based Violence Online and Cyberbullying. *Masyarakat, Kebudayaan dan Politik, 35(4),* 450–465.

FBI. (2024, March 25). *2023 Internet Crime Report.* Retrieved from Internet Crime Complaint Center (IC3): https://www.ic3.gov/Media/PDF/AnnualReport/2023_IC3Report.pdf

FHEHealth. (2023, January 19). *What Are the Mental Effects of Public Exposure and Lack of Privacy?* Retrieved from FHEHealth Restore: https://restore-mentalhealth.com/public-privacy-mental-health-impact/

Fischer, S., & Hawkins, E. (2023, January 16). *Polarization Eats the Developed World.* Retrieved from Axios.com: https://www.axios.com/2023/01/16/political-polarization-developed-world

FlexiSpy. (2024, July 29). *FlexiFLESH.* Retrieved from FlexiSpy: https://www.flexispy.com//en/best-sex-toy-spy-app.htm?a_aid=cb523eda

Florimbio, A. R., Brem, M. J., Garner, A. R., Grigorian, H. L., & Stuart, G. L. (2018). Alcohol-Related Sex Expectancies Explain the Relation between Alcohol Use and Sexting among College Students. *Computers in Human Behavior, 88,* 205–209, https://doi.org/10.1016/j.chb.2018.07.005

Floyd, C. G., & Grubbs, J. B. (2022). Context Matters: How Religion and Morality Shape Pornography Use Effects. *Current Sexual Health Reports, 14,* 82–98, https://doi.org/10.1007/s11930-022-00329-8

Foldes, L. (2024, July 14). *Sex Workers Built the Internet.* Retrieved from The New School: https://parsons.edu/dt-2022/sex-workers-built-the-internet/#:~:text=Sex%20

workers%20have%20been%20pivotal,spaces%20to%20work%20and%20 communicate

Fontes, L. A., & Miller, P. (2022, June 8). *10 Tactics of Coercive Control, Torture within a Family*. Retrieved from DomesticShelters: https://www.domesticshelters.org/articles/ identifying-abuse/10-tactics-of-coercive-control-torture-within-a-family

Freya, S. (2023, December 3). *Think Selling Panties Online is Easy? Think Again!* Retrieved from Medium: https://medium.com/@freyatheferalhousewife/think-selling-panties-online-is-easy-think-again-50e354ef1fd2

FTND. (2024, July 2). *10 Negative Effects of Porn on Your Brain, Body, Relationships, and Society*. Retrieved from Fight the New Drug: https://fightthenewdrug.org/10-reasons-why-porn-is-unhealthy-for-consumers-and-society/

Garga, S., Thomas, M., Bhatia, A., Sullivan, A., John-Leader, F., & Pit, S. (2021). Geosocial Networking Dating App Usage and Risky Sexual Behavior in Young Adults Attending a Music Festival: Cross-Sectional Questionnaire Study. *Journal of Medical Internet Research, 23(4)*, https://doi.org/10.2196/21082

Geiger, A. (2018, June 4). *How Americans Have Viewed Government Surveillance and Privacy since Snowden Leaks*. Retrieved from Pew Research: https://www.pewresearch. org/short-reads/2018/06/04/how-americans-have-viewed-government-surveillance-and-privacy-since-snowden-leaks/

George, A. (2019, March 14). *Margaret Hamilton Led the NASA Software Team That Landed Astronauts on the Moon*. Retrieved from Smithsonian Magazine: https:// www.smithsonianmag.com/smithsonian-institution/margaret-hamilton-led-nasa-software-team-landed-astronauts-moon-180971575/

Ghosh, S. C. (2017). Dinesh Moorjani and Hatch Labs. *Harvard Business School Case, 818–026.*

Gillespie, T. (2022). Do Not Recommend? Reduction as. Form of Content Moderation. *Social Media + Society, 8(3)*, https://doi.org/10.1177/20563051221117552

Glover Blackwell, A. (2017). *The Curb-Cut Effect*. Retrieved from Stanford Social Innovation Review: https://ssir.org/articles/entry/the_curb_cut_effect

Godawatte, K. R. (2019). Dark Web along with the Dark Web Marketing and Surveillance. *20th International Conference on Parallel and Distributed Computing, Applications and Technologies (PDCAT)*, 483–485.

Goerlich, S. (2022). *With Sprinkles on Top: Everything Vanilla People and Their Kinky Partners Need to Know to Communicate, Explore, and Connect*. Louisville, CO: Sounds True.

Gonsalves, P. (2022, March 9). *Self-Disclosure and Social Media: Review Identifies Two-Way Relationship with Mental Health*. Retrieved from The Mental Elf: https:// www.nationalelfservice.net/treatment/digital-health/self-disclosure-social-media/

Goode, E., & Ben-Yehuda, N. (2009). *Moral Panics: The Social Construction of Deviance*. Oxford, UK: Wiley-Blackwell.

Goodmark, L. (2019, July 23). *Stop Treating Domestic Violence Differently from Other Crimes*. Retrieved from The New York Times: https://www.nytimes.com/2019/07/23/ opinion/domestic-violence-criminal-justice-reform-too.html

Gordon-Messer, D. B. (2013). Sexting among Young Adults. *The Journal of Adolescent Health: Official Publication of the Society for Adolescent Medicine, 52(3)*, 301–306.

Grand View Research. (2023). *Online Dating Market Size, Share & Growth Report, 2030*. Grand View Research.

Grey, J. (2024, February 12). *What Should Your Sex Toys Be Made Of?* Retrieved from Wired. com: https://www.wired.com/story/how-to-choose-sex-toy-materials/#:~:text=Silicone% 20is%20the%20most%20widely,I've%20vetted%20each%20one

Griffith, E. (2019, December 20). *Pornhub Reveals Explicit Traffic Numbers*. Retrieved from PC Mag: https://www.pcmag.com/news/pornhub-reveals-explicit-traffic-numbers

Gritters, J. (2019, September). *App-Based Dating Is Here to Stay: Here's How It's Rewiring the Courtship Process*. Retrieved from Experience Magazine: https://expmag.com/2019/09/app-based-dating-is-here-to-stay-heres-how-its-rewiring-the-courtship-process/

Grubbs, J. B., Exline, J. J., Pargament, K. I., Volk, F., & Lindberg, M. J. (2017). Internet Pornography Use, Perceived Addiction, and Religious/Spiritual Struggles. *Archives of Sexual Behavior, 46(6)*, 1733–1745, https://doi.org/10.1007/s10508-016-0772-9

Grubbs, J. B., Wright, P. J., Braden, A. L., Wilt, J. A., & Kraus, S. W. (2019). Internet Pornography Use and Sexual Motivation: A Systematic Review and Integration. *Annals of the International Communication Association, 43(2)*, 117–155, https://doi.org/10.1080/23808985.2019.1584045

Gruzd, A., & Hernandez-Garcia, A. (2018). Privacy Concerns and Self-Disclosure in Private and Public Uses of Social Media. *Cyberpsychology, Behavior and Social Networking, 21(7)*, https://www.liebertpub.com/doi/10.1089/cyber.2017.0709

Gu, Y., & Wang, Z. (2022). Income Inequality and Global Political Polarization: The Economic Origin of Political Polarization in the World. *Journal of Chinese Political Science, 27(2)*, 375–398.

Gupta, R. (2024, January 1). *LAION and the Challenges of Preventing AI-Generated CSAM*. Retrieved from TechPolicy.press: https://www.techpolicy.press/laion-and-the-challenges-of-preventing-ai-generated-csam/

Hamilton, V., Kaptchuk, G., McDonald, A., & Redmiles, E. (2023). *Safer Digital Intimacy for Sex Workers and Beyond: A Technical Research Agenda*. Retrieved from IEEE Security & Privacy: https://cs-people.bu.edu/kaptchuk/publications/sw-threat-modeling-2.pdf

Harris, B., & Woodlock, D. (2023). *Technology and Domestic Violence and Family Violence: Victimisationm Perpetration, and Responses*. London, UK: Routledge.

Harwood, J. D. (2014). Constantly Connected—the Effects of Smart-Devices on Mental Health. *Computers in Human Behavior, 34*, 267–272.

Harysi, M. N. (2020). Building Governance Capability in Online Communities: A Social Network Perspective. *Proceedings of the 53rd Hawaii International Conference on System Sciences*.

Hassan, S. (1990). *Combatting Cult Mind Control*. New York, NY: Park Street Press.

Hauser, B. (2024, February 7). *Why Generation Z Is Having Less Sex*. Retrieved from Technician: https://www.technicianonline.com/news/why-generation-z-is-having-less-sex/article_ff14868c-c55f-11ee-aec7-8ba8cdd38686.html

Hayrapetyan, D. (2022). The Fallacy of Personal Validation (the Forer Effect) in the System of Behavioral Finance Biases. *Modern Psychology, 5(1(10))*, 56–62.

Heid, M. (2013, July 10). *How Hot Women Help You De-Stress*. Retrieved from Men's Health: https://www.menshealth.com/health/a19544656/how-hhot-women-help-you-de-stress/

Helm, B., Holt, T., Scrivens, R., & Frank, R. (May 2022). Examining Incel Subculture on Reddit. *Journal of Crime and Justice*, https://doi.org/10.1080/0735648X.2022.2074867

Henion, A., & Finn, M. (2016, August 16). *Prostitution Has Gone Online—and Pimps Are Thriving*. Retrieved from MSU Today: https://msutoday.msu.edu/news/2016/prostitution-has-gone-online-and-pimps-are-thriving#:~:text=Technology%20has%20reshaped%20the%20contours,public%2C%20mainly%20Craigslist%20and%20Backpage

Henry, L. (2014, April 28). *Investigation Online: Gathering Information to Assess Risk*. Retrieved from Model View Culture: https://modelviewculture.com/pieces/investigation-online-gathering-information-to-assess-risk

Henry, N., Flynn, A., & Powell, A. (2019, March). *Image-Based Sexual Abuse: Victims and Perpetrators*. Retrieved from Australian Institute of Criminology: https://www.aic.gov.au/sites/default/files/2020-05/imagebased_sexual_abuse_victims_and_perpetrators.pdf

Henry, N., & Powell, A. (2014). The Dark Side of the Virtual World. In N. Henry, & A. Powell, *Preventing Sexual Violence: Interdisciplinary Approaches to Overcoming a Rape Culture* (pp. 84–101). Palgrave Macmillan.

Hernandez, D. (2014, August 8). *Tech Time Warp of the Week: In the 60's, There Was a Proto-Tinder That Ran on a 5-Ton Mainframe.* Retrieved from Wired: https://www.wired.com/2014/08/tech-time-warp-ibm-1401-dating/

Herrera, A. (2018). Curator's Gallery Tour. In T. Kren, J. Burke, S. J. Campbell, A. Herrera, & T. DePasquale, *The Renaissance Nude.* Los Angeles, CA: J. Paul Getty Museum.

HHS. (2023, May 3). *New Surgeon General Advisory Raises Alarm about the Devastating Impact of the Epidemic of Loneliness and Isolation in the United States.* Retrieved from U.S. Department of Health and Human Services: https://www.hhs.gov/about/news/2023/05/03/new-surgeon-general-advisory-raises-alarm-about-devastating-impact-epidemic-loneliness-isolation-united-states.html

Hiebert, A., & Kortes-Miller, K. (2021). Finding Home in Online Community: Exploring TikTok as a Support for Gender and Sexual Minority Youth throughout COVID-19. *Journal of LGBT Youth,* https://doi.org/10.1080/19361653.2021.2009953

Hogge, B. (2011). *Barefoot into Cyberspace: Adventures in Search of Techno-Utopia.* Barefoot Publishing Limited.

Holladay, K. R., & Lardier, D. T. (2021). The Trauma of Cyber-Sexual Assault: Heightened Dimensions of Emotional Disregulation among Survivors. *The Practitioner Scholar: Journal of the International Trauma Training Institute, 3,* 60–77.

Holtzhausen, N., Fitzgerald, K., Thakur, I., Ashley, J., Rolfe, M., & Pit, S. W. (2020). Swipe-Based Dating Applications Use and Its Association with Mental Health Outcomes: A Cross-Sectional Study. *BMC Psychology, 8,* https://bmcpsychology.biomedcentral.com/articles/10.1186/s40359-020-0373-1

HRC Foundation. (2024, July 21). *Map: Attacks on Gender Affirming Care by State.* Retrieved from Human Rights Campaign: https://www.hrc.org/resources/attacks-on-gender-affirming-care-by-state-map

Huber, J. (2018, June 24). *Loss of Privacy Has "Four Psychological Effects".* Retrieved from KTRH: https://ktrh.iheart.com/alternate/amp/2018-06-22-loss-of-privacy-has-four-psychological-effects/

Hutchison, J. (2019). Culture, Communication, and an Information Age Madonna. *IEEE Professional Communication Society Newsletter, 45(3).*

Huyler, D. (2021). The Case for Work from Home. *New Horizons in Adult Education and Human Resource Development, 33,* 1–3.

IBM. (2024). *The IBM 1401.* Retrieved from IBM: https://www.ibm.com/history/1401

Igo, S. (2018). *The Known Citizen: A History of Privacy in Modern America.* Harvard University Press.

Ilascu, I. (2021, January 9). *Hacker Used Ransomware to Lock Victims in Their IOT Chastity Belt.* Retrieved from BleepingComputer.com: https://www.bleepingcomputer.com/news/security/hacker-used-ransomware-to-lock-victims-in-their-iot-chastity-belt/

Internet Filter. (2006). *Internet Pornography Statistics.* Retrieved from Internet Filter: http://internet-filterreview.toptenreviews.com/internet-pornography-statistics.html

Internet Live Stats. (2019). *Total Number of Websites.* Retrieved from Internet Live Stats: https://www.internetlivestats.com/total-number-of-websites/

Iroegbu, M., O'Brien, F., Muñoz, L. C., & Parsons, G. (2024). Investigating the Psychological Impact of Cyber-Sexual Harassment. *Journal of Interpersonal Violence,* 1–22, https://doi.org/10.1177/08862605241231615

Jackson, C., & Ballard, N. (2018, May 1). *Over Half of Americans Report Feeling Like No One Knows Them Well.* Retrieved from Ipsos: https://www.ipsos.com/en-us/news-polls/us-loneliness-index-report

James, E. L. (2023, March 19). *The Long and Satisfying 28,000-Year History of the Dildo*. Retrieved from Barcelona-Metropolitan: https://www.barcelona-metropolitan.com/features/history/the-28-000-year-history-of-the-dildo/

Jansen, S., & Martin, B. (2004). Exposing and Opposing Censorship: Backfire Dynamics in Freedom-of-Speech Struggles. *Pacific Journalism Review, 10*, 29.

Jiang, B. K. (2021). Mechanisms and Attributes of Echo Chambers in Social Media. *ArXiv*.

Johanssen, J. (2022). *Fantasy, Online Misogyny, and the Manosphere: Male Bodies of Dis/Inhibition*. New York, NY: Routledge.

Johnson, M. B. (2022, February 20). *Mandated Reporting and the Bullying Loophole*. Retrieved from Medium.com: https://medium.com/south-of-certainty/mandated-reporting-and-the-bullying-loophole-7e5ac1c6f3fc

Jones, A. (2020). *Camming: Money, Power, and Pleasure in the Sex Work Industry*. New York, NY: NYU Press.

Jones, C., & Bergen, B. (2024). Does GPT-4 pass the Turing test? *Proceedings of the 2024 Conference of the North American Chapter of the Association for Computational Linguistics: Human Language Technologies (Volume 1: Long Papers)* (pp. 5183–5210). Mexico City, Mexico: Association for Computational Linguistics.

Jourard, S. M. (1966). Some Psychological Aspects of Privacy. *Law and Contemporary Problems (Spring)*, 307–318.

Julian, K. (2018, December). *Why Are Young People Having So Little Sex?* Retrieved from The Atlantic: https://www.theatlantic.com/magazine/archive/2018/12/the-sex-recession/573949/

Kaplan, M. (2021, November 12). *$4 a Minute for Fetishes: How the 1-900 Phone-Sex Industry Changed America*. Retrieved from New York Post: https://nypost.com/2021/11/12/how-the-1-900-phone-sex-industry-changed-america/

Kato, B. (2023, July 14). *Most Tinder Users Are in Relationships or Married: "Game of Deception"*. Retrieved from New York Post: https://nypost.com/2023/07/14/majority-of-tinder-users-are-in-relationships-or-married-survey/

Kauffman, J. (2019). *Hippie Food: How Back-to-the-Landers, Longhairs, and Revolutionaries Changed the Way We Eat*. William Morrow.

Kemper, B. (2022). AI and Stochastic Terrorism—Should It Be Done? *IEEE International Symposium on Software Reliability Engineering Workshops (ISSREW)*, 347–356.

KFF. (2013, January). *See No Evil: How Internet Filters Affect the Search for Online Health Information*. Retrieved from Kaiser Family Foundation: https://www.kff.org/wp-content/uploads/2013/01/see-no-evil-how-internet-filters-affect-the-search-for-online-health-information-executive-summary.pdf

Kierkegaard, S. (2011). To Block or Not to Block—European Child Porno Law in Question. *Computer Law Security Review, 27*, 573–584.

Killen, M., Raz, K. L., & Graham, S. (2021). Reducing Prejudice through Promoting Cross-Group Friendships. *Review of General Psychology, 26(3)*, https://doi.org/10.1177/10892680211061262

King, J. L., Gurbaxani, V., Kraemer, K. L., McFarlan, F. W., Raman, K. S., & Yap, C. S. (1994). Institutional Factors in Information Technology Innovation. *Information Systems Research, 5(2)*, 139–169.

Kinstler, L. (2019, January). *Finding Lena, the Patron Saint of JPEGs*. Retrieved from Wired: https://www.wired.com/story/finding-lena-the-patron-saint-of-jpegs/

Klettke, B. H. (2019). Sexting and Psychological Distress: The Role of Unwanted and Coerced Sexts. *Cyberpsychology, Behavior and Social Networking, 22(4)*, 237–242.

Kloess, J., & van der Bruggen, M. (2021). Trust and Relationship Development among Users in Dark Web Child Sexual Exploitation and Abuse Networks: A Literature Review from a Psychological and Criminological Perspective. *Trauma, Violence & Abuse, 24(3)*, 1220–1237.

Knight, M. E. (2022, May 6). *#Seggsed: Sex, Safety, and Censorship on TikTok* (Masters thesis, San Diego State University). Retrieved from MikaylaKnight.com: https://mikaylaknight.com/wp-content/uploads/2023/01/knight_mikayla-1.pdf

Knowles, E. S., & Linn, J. A. (2004). The Importance of Resistance to Persuasion. In E. S. Knowles, & J. A. Linn, *Resistance and Persuasion* (pp. 1–10). Mahway, NJ: Lawrence Erlbaum Associates.

Kowalski, R. T. (2018). Bullying and Cyberbullying in Adulthood and the Workplace. *The Journal of Social Psychology, 158*, 64–81.

Kranich, N. (2004). Why Filters Won't Protect Children or Adults. *Library Administration & Management, 18(1)*, 14–18, https://www.ala.org/advocacy/intfreedom/filtering/whyfilterswontprotect

Kraut, R. P. (1998). Internet Paradox: A Social Technology That Reduces Social Involvement and Psychological Well-Being? *The American Psychologist, 53(9)*, 1017–1031.

Kumar, A. N. (2018). Empirical Analysis of Supervised Machine Learning Techniques for Cyberbullying Detection. *International Conference on Innovative Computing and Communications*.

Laestadius, L. B.-C. (2022). Too Human and Not Human Enough: A Grounded Theory Analysis of Mental Health Harms from Emotional Dependence on the Social Chatbot Replika. *New Media & Society, 26(10)*, 5923–5941, https://doi.org/10.1177/14614448221142007

LastPass. (2022). *Psychology of Passwords 2022*. Retrieved from LastPass: https://www.lastpass.com/resources/ebook/psychology-of-passwords-2022

Lawrence, F. M. (2022). "The Remedy to Be Applied Is More Speech": Rights, Responsibilities and Obligations of Free Expression at Law Schools. *Hofstra Law Review, 51(419)*, https://hofstralawreview.org/wp-content/uploads/2023/07/HLR-51.2-Lawrence.pdf

Lee, S. (2016, February 14). *The History of Online Dating from 1695 to Now*. Retrieved from Huffington Post: https://www.huffpost.com/entry/timeline-online-dating-fr_b_9228040

Lefferts, D., & Dempsey, L. (2013, March 21). *Q&A: "Spontaneous Happiness" with Andrew Weil*. Retrieved from USA Today: https://www.usatoday.com/story/life/books/2013/03/21/andrew-weil-interview/2006409/

Lehmiller, J. (2022, June 26). *Gen Z Aren't Having the Sex You Think: Here's Why*. Retrieved from Lovehoney: https://www.lovehoney.com/blog/gen-z-are-having-less-sex-here-is-why.html

Levy, D. (2007). *Love + Sex with Robots*. New York, NY: Harper Perinneal.

Ley, M., & Rambukkana, N. (2021). Touching at a Distance: Digital Intimacies, Haptic Platforms, and the Ethics of Consent. *Science and Engineering Ethics, 27(5)*, https://doi.org/10.1007/s11948-021-00338-1

Lieberman, H. (2017). *Buzz: The Stimulating History of the Sex Toy*. Pegasus Books.

Light, L. L., Panicker, S., Abrams, L., & Huh-Yoo, J. (2024). Ethical Challenges in the Use of Digital Technologies in Psychological Science: Introduction to the Special Issue. *American Psychologist, 79(1)*, 1–8.

Lima, M. L., Marques, S., Muiños, G., & Camilo, C. (2017). All You Need Is Facebook Friends? Associations between Online and Face-to-Face Friendships and Health. *Personality and Social Psychology, 8*, https://doi.org/10.3389/fpsyg.2017.00068

Linden, M. (2014). Telework Research and Practice: Impacts on People with Disabilities. *Work, 48(1)*, 65–67.

Littlewood, A. (2003). Cyberporn and Moral Panic: An Evaluation of Press Reactions to Pornography on the Internet. *Library and Information Research, 27*, 8–18.

Lomas, A. (2017, September 29), *https://www.lovense.com/sex-blog/sex-toys/lovense-hack*. Retrieved from Pen Test Partners: https://www.pentestpartners.com/security-blog/screwdriving-locating-and-exploiting-smart-adult-toys/

Lomas, A. (2020, October 6). *Smart Male Chastity Lock Cock-Up*. Retrieved from Pen Test Partners: https://www.pentestpartners.com/security-blog/smart-male-chastity-lock-cock-up/

Lovense. (2024, July 29). *Burrowing into a Butt Plug's Bluetooth-the Lovense Hack*. Retrieved from Lovense Blog: https://www.lovense.com/sex-blog/sex-toys/lovense-hack

Lyytinen, K., & Rose, G. M. (2003). Disruptive Information System Innovation: The Case of Internet Computing. *Information Systems Journal, 13*, 301–330.

Maheu, M. (2024, April 30). *What Is an Echo Chamber in Social Media? Supporting Mental Health on TikTok & Instagram*. Retrieved from Telehealth.org: https://telehealth.org/what-is-an-echo-chamber-in-social-media-supporting-mental-health-on-tiktok-instagram/

Mahmoud, T. A.-E.-H. (2012). A Highly Efficient Content Based Approach to Filter Pornography Websites. *International Journal of Computer Vision and Image Processing, 2*, 75–90.

Maiberg, E. (2024, January 29). *Microsoft Closes Loophole That Created AI Porn of Taylor Swift*. Retrieved from 404 Media: https://www.404media.co/microsoft-closes-loophole-that-created-ai-porn-of-taylor-swift/

Makin, D., & Ireland, L. (2019). The Secret Life of PETs. *Policing: An International Journal, 43*, 121–136.

Malatino, K. (2024, May 9). *Analysis of Millions of Posts Shows That Users Seek Out Echo Chambers on Social Media*. Retrieved from Phys.org: https://phys.org/news/2024-05-analysis-millions-users-echo-chambers.html

MandatedReporter.com. (2024, July 28). *Are You a Mandated Reporter of Domestic Violence?* Retrieved from MandatedReporter.com: https://mandatedreporter.com/domestic-violence/

Manne, F. (2019). *An Aesthetic Comparison of Erotic Art Verses Pornographic Art* (Doctoral dissertation, School of the Art Institute of Chicago). Retrieved from https://digitalcollections.saic.edu/_flysystem/fedora/2022-04/201906_ManneF_MFALowRes.pdf

Mara, M.-H., & Wandt, A. S. (2019). Enabling Mass Surveillance: Data Aggregation in the Age of Big Data and the Internet of Things. *Journal of Cyber Policy, 4(2)*, 160–177, https://doi.org/10.1080/23738871.2019.1590437

Masson, E. M. (1997). The Women's Christian Temperance Union 1874–1898: Combating Domestic Violence. *William & Mary Journal of Women and the Law, 3(1)*, https://scholarship.law.wm.edu/cgi/viewcontent.cgi?referer=&httpsredir=1&article=1273&context=wmjowl#:~:text='Me%20temperance%20movement%20became%20the,supra%20note%203%2C%20at%2049

Matthews, J., & Goerzen, M. (2019). Black Hat Trolling, White Hat Trolling, and Hacking the Attention Landscape. *Companion Proceedings of The 2019 World Wide Web Conference*.

McArthur, N., & Twist, M. L. (2017). People Whose Primary Sexual Identity Comes through the Use of Technology. *Sexual and Relationship Therapy*, 1468–1749, https://doi.org/10.1080/14681994.2017.1397950

McCain, A. (2023, January 11). *How Fast Is Technology Advancing? [2023]: Growing, Evolving, and Accelerating at Exponential Rates*. Retrieved from Zippia.com: https://www.zippia.com/advice/how-fast-is-technology-advancing/

McCloud, T. (2022, October 24). *School Seeking Access to Personal Devices Sparks Outrage Online: "Hard No"*. Retrieved from Newsweek: https://www.newsweek.com/school-seeking-access-personal-devices-sparks-outrage-online-hard-no-1754368

McCullen, A. (2022, December 7). *Panopticon States and the Hawthorne Effect-Eye Am Watching*. Retrieved from The Innovation Show: https://theinnovationshow.io/panopticon-states-and-the-hawthorne-effect-eye-am-watching/#:~:text=Foucault%20wrote%2C%20%E2%80%9Cthe%20major%20effect,known%20as%20The%20Hawthorne%20Effect

McGlaun, S. (2013, April 10). *Survey Shows 62% of Teens Want to Buy the iPhone*. Retrieved from SlashGear: https://www.slashgear.com/survey-shows-62-of-teens-want-to-buy-the-iphone-10277238/

McInroy, L. B., & Craig, S. L. (2020). "It's Like a Safe Haven Fantasy World": Online Fandom Communities and the Identity Development Activities of Sexual and Gender Minority Youth. *Psychology of Popular Media, 9(2)*, 236–246, http://dx.doi.org/10.1037/ppm0000234

McKee, A., Dawson, A., & Kang, M. (2023). The Criteria to Identify Pornography That Can Support Healthy Sexual Development for Young Adults: Results of an International Delphi Panel. *International Journal of Sexual Health, 35(1)*, 1–12, https://doi.org/10.1080/19317611.2022.2161030

McKee, A., Litsou, K., Byron, P., & Ignham, R. (2022). *What Do We Know about the Effects of Pornography after Fifty Years of Academic Research?* New York, NY: Routledge.

Melville, N., & Ramirez, R. (2008). Information Technology Innovation Diffusion: An Information Requirements Paradigm. *Information Systems Journal, 18*, 247–273.

Miller, D., & Kitzinger, J. (1998). AIDS, the Policy Process and Moral Panics. In D. Miller, J. Kitzinger, & P. Beharrell, *The Circuit of Mass Communication* (pp. 213–223). London, UK: Sage.

Mohan, S. G. (2017). The Impact of Toxic Language on the Health of Reddit Communities. *Advances in Artificial Intelligence*, 51–56.

Molyneaux, R., Mirembe, E., Leicester, S., Schley, C., & Alisic, E. (2024). Digital Disclosures: Exploring the Role of Online Mental Health Services in Supporting Young People Who Disclose Violence or Maltreatment. *Child Protection and Practice, 1*, https://doi.org/10.1016/j.chipro.2024.100016

Moraff, L. (2022, June 27). *How Online Censorship Harms Sex Workers and LGBTQ Communities*. Retrieved from ACLU: https://www.aclu.org/news/civil-liberties/how-online-censorship-harms-sex-workers-and-lgbtq-communities

Morales, J. (2024, July 22). *Microsoft's Secret AI Publishing Deal Sparks Outrage among Academics*. Retrieved from CCN.com: https://www.ccn.com/news/technology/microsoft-taylor-francis-secret-ai-publishing-deal-outrages-academics/

Mori, C. C. (2020). The Prevalence of Sexting Behaviors among Emerging Adults: A Meta-Analysis. *Archives of Sexual Behavior, 49*, 1103–1119.

Morrish, L. (2023, June 29). *Instagram Is Removing Sex-Positive Accounts without Warning*. Retrieved from Wired: https://12ft.io/proxy?q=https%3A%2F%2Fwww.wired.com%2Fstory%2Finstagram-removing-sex-positive-accounts-without-warning%2F

Moschella, D. (1997). *Waves of Power: Dynamics of Global Technology Leadership 1964–2010*. Amacom Books.

Musto, J., Fehrenbacher, A. E., Hoefinger, H., Mai, N., Macioti, P. G., Bennachie, C., . . . D'Adamo, K. (2021). Anti-Trafficking in the Time of FOSTA/SESTA: Networked Moral Gentrification and Sexual Humanitarian Creep. *Social Sciences, 10(2)*, https://doi.org/10.3390/socsci10020058

Nadal, K. L. (2021, December 27). *Why Representation Matters and Why It's Still Not Enough*. Retrieved from Psychology Today: https://www.psychologytoday.com/us/blog/psychology-the-people/202112/why-representation-matters-and-why-it-s-still-not-enough

Naftulin, J. (2021, March 26). *Young People Are Vaving Less Casual Sex and Spending More Time Scrolling on Social Media*. Retrieved from Business Insider: https://www.businessinsider.com/teens-less-casual-sex-generation-parents-did-2021-3#:~:text=Millennials%20and%20Gen%20Z%20are,parents%20for%20longer%20may%20contribute

NASW, ASWB, CSWE, & CSWA. (2024). *Standards for Technology in Social Work Practice*. Retrieved from SocialWorkers.org: https://www.socialworkers.org/Practice/NASW-Practice-Standards-Guidelines/Standards-for-Technology-in-Social-Work-Practice

NCDAV. (2024, June 19). *National Statistics*. Retrieved from National Coalition against Domestic Violence: https://ncadv.org/STATISTICS

NCMEC. (2024, July 28). *Frequently Asked Questions*. Retrieved from National Center for Missing and Exploited Children: https://report.cybertip.org/faqs

NCOSE. (2024, June 19). *2023 Dirty Dozen List*. Retrieved from National Center on Sexual Exploitation: https://endsexualexploitation.org/dirtydozenlist-2023/

Nelson, K. M., & Rothman, E. F. (2020). Should Public Health Professionals Consider Pornography a Public Health Crisis? *American Journal of Public Health*, https://ajph.aphapublications.org/doi/10.2105/AJPH.2019.305498

Neves, S. (2021). *Compulsive Sexual Behaviors: A Psycho-Sexual Treatment Guide for Clinicians*. London, UK: Routledge.

Newman, M. S. (2019, June 19). *On the Unsung Chinese and Korean History of Movable Type*. Retrieved from LitHub: https://lithub.com/so-gutenberg-didnt-actually-invent-the-printing-press/#:~:text=Do%20this%20many%20times%2C%20and,printing%20of%20the%20aforementioned%20Bible

Nicholas, G. (2022, April 26). *Shedding Light on Shadowbanning*. Retrieved from Center for Democracy & Technology: https://cdt.org/insights/shedding-light-on-shadowbanning/#:~:text=Our%20survey%20found%20that%20nearly,%2C%20or%20non%2Dcis%20gendered

Nickerson, R. (1998). Confirmation Bias: A Ubiquitous Phenomenon in Many Guises. *Review of General Psychology, 2*, 175–220.

NIJ. (2023, December 18). *Five Things about the Role of Social Networks in Domestic Radicalization*. Retrieved from National Institute of Justice: https://nij.ojp.gov/topics/articles/five-things-about-role-social-networks-domestic-radicalization

Noel, K., & Ellison, B. (2020). Inclusive Innovation in Telehealth. *NPJ Digital Medicine, 3*, https://doi.org/10.1038/s41746-020-0296-5

Nooney, L. (2014, December 2). *The Odd History of the First Erotic Computer Game*. Retrieved from The Atlantic: https://www.theatlantic.com/technology/archive/2014/12/the-odd-history-of-the-first-erotic-computer-game/383114/

Norris, P. (2021). Cancel Culture: Myth or Reality? *Political Studies, 71*, 145–174.

NSWP. (2024, July 14). *Digital Security: The Smart Sex Worker's Guide*. Retrieved from Global Network of Sex Work Projects: https://www.nswp.org/sites/default/files/sg_to_digital_security_eng.pdf

NYU. (2024, June 11). *I Always Feel Like My Apps Are Watching Me*. Retrieved from NYU.edu: https://www.nyu.edu/life/information-technology/safe-computing/protect-your-privacy/i-always-feel-like-my-apps-are-watching-me.html#:~:text=This%20type%20of%20data%20collection,political%20parties%2C%20and%20government%20agencies

Oatman-Stanford, H. (2014, July 24). *Naughty Nuns, Flatulent Monks, and Other Surprises of Sacred Medieval Manuscripts*. Retrieved from Collectors Weekly: https://www.collectorsweekly.com/articles/naughty-nuns-flatulent-monks-and-other-surprises-of-sacred-medieval-manuscripts/

O'Donnell, J. (2022). *Gamergate and Anti-Feminism in the Digital Age*. London, UK: Palgrave Macmillan.

Owsianik, J. (2018, March 27). *See Visions of Cybersex Suits and Teledildonics from the 1990s*. Retrieved from FutureofSex: https://futureofsex.net/remote-sex/see-visions-cybersex-suits-teledildonics-1990s/

Palmer, K. (2024, July 29). *Taylor & Francis AI Deal Sets "Worrying Precedent" for Academic Publishing*. Retrieved from Inside Higher Ed: https://www.insidehighered.com/news/faculty-issues/research/2024/07/29/taylor-francis-ai-deal-sets-worrying-precedent

Palumbo, J. (2019, August 28). *How Renaissance Artists Brought Pornography to the Masses*. Retrieved from Artsy: https://www.artsy.net/article/artsy-editorial-renaissance-artists-brought-pornography-masses

Pan, X., Hou, Y., & Wang, Q. (2023). Are We Braver in Cyberspace? Social Media Anonymity Enhances Moral Courage. *Computers in Human Behavior, 148*, https://doi.org/10.1016/j.chb.2023.107880

Pangilinan, M. (2023, June 19). *Global Civil Unrest on the Rise as Cost-of-Living Crisis Intensifies*. Retrieved from Insurance Business Magazine: https://www.insurancebusinessmag.com/us/risk-management/news/global-civil-unrest-on-the-rise-as-costofliving-crisis-intensifies-449683.aspx#:~:text=The%20world%20is%20experiencing%20a,29%2C535%20in%20the%20previous%20year

Pantumsinchai, P. (2018). Armchair Detectives and the Social Construction of Falsehoods: An Actor–Network Approach. *Information, Communication & Society, 21*, 761–778.

Park, J. (2024, July 19). *5 Things Parents Need to Know about Student Data Privacy*. Retrieved from Student Privacy Compass: https://studentprivacycompass.org/5-things-parents-need-to-know-about-student-data-privacy/

Patchin, J., & Hinduja, S. (2018). Sextortion among Adolescents: Results from a National Survey of U.S. Youth. *Sexual Abuse: A Journal of Research and Treatment, 32*, 30–54.

PBS News. (2023, January 8). *Why Americans Are Lonelier and Its Effects on Our Health*. Retrieved from PBS News: https://www.pbs.org/newshour/show/why-americans-are-lonelier-and-its-effects-on-our-health#:~:text=You%20know%2C%20some%20surveys%20reveal,worse%20than%20rates%20of%20obesity

PEN. (2024, June 19). *State Laws & Online Harassment*. Retrieved from Pen America Online Harassment Field Manual: https://onlineharassmentfieldmanual.pen.org/state-laws-online-harassment/

Penzeymoog, E. (2021). *Design for Safety*. Book Apart.

Perry, S. L. (2017). Pornography Use and Marital Separation: Evidence from Two-Wave Panel Data. *Archives of Sexual Behavior, 47*, https://doi.org/10.1007/s10508-017-1080-8

Petley, J. (2012). "Are We Insane?" the "Video Nasty" Moral Panic. *Random Structures and Algorithms, 43*, 35–57.

Petry, N. M., Zajac, K., & Ginley, M. K. (2018). Behavioral Addictions as Mental Disorders: To Be or Not to Be? *Annual Review of Clinical Psychology, 14*, 399–423, https://doi.org/10.1146/annurev-clinpsy-032816-045120

Petty, M. (2017, October 21). *Welcome to the World of Victorian Match.com Where Lovers Used This to Communicate*. Retrieved from Express.co.uk: https://www.express.co.uk/life-style/life/869311/Match-com-1800s-dating-victorian-times-telegraph-operators-Radio-4-Wired-Love

Pickens, S., & Solak, J. (2005). National Provider Identifier (NPI) Planning and Implementation Fundamentals for Providers and Payers. *Journal of Healthcare Information Management: JHIM, 19(2)*, 41–47.

Pitcho-Prelorentzos, S., Heckel, C., & Ring, L. (2020). Predictors of Social Anxiety among Online Dating Users. *Computers in Human Behavior, 110*, https://doi.org/10.1016/j.chb.2020.106381

Plaat, K. V. (2024, July 21). *The Banning of Sex Ed on Social Media*. Retrieved from The Porn Conversation: https://thepconversation.org/community-page-blogs/the-banning-of-sex-ed-on-social-media

Plato. (2016). *The Allegory of the Cave, Translated by Shawn Eyer*. Washington DC: Plumbstone Books.

Playboy. (1972, November). *Lenna Sjooblom, Miss November*. Playboy, 139, 141–143.

Poddster. (2023, September 22). *Only 11% of Podcasts Make It to 50 Episodes*. Retrieved from LinkedIn: www.linkedin.com/pulse/only-11-podcasts-make-50-episodes-poddster/

Ponemon. (2020, February). *The 2020 State of Password and Authenticaion Security Behaviors Report*. Retrieved from Yubico.com: https://resources.yubico.com/53 ZDUYE6/as/q5pmcf-fn3ls-b436le/2020_State_of_Password_and_Authentication_Security_ Behaviors_Report

PornHub. (2022, July 21). *Geo Blocking Explained*. Retrieved from PornHub.com: https://www.pornhub.com/blog/geo-blocking-explained

PornHub. (2023). *PornHub Year in Review 2022*. Retrieved from PornHub.com: https://www.pornhub.com/insights/2022-year-in-review

Poushter, J., & Kent, N. (2020, June 25). *The Global Divide on Homosexuality Persists*. Retrieved from Pew Research Center: https://www.pewresearch.org/global/2020/06/25/global-divide-on-homosexuality-persists/

Powell, L. (2023, September 28). *The Psychology of Privacy: Why Do We Value It?* Retrieved from Medium: https://medium.com/@th3Powell/the-psychology-of-privacy-why-do-we-value-it-677d74d42689

Power, J., Moor, L., Anderson, J., Waling, A., James, A., Shackleton, N., . . . Dowsett, G. W. (2022). Traversing TechSex: Benefits and Risks in Digitally Mediated Sex and Relationships. *Sexual Health, 19(1)*, https://doi.org/10.1071/SH21220

Prause, N., & Pfauss, J. G. (2015). Viewing Sexual Stimuli Associated with Greater Sexual Responsiveness, Not Erectile Dysfunction. *Sexual Medicine, 3(2)*, https://doi.org/10.1002/sm2.58

Psychologs. (2023, October 28). *Understanding the Pyschology behind Privacy*. Retrieved from Psychologs.com: https://www.psychologs.com/understanding-the-psychology-behind-privacy/?amp=1#origin=https%3A%2F%2Fwww.google.com%2 F&cap=swipe,education&webview=1&dialog=1&viewport=natural&visibilityState= prerender&prerenderSize=1&viewerUrl=https%3A%2F%2Fwww.google.com%2

Putnam, C. R. (2016). Human-Centered Design in Practice. *Journal of Technical Writing and Communication, 46*, 446–470.

Quinn. (2024, February 26). *The 8 Best Feminist Porn Sites to Help You Get Off Ethically*. Retrieved from Quinn: https://www.tryquinn.com/blog/feminist-porn-sites

Rafiq, F. (2023, July 6). *100 Mind-Blowing Facts Related to Technology That Will Leave You Astonished*. Retrieved from Wome in Technology: https://medium.com/womenintechnology/100-mind-blowing-facts-related-to-technology-that-will-leave-you-astonished-46cda3f56718

Raustiala, K., & Sprigman, C. J. (2019). The Second Digital Disruption: Streaming & the Dawn of Data-Driven Creativity. *The New York University Law Review, 94(6)*, https://nyulawreview.org/issues/volume-94-number-6/the-second-digital-disruption-streaming-and-the-dawn-of-data-drive-creativity/

Reddit. (2024, July 21). *r/AutoModerator*. Retrieved from Reddit.com: https://www.reddit.com/r/AutoModerator/wiki/library/#wiki_user_shadowban_list

Reed, B. (1999, September 30). *The Porn Pioneers*. Retrieved from The Guardian: https://www.theguardian.com/technology/1999/sep/30/onlinesuppleme

Rees, M. (2022, October 14). *What Are the Symptoms of Methamphetamine Withdrawal?* Retrieved from Medical News Today: https://www.medicalnewstoday.com/articles/meth-withdrawal-symptoms

Rich, M., & Satariano, A. (2025, May 15). *Top Priority for Pope Leo: Warn the World of the A.I. Threat*. Retrieved from The New York Times: https://www.nytimes.com/2025/05/15/world/europe/pope-leo-artificial-intelligence.html

Roberts, E. (2001, January). *History of Pornography and Technology.* Retrieved from Stanford: https://cs.stanford.edu/people/eroberts/cs201/projects/2000-01/pornography/technology.htm

Rodrigues, D., Lopes, D., Alexopoulos, T., & Goldenberg, L. (2017). A New Look at Online Attraction: Unilateral Initial Attraction and the Pivotal Role of Perceived Similarity. *Computers in Human Behavior, 74*, 16–25.

Rogers, L. (2024, February 14). *The Platformisation of Sex Work: Affordances, Challenges, Precarities.* Retrieved from Feminist Futures Programme: https://autonomy.work/portfolio/the-platformisation-of-sex-work-affordances-challenges-precarities/

Romano, A. (2018, July 2). *A New Law Intended to Curb Sex Trafficking Threatens the Future of the Internet as We Know It.* Retrieved from Vox.com: https://www.vox.com/culture/2018/4/13/17172762/fosta-sesta-backpage-230-internet-freedom

Romkey, J. (2017). Toast of the IoT: The 1990 *Interop Internet Toaster. IEEE Consumer Electronics Magazine, 6*, 116–119.

Roosen, C. (2022, August 1). *The Widest Possible Definition of Technology Includes Nebulous Things Like Laws, Processes, Language and Ideas.* Retrieved from Christopher Roosen: https://www.christopherroosen.com/blog/2022/8/1/a-wide-definition-of-technology

Rosean, L., Matic, J., & Samardžija, J. (2019). The Propensity for Dating Apps Usage and the Millennials' Interpersonal Skills Development. *Medijska istraživanja: znanstveno-stručni časopis za novinarstvo i medije, 29(2)*, 95–114, https://doi.org/10.22572/mi.29.2.4

Rosen, D. (2023). Pornography and the Erotic Phantasmagoria. *Sexuality & Culture, 27(1)*, 242–265.

Rosenfeld, M., Thomas, R. J., & Hausen, S. (2019). Disintermediating Your Friends: How Online Dating in the United States Displaces Other Ways of Meeting. *Proceedings of the National Academy of Sciences*, https://web.stanford.edu/~mrosenfe/Rosenfeld_et_al_Disintermediating_Friends.pdf

Ross, G. (2015). Innovation and Information Technology. *Management Information Systems, 7*.

Saliba, E., & Castano, A. E.-H. (2023, October 3). *Mobile Apps Fueling AI-Generated Nudes of Young Girls: Spanish Police.* Retrieved from ABC News: https://abcnews.go.com/US/mobile-apps-fueling-ai-generated-nudes-young-girls/story?id=103563734

Samuels, M. (2020, January 9). *Pornography Is Not a "Public Health Crisis".* Retrieved from Boston University School of Public Health: https://www.bu.edu/sph/news/articles/2020/pornography-is-not-a-public-health-crisis/#:~:text=Since%202016%2C%20 17%20states%20have,to%20infidelity%20to%20sex%20trafficking

Sanders, J. (2023, October 12). *How Much Can You Really Earn on OnlyFans.* Retrieved from Follower.co: https://follower.co/guides/how-much-can-you-really-earn-on-onlyfans/

Santoro, H. (2022, December 12). *How Anti-LGBTQ+ Rhetoric Fuels Violence.* Retrieved from Scientific American: https://www.scientificamerican.com/article/how-anti-lgbtq-rhetoric-fuels-violence/

Sarnoto, A. Z., Hayatina, L., & Rahmawati, S. T. (2024). Ideological Radicalization among Adolescents: Multidimensional Analysis and Prevention Strategies. *Jurnal Ilmu Pendidikan dan Humaniora, 13(3)*, 141–151.

Sbarra, D. B. (2019). Smartphones and Close Relationships: The Case for an Evolutionary Mismatch. *Perspectives on Psychological Science, 14(4)*, https://doi.org/10.1177/1745691619826535

Schmidt, F. (2023, April 20). *Avoiding Censorship: How to Move Anonymously on the Internet.* Retrieved from Global Investigative Journalism Network: https://gijn.org/stories/avoiding-censorship-moving-anonymous-internet/

Schneider, F. Z. (2017). Social Media Ostracism: The Effects of Being Excluded Online. *Computers in Human Behavior, 73*, 385–393.

Schneier, B. (2019, December 12). *Scaring People into Supporting Backdoors*. Retrieved from Schneier on Security: https://www.schneier.com/blog/archives/2019/12/scaring_people_html

Schonfeld, A., McNiel, D., Toyoshima, T., & Binder, R. (2023). Cyberbullying and Adolescent Suicide. *The Journal of the American Academy of Psychiatry and the Law, 29(2)*, https://doi.org/10.29158/JAAPL.220078-22

Seariac, H. (2023, April 7). *Falling in Love with Your Friend Might Be More Popular Than Finding Love on Dating Apps*. Retrieved from Deseret News: https://www.deseret.com/2023/4/27/23700974/do-dating-apps-actually-work/

Selva, J. (2018, March 8). *What is Albert Ellis' ABC Model in CBT Theory?* Retrieved from Positive Psychology: https://positivepsychology.com/albert-ellis-abc-model-rebt-cbt/

Seymour, W., & Lupton, D. (2004). Holding the Line Online: Exploring Wired Relationships for People with Disabilities. *Disability & Society, 19*, 291–305.

Shahbaz, A., Funk, A., & Vesteirnsson, K. (2022). *Freedom on the Net 2022: Countering an Authoritarian Overhaul of the Internet*. Retrieved from Freedom House: https://freedomhouse.org/sites/default/files/2022-10/FOTN2022Digital.pdf

Sharabi, L. (2020). Exploring How Beliefs about Algorithms Shape (Offline) Success in Online Dating: A Two-Wave Longitudinal Investigation. *Communication Research, 48*, 931–952.

Sharabi, L. (2022). Finding Love on a First Data: Matching Algorithms in Online Dating. *Harvard Data Science Reivew, 4(1)*, https://doi.org/10.1162/99608f92.1b5c3b7b

Sharath, L. (2016). *Stories and Myths Around the Erotic Sculptures of Khajuraho*. Retrieved from lakshmisharath.com: https://lakshmisharath.com/stories-erotic-sculptures-of-khajuraho/

Shen, Q., & Rose, C. (2019). The Discourse of Online Content Moderation: Investigating Polarized User Responses to Changes in Reddit's Quarantine Policy. *Proceedings of the Third Workshop on Abusive Language Online*.

Shepherd, J. (2024, April 25). *21 Essential Meta Statistics You Need to Know in 2024*. Retrieved from Social Shepherd: https://thesocialshepherd.com/blog/meta-statistics#:~:text=Meta's%20most%20popular%20platform%20boasted,in%20the%20years%20to%20come

Sheridan, M. (2024, June 17). *Doxxing Statistics in 2024: 11 Million Americans Have Been Victimized*. Retrieved from SafeHome.org: https://www.safehome.org/family-safety/doxxing-online-harassment-research/

Shipman, D., & Martin, T. (2019). Clinical and Supervisory Considerations for Transgender Therapists: Implications for Working with Clients. *Journal of Marital and Family Therapy, 45(1)*, 92–105.

Shor, E., & Seida, K. (2021). *Aggression in Pornography: Myths and Realities*. New York, NY: Routledge.

Shostack, A. (2014). *Threat Modeling: Designing for Security*. Wiley.

Silva, C. (2025, April 10). *Teens Really Love Their iPhones, New Survey Shows*. Retrieved from Mashable.com: https://mashable.com/article/teens-really-love-their-iphones

Simmons, M., & Lee, J. S. (2020). Catfishing: A Look into Online Dating and Impersonation. *Social Computing and Social Media*. Design, Ethics, User Behavior, and Social Network Analysis: 12th International Conference, SCSM 2020, Held as Part of the 22nd HCI International Conference, HCII 2020, Copenhagen, Denmark, July 19–24, 2020, Proceedings, Part I, pp. 349–358. https://doi.org/10.1007/978-3-030-49570-1_24

SNPM. (2024, July 11). *Go West, Young Woman! An Exploration of Mail-Order Brides in America*. Retrieved from Smithsonian National Postal Museum: https://postalmuseum.si.edu/research-articles/go-west-young-woman/how-did-couples-find-each-other

Sokol, R. (2018, February 13). *Ask the Lawyer: Are Porn Actors Now Required to Wear Condoms?* Retrieved from Daily Breeze: https://www.dailybreeze.com/2018/02/13/ask-the-lawyer-are-porn-actors-now-required-to-wear-condoms/

Solove, D. J. (2006). A Taxonomy of Privacy. *University of Pennsylvania Law Review, 154(3)*, 477–560.

Southerton, C. M. (2020). Restricted Modes: Social Media, Content Classification and LGBTQ Sexual Citizenship. *New Media & Society, 23*, 920–938.

Standage, T. (2014). *The Victorian Internet: The Remarkable Story of the Telegraph and the Nineteenth Century's On-Line Pioneers.* USA: Bloomsbury.

Stardust, Z. A. (2023). Sex Tech Entrepreneurs: Governing Intimate Data in Start-Up Culture. *New Media & Society, 26(12).* https://doi.org/10.1177/14614448231164408

Stock Analysis. (2024a). *Bumble Inc. (BMBL).* Retrieved from Stock Analysis: https://stockanalysis.com/stocks/bmbl/financials/

Stock Analysis. (2024b). *Match Group, Inc. (MTCH).* Retrieved from Stock Analysis: https://stockanalysis.com/stocks/mtch/revenue/

Stock Analysis. (2024c). *Spark Networks SE (LOVLQ).* Retrieved from Stock Analysis: https://stockanalysis.com/stocks/lovlq/financials/

StopBullying.gov. (2024, Feburary 27). *Report Cyberbullying.* Retrieved from Stop Bullying.gov: https://www.stopbullying.gov/cyberbullying/how-to-report#:~:text=In%20many%20states%2C%20schools%20are,and%20ways%20of%20reporting%20cyberbullying

Stouffer, C. (2023, June 27). *139 Password Statistics to Help You Stay Safe in 2024.* Retrieved from Norton: https://us.norton.com/blog/privacy/password-statistics

Swan, M. (2012). Sensor Mania! The Internet of Things, Wearable Computing, Objective Metrics, and the Quantified Self 2.0. *Journal of Sensor and Actuator Networks, 1*, 217–253.

Switzky, L. (2020). ELIZA Effects: Pygmalion and the Early Development of Artificial Intelligence. *Shaw, 40(1)*, 50–68.

Ta, V. G. (2020). User Experiences of Social Support from Companion Chatbots in Everyday Contexts: Thematic Analysis. *Journal of Medical Internet Research, 22.*

Take, K. G. (2022). "It Feels Like Whack-a-Mole": User Experiences of Data Removal from People Search Websites. *Proceedings on Privacy Enhancing Technologies, 2022*, 159–178.

Tarafdar, M., Maier, C., Laumer, S., & Weitzel, T. (2020). Explaining the Link between Technostress and Technology Addiction for Social Networking Sites: A Study of Distraction as a Coping Behavior. *Information Systems Journal, 30(1)*, 96–124.

Tassin, P. (2018, January 12). *eHarmony Agrees to $2.3M Settlement over Auto-Renewal Terms.* Retrieved from Top Class Actions: https://topclassactions.com/lawsuit-settlements/lawsuit-news/eharmony-agrees-2-3m-settlement-auto-renewal-terms/comment-page-4/

Taylor, J. (2024, July 20). *We Unleashed Facebook and Instagram's Algorithms on Blank Accounts: They Served Up Sexism and Misogyny.* Retrieved from The Guardian: https://www.theguardian.com/technology/article/2024/jul/21/we-unleashed-facebook-and-instagrams-algorithms-on-blank-accounts-they-served-up-sexism-and-misogyny

Temming, M. (2019, February 12). *Robots Are Becoming Classroom Tutors: But Will They Make the Grade?* Retrieved from Science News: https://www.sciencenews.org/article/robots-are-becoming-classroom-tutors-will-they-make-grade

Thales. (2024, April 16). *Bots Now Make Up Nearly Half of All Internet Traffic Globally.* Retrieved from Thalesgroup.com: https://www.thalesgroup.com/en/worldwide/security/press_release/bots-now-make-nearly-half-all-internet-traffic-globally

The Guardian. (2024, March 31). *Institute Bans Use of Playboy Test Image in Engineering Journals.* Retrieved from The Guardian: https://www.theguardian.com/technology/2024/mar/31/tech-publisher-bans-playboy-centrefold-test-image-from-its-journals#:~:text=From%20that%20beginning%2C%20the%20photo,call%20time%20on%20the%20photo

Theopilus, Y., Al Mahmud, A., Davis, H., & Octavia, J. R. (2024). Digital Interventions for Combating Internet Addiction in Young Children: Qualitative Study of Parent and Therapist Perspectives. *JMIR Pediatrics and Parenting, 7*, https://pediatrics.jmir.org/2024/1/e55364/

Thomas, K. A. (2021). Hate, Harassment, and the Changing Landscape of Online Abuse. *IEEE Symposium on Security and Privacy (SP)*, 247–267.

Thomas, S. E. (2018). "What Should I Do?": Young Women's Reported Dilemmas with Nude Photographs. *Sexuality Research and Social Policy, 15*, https://doi.org/10.1007/s13178-017-0310-0

Tierney, J. (1994, January 9). *Porn, the Low-Slung Engine of Progress*. Retrieved from The New York Times: https://www.nytimes.com/1994/01/09/arts/porn-the-low-slung-engine-of-progress.html?unlocked_article_code=1.0U0.eFFl.opPXM88NBs3M&smid=url-share

TISP. (2023, May 30). *Revenge Porn: The Latest Research and Law Enforcement Efforts*. Retrieved from Training Institute of Strangulation Prevention: https://www.strangulationtraininginstitute.com/revenge-porn-the-latest-research-and-law-enforcement-efforts/

Tran, A., Suharlim, C., Mattie, H., Davison, K., Agénor, M., & Austin, S. B. (2019). Dating App Use and Unhealthy Weight Control Behaviors among a Sample of U.S. Adults: A Cross-Sectional Study. *Journal of Eating Disorders, 7(16)*, https://jeatdisord.biomedcentral.com/articles/10.1186/s40337-019-0244-4

Trevisan, F. (2020). "Do You Want to Be a Well-Informed Citizen, or Do You Want to Be Sane?" Social Media, Disability, Mental Health, and Political Marginality. *Social Media + Society, 6(1)*, https://doi.org/10.1177/2056305120913909

Trout, H. (2021, December 22). *The Bathhouse Battle of 1984*. Retrieved from San Francisco AIDS Foundation: https://www.sfaf.org/collections/beta/the-bathhouse-battle-of-1984/

Tsai, H. J. (2016). Understanding Online Safety Behaviors: A Protection Motivation Theory Perspective. *Computer Security, 59*, 138–150.

Tsai, J. S. (2018). Is Online Partner-Seeking Associated with Increased Risk of Condomless Sex and Sexually Transmitted Infections among Individuals Who Engage in Heterosexual Sex? *A Systematic Narrative Review. Archives of Sexual Behavior, 48*, 533–555.

Turrecha, L. (2021, May 23). *Defining Privacy Tech*. Retrieved from Medium: https://medium.com/privacy-technology/defining-privacy-tech-ae7b022888ec

Twist, M., & McArthur, N. (2020). Introduction to Special Issue on Digihealth and Sexual Health. *Sexual and Relationship Therapy, 35(2)*, 131–136.

University of Sidney. (2023, June 13). *Experts Recommend Criteria to Identify Ethical Pornography*. Retrieved from University of Sidney: https://www.sydney.edu.au/news-opinion/news/2023/06/13/experts-recommend-criteria-to-identify-ethical-pornography.html

Urban Institute. (2024, June 23). *Digitizing Abuse*. Retrieved from Urban Institute: https://www.urban.org/digitizing-abuse-infographic

U.S. Federal Trade Commission. (2019, September 25). *FTC Sues Owner of Online Dating Service Match.com for Using Fake Love Interest Ads to Trick Consumers into Paying for a Match.com Subscription*. Retrieved from Federal Trade Commission: https://www.ftc.gov/news-events/news/press-releases/2019/09/ftc-sues-owner-online-dating-service-matchcom-using-fake-love-interest-ads-trick-consumers-paying

USCOP. (1970). *President's Commission on Obscenity and Pornography*. Retrieved from HathiTrust: https://catalog.hathitrust.org/Record/001354117/Cite

USG. (2024, July 10). *A Brief History of the Internet*. Retrieved from University System of Georgia Online Library Learning System: https://www.usg.edu/galileo/skills/unit07/internet07_02.phtml

Uzer, A. (2024, March 4). *Close Banner Advertisement This Ad is Displayed Using Third Party Content and We Do Not Control Its Accessibility Features: Sex | Expert Reviewed the Ultimate Guide to Sexting, with Examples (Plus, How to Sext)*. Retrieved from Mind-BodyGreen: https://www.mindbodygreen.com/articles/sexting-guide-with-examples

Valkenburg, P. J. (2016). Adolescents and Pornography: A Review of 20 Years of Research. *Journal of Sex Research, 53(4–5)*, 509–531.

Vandenbosch, L., Beyens, I., Vangeel, L., & Eggermont, S. (2016). Online Communication Predicts Belgian Adolescents' Initiation of Romantic and Sexual Activity. *European Journal of Pediatrics, 175*, 509–516, https://doi.org/10.1007/s00431-015-2666-6

Verdiell, M. (2018). *The IBM 1401 Mainframe Runs "Edith"*. Retrieved from Curiousmarc.com: https://www.curiousmarc.com/computing/ibm-1401-mainframe/ibm-1401-edith

Vittert, L. (2023, September 26). *AI Girlfriends Are Ruining an Entire Generation of Men*. Retrieved from The Hill: https://thehill.com/opinion/technology/4218666-ai-girlfriends-are-ruining-an-entire-generation-of-men/

Vogels, E. A., & McClain, C. (2023, February 2). *Key Findings about Online Dating in the U.S.* Retrieved from Pew Research Center: https://www.pewresearch.org/short-reads/2023/02/02/key-findings-about-online-dating-in-the-u-s/

von Behr, I., Reding, A., Edwards, C., & Gribbon, L. (2013). *Radicalisation in the Digital Era the Use of the Internet in 15 Cases of Terrorism and Extremism*. Retrieved from RAND.org: https://www.rand.org/content/dam/rand/pubs/research_reports/RR400/RR453/RAND_RR453.pdf

Wagner, T., & Blewer, A. (2019). "The Word Real Is No Longer Real": Deepfakes, Gender, and the Challenges of AI-Altered Video. *Open Information Science, 3*, 32–46.

Walker, A. M., & DeVito, M. A. (2020). "'More Gay' Fits in Better": Intracommunity Power Dynamics and Harms in Online LGBTQ + Spaces. *Proceedings of the 2020 CHI Conference on Human Factors in Computing Systems*, 1–15.

Walsh, J. P., & Hill, D. (2022). Social Media, Migration and the Platformization of Moral Panic: Evidence from Canada. *Convergence: The International Journal of Research into New Media Technologies, 29(3)*, https://doi.org/10.1177/13548565221137002

Walther, J. B. (2007). Selective Self-Presentation in Computer-Mediated Communication: Hyperpersonal Dimensions of Technology, Language, and Cognition. *Computers in Human Behavior, 23(5)*, 2538–2557.

Wang, F., & Zhou, X. (2023). Persuasive Schemes for Financial Exploitation in Online Romance Scam: An Anatomy on Sha Zhu Pan (杀猪盘) in China. *Victims & Offenders, 18*, 915–942.

Waugh, R. (2017, January 25). *Huge Bronze Strap-on Dildos and Jade Butt Plugs Found in Ancient Chinese Tombs*. Retrieved from Metro U.K.: https://metro.co.uk/2017/01/25/huge-bronze-strap-on-dildos-and-jade-butt-plugs-found-in-ancient-chinese-tombs-6404702/

WebPurify. (2023, March 31). *Fake Dating App Pictures: What Are Brands Doing to Stop the Next "Tinder Swindlers"?* Retrieved from WebPurify: https://www.webpurify.com/blog/fake-dating-app-pictures/

Weinberg, M. S., Irizarry, Y., & Williams, C. (2010). Pornography, Normalization, and Empowerment. *Archives of Sexual Behavior, 39*, 1389–1401, https://doi.org/10.1007/s10508-009-9592-5

Weir, K. (2025, April 15). *This Is How Meta AI Staffers Deemed More Than 7 Million Books to Have No "Economic Value"*. Retrieved from Vanity Fair: https://www.vanityfair.com/news/story/meta-ai-lawsuit?srsltid=AfmBOoq2EOadU9v4_LahMtC7-G8EnsJtQSmEU9skoQKN9gv9uTXAir1q

Weizenbaum, J. (1983). ELIZA—a Computer Program for the Study of Natural Language Communication between Man and Machine. *Communications of the ACM, 26(1)*, 23–28.

Westfall, C. (2023, October 4). *As AI Usage Increases At Work, Searches For "AI Girlfriend" Up 2400%*. Retrieved from Forbes: https://www.forbes.com/sites/chriswestfall/2023/09/29/as-ai-usage-increases-at-work-searches-for-ai-girlfriend-up-2400/?sh=412af8ad403b

Westin, A. F. (1968). Privacy and Freedom. *Washing and Lee Law Review, 25(1)*, https://scholarlycommons.law.wlu.edu/wlulr/vol25/iss1/20/

Whittaker, E., & Kowalski, R. M. (2015). *Cyberbullying Via Social Media. Journal of School Violence, 14*, 11–29.

Whitty, M. (2013). The Scammers Persuasive Techniques Model Development of a Stage Model to Explain the Online Dating Romance Scam. *British Journal of Criminology, 53*, 665–684.

Whitty, M. (2015). Anatomy of the Online Dating Romance Scam. *Security Journal, 28*, 443–455.

Wikipedia. (2024). *Hunter Moore*. Retrieved from Wikipedia: https://en.wikipedia.org/wiki/Hunter_Moore

Wilson, E. (2019, September 22). *Are Dating Apps Affecting Face-to-Face Interactions?* Retrieved from Medium: https://medium.com/the-public-ear/are-dating-apps-affecting-face-to-face-interactions-801c7e19c986

Winston, A. (2024, March 13). *There Are Dark Corners of the Internet: Then There's 764*. Retrieved from Wired.com: https://www.wired.com/story/764-com-child-predator-network/

Winter, C., Neumann, P., Meleagrou-Hitches, A., Ranstorp, M., Vidino, L., & Fürst, J. (2020). Online Extremism: Research Trends in Internet Activism, Radicalization, and Counter-Strategies. *International Journal of Conflict and Violence, 14(2)*, https://doi.org/10.4119/ijcv-3809

Witte, K. (1992). Putting the Fear Back into Fear Appeals: The Extended Parallel Process Model. *Communication Monographs, 59*, 329–349.

Wockhardt Hospitals. (2024, April 4). *A Psychiatrist Explains the Benefits of Turning Off Your Phone for Mental Health*. Retrieved from Wockhardt Hospitals Life Wins: https://www.wockhardthospitals.com/articles/mental-health/psychiatrist-explains-how-turning-off-phone-notifications-can-improve-your-mental-health/

WPR. (2024, July 15). *Countries Where Prostitution is Legal 2024*. Retrieved from World Population Review: https://worldpopulationreview.com/country-rankings/countries-where-prostitution-is-legal

Wright, J. (2023, January 9). *Inside Japan's Long Experiment in Automating Elder Care*. Retrieved from MIT Technology Review: https://www.technologyreview.com/2023/01/09/1065135/japan-automating-eldercare-robots/

Wright, P. T. (2023). But Do Porn Sites Get More Traffic than TikTok, OpenAI, and Zoom? *The Journal of Sex Research, 60*, 763–767.

Yang, Y. L. (2021). Anthropomorphism and Customers' Willingness to Use Artificial Intelligence Service Agents. *Journal of Hospitality Marketing & Management, 31*, 1–23.

Ybarra, M., Price-Feeney, M., Lenhart, A., & Zickuhr, K. (2017, January 18). *Intimate Partner Digital Abuse*. Retrieved from Data & Society Research Institute: https://datasociety.net/pubs/oh/Intimate_Partner_Digital_Abuse_2017.pdf

YesOnB. (2024, July 9). *The Los Angeles County Medical Association Say Vote Yes On B*. Retrieved from YesOnB.info: https://web.archive.org/web/20121102171022/http://www.yesonb.info/

Zhang, T., Morris, N. P., McNiel, D. E., & Binder, R. (2023). Elder Financial Exploitation in the Digital Age. *Journal of the American Academy of Psychiatry and the Law Online, 51(2)*, https://jaapl.org/content/51/2/173

Zhang, W. (2022). How Design in the 19th and 20th Centuries has Helped Connect Humans Across Nations and Cultures. *Highlights in Business, Economics and Management, 4,* 350–354, https://doi.org/10.54097/hbem.v4i.3524

Zlatolas, L. N., Welzer, T., Hölbl, M., Heričko, M., & Kamišalić, A. (2019). A Model of Perception of Privacy, Trust, and Self-Disclosure on Online Social Networks. *Entropy, 21(8),* https://doi.org/10.3390/e21080772

Zytko, D. G. (2018). The (Un)Enjoyable User Experience of Online Dating Systems. In *Funology 2: From Usability to Enjoyment* (pp. 61–75). Springer.

Index

Note: Page numbers in *italics* indicate a figure and page numbers in **bold** indicate a table on the corresponding page.

For Product Safety Concerns and Information please contact our EU
representative GPSR@taylorandfrancis.com
Taylor & Francis Verlag GmbH, Kaufingerstraße 24, 80331 München, Germany

www.ingramcontent.com/pod-product-compliance
Lightning Source LLC
Chambersburg PA
CBHW052003270326
41929CB00015B/2766

*9 7 8 1 0 3 2 4 8 8 5 1 6 *